FEMALE GOTHIC HISTORIES

SERIES PREFACE

Gothic Literary Studies is dedicated to publishing groundbreaking scholarship on Gothic in literature and film. The Gothic, which has been subjected to a variety of critical and theoretical approaches, is a form which plays an important role in our understanding of literary, intellectual and cultural histories. The series seeks to promote challenging and innovative approaches to Gothic which question any aspect of the Gothic tradition or perceived critical orthodoxy. Volumes in the series explore how issues such as gender, religion, nation and sexuality have shaped our view of the Gothic tradition. Both academically rigorous and informed by the latest developments in critical theory, the series provides an important focus for scholarly developments in Gothic studies, literary studies, cultural studies and critical theory. The series will be of interest to students of all levels and to scholars and teachers of the Gothic and literary and cultural histories.

SERIES EDITORS

EDITORIAL BOARD

Female Gothic Histories
Gender, History and the Gothic

Diana Wallace

UNIVERSITY OF WALES PRESS
CARDIFF
2013

www.uwp.co.uk

British Library CIP Data
A catalogue record for this book is available from the British Library.

ISBN   978-0-7083-2574-2
e-ISBN   978-0-7083-2575-9

Typeset in Wales by Eira Fenn Gaunt, Cardiff
Printed by CPI Antony Rowe, Chippenham, Wiltshire

CONTENTS

We need, as I argue in this book, a new theory of historical fiction and a meta-narrative of its development which takes more seriously its intimate relationship with the Gothic. Such an account would allow us more accurately to assess the contribution women writers have made to the genre and, conversely, its central importance to thinking about women and history. I use the term 'historical fiction' deliberately here, rather than 'historical novel', because looking at short fiction problematises many of the assumptions frequently made about both historical novels and the Gothic.

As I argued in *The Woman's Historical Novel: British Women Writers, 1900–2000* (2005), women's historical fiction has its roots in the Gothic novel which precedes the work of Sir Walter Scott. Despite evidence to the contrary, Scott is still commonly positioned as the progenitor of the historical novel, even in such recent texts as Jerome de Groot's *The Historical Novel* (2010). *Female Gothic Histories* extends the project of my earlier book in order to offer an alternative account of historical fiction as it has been developed and used by women. It traces a female genealogy of Gothic historical fiction from Sophia Lee's *The Recess* (1783–5) in the late eighteenth century through the short fictions of Elizabeth Gaskell and Vernon Lee, to the work of Daphne du Maurier which inspired the 'modern Gothics' of the 1960s, and finally to its most recent manifestation in the hugely popular novels of Sarah Waters in the twenty-first century.

Such a long time span – covering two and a half centuries – offers both benefits and problems. On the benefit side it provides a slice of the 'long history' which historians such as Gerda Lerner and Mary Beard have suggested is necessary if we are to understand what Beard called 'woman as force in history'.[1] Beard suggests in particular the need to go back beyond nineteenth-century ideologies which so often shape our thinking about women. Indeed, I would argue that one of the most valuable aspects of historical fiction is precisely its ability to direct our vision into the past, and to enable an imaginative engagement with other possibilities.

On the other hand, such a long view creates real problems in an age when academics are increasingly specialised. Given that my own period specialism is the early twentieth century, it seems a dangerous thing to strike back as far as the late eighteenth century. It is, however, both important and invigorating to do such work. This book is therefore indebted to the important work done by other feminist literary critics on the beginnings of the historical novel, the national tale and the Gothic in the late eighteenth and early nineteenth century. Perhaps most importantly it builds on Ellen Moers's eclectic and innovative *Literary Women* (1976), written during the early years of 'women's liberation'.[2] It was Moers who first coined the term 'Female Gothic' and, although she did not discuss historical fiction as such, she was intensely aware of the importance of history: 'If ever there was a time which teaches that one must know the history of women to understand the history of literature', she wrote, 'it is now.'[3] The same is still true today and, despite its now well-documented limitations and omissions, her ground-breaking work remains an important inspiration.

Notes to the Preface

[1] Mary R. Beard, *Woman as Force in History* (New York: Macmillan, 1946).
[2] Ellen Moers, *Literary Women* (1976; London: The Women's Press, 1978).
[3] Ibid., p. xiii.

ACKNOWLEDGEMENTS

This book has been a long time in the writing and I would like to thank several colleagues and friends for their support and assistance. Jane Aaron read most of the work in progress and has been a huge source of support throughout. I am indebted to Jeni Williams, who gave astute and tactful feedback on several chapters, and to Gavin Edwards, Marion Shaw and Kevin Mills, who read individual chapters and offered sage advice. I'd like to thank Meredith Miller for a useful conversation about the ways in which the Gothic can be seen as a kind of theory; Angela Wright for allowing me to see her work in progress on Sophia Lee's translation of *Varbeck*; Jonathan Durrant for lending me books on witches; Rebecca Moore for conversations about Daphne du Maurier; Linda Graves, Lesley Hargreaves and the Inter-library loan team at the University of Glamorgan for their patience and persistence in obtaining material; and Rhiannon Sargent for support in the final stages. My students on The Female Gothic and Gothic Histories modules at Glamorgan University have been another source of inspiration. Thank you to Andrew Smith for inviting me to contribute this volume to the series; to Sarah Lewis, who has been an endlessly patient editor in the face of repeated delays; and to UWP's anonymous reader for her astute comments. I'd also like to thank the postgraduates who organised the PGCWWN Theory and Practice Networking day at Leicester University in October 2010, and those who attended my workshop on historical fiction.

I am grateful to Sarah Waters and her literary agents, Greene & Heaton, for kind permission to quote extracts from her novels, *Affinity* © 1999, *Fingersmith* © 2002 and *The Little Stranger* © 2009; to the Curtis Brown Group Ltd for kind permission to quote from the novels of Daphne du Maurier: *Jamaica Inn* © 1936, *Rebecca* ©

1938, *The King's General* © 1946, *My Cousin Rachel* © 1951, *Myself When Young* © 1977, *The Rebecca Notebook: And Other Memories* © 1981; and to the Curtis Brown Group Ltd, London on behalf of the Chichester Partnership, for kind permission to quote from the Introduction to *Northanger Abbey* by Jane Austen © 1948.

Finally, my family have, as ever, been my biggest source of support and encouragement, and I would like to thank my parents, Anne and Nigel Wallace, my sisters, Linda Schjoett and Dawn Percival, and, most of all, Jarlath and Seán.

For Jarlath and Seán

1

Introduction

∽

The history of England is the history of the male line, not of the female.

Virginia Woolf, 'Women and Fiction' (1929)[1]

If the rationale of History is ultimately to remind us of everything that has happened and to take it into account, we must make the interpretation of the forgetting of female ancestries part of History and re-establish its economy.

Luce Irigaray, *Thinking the Difference* (1989)[2]

From the late eighteenth century, women writers, aware of their exclusion from traditional historical narratives, have used Gothic historical fiction as a mode of historiography which can simultaneously reinsert them into history and symbolise their exclusion. If the Gothic with its blatant flouting of realism is always already, as I will suggest here, a kind of metafiction *avant la lettre*, then Gothic historical fiction, the subject of my study, can be seen as a kind of metahistory, a way of theorising or producing a philosophy of history.[3] In the hands of women writers, Gothic historical fiction has offered a way of 'interpreting', or symbolising, what Luce Irigaray calls 'the forgetting of female ancestries' and of re-establishing them within 'History'.[4]

In doing so these novels throw into question what exactly we mean by 'History', or indeed, 'history', or 'the past'. That is, how do we shape accounts of what happened in the past (the events of 'history') into narratives ('History')? How does our understanding of gender influence such processes? What happens to those accounts when women are either left out, or added in? And, if the 'economy' (to borrow Irigaray's term) of 'History' is based on the assumption that public and political events have more 'value' than private and domestic events, and are more worth recording, how can we re-value, or re-imagine, women's unrecorded experience in the past?

Furthermore, if (married) women were for over two centuries regarded as 'civilly dead', what kinds of ghostly traces can we retrieve from the texts of history? Mary Beard traces back to 1765 the notion that 'women were a subject sex or nothing at all – in any past or the total past,' attributing its genesis to Sir William Blackstone's influential statement of the legal position of married women:

> By marriage, the husband and wife are one person in law; that is, the very being or legal existence of the woman is suspended during the marriage, or at least is incorporated and consolidated into that of the husband; under whose wing, protection and *cover*, she performs every thing.[5]

This legal concept of the married woman as 'civilly dead' led, Beard argues, to what she calls the 'haunting idea' that woman in the past was 'a being always and everywhere subject to *male* man or as a ghostly creature too shadowy to be even that real'.[6] The language of spectrality used by Beard here suggests the particular power of the Gothic to express the erasure of women in history, something which may not be expressible in other kinds of language or in the traditional forms of historiographic narratives. This suggests one reason why the Gothic has been such an important mode of writing for women, and why, from Ellen Moers's *Literary Women* (1976) on, it has occupied such a central place in feminist literary criticism.

From the late seventeenth century, with the publication of Madame de Lafayette's *The Princess of Clèves* (1678), fiction has been one of the primary ways in which women writers have written

history, and written themselves into 'History'. The invisibility of
women within mainstream history, and as historians, obscures the
fact that women have not only participated in historical events but
engaged with history for as long as we have had historical records.
The problem has been that, in Mary Spongberg's words,

> [women's] historical endeavours have not been regarded as 'proper'
> history. Women who attempted to write history were rarely con-
> sidered 'real' historians: rather they have been characterised as biog-
> raphers, *historical novelists*, political satirists, genealogists, writers of
> travellers' tales, collectors of folklore and antiquarians.[7]

History, Bonnie G. Smith argues, has been 'gendered male by tradition, accident and circumstance' since its professionalisation in the
early nineteenth century.[8] More than that, Christina Crosby has
suggested, the construction of history as 'man's truth' required 'that
"woman" be *outside history*, above, below, or beyond properly historical and political life'.[9]

Yet women's enforced position 'outside history', as what Crosby
calls 'the unhistorical other of history',[10] has often made them
sceptical about mainstream historical narratives in ways which have
proven fruitful for their fiction. The recognition that history which
does not include women's experience is, in Virginia Woolf's words,
'a little queer . . . unreal, lopsided',[11] has alerted women writers to
the ways in which any historical narrative is always constructed from
a particular (subjective) point of view. There is not one 'History',
their fiction suggests, but plural and contradictory histories. It is
in fiction that women writers have been able to be most subversive
in their critiques of traditional historiography and its effects. In this
sense women's historical fiction has fulfilled Joan Wallach Scott's
stipulation that women's history should be not just an 'addition
of information previously ignored . . . but an analysis of the effects
of dominant understandings of gender in the past'.[12] Despite this,
fiction has not been regarded as '"proper" history'.

Furthermore, if the historical novel as a genre appears oxy-
moronic in its yoking of supposedly antithetical opposites – 'fact'
and 'fiction', 'history' and 'literature', the new ('novel') and the
old ('history') – then the Gothic historical novel is even more

problematic. With its associations with the supernatural, the Gothic is even more at odds with our notion of history than the realist novel which at least appears to represent the 'real'. Like so many other binary oppositions, these two terms are defined in opposition to each other. To say something is 'Gothic' is at once to imply that it is obsessed with the return of the past, and to define it as un-historical, not 'proper history', fantasy rather than fact. Conversely, historical fiction proper is defined partly by its eschewing of the fantastic, the supernatural, and (ironically) the 'fictional' in the sense of the invented or imaginary.

The Gothic historical novel seems to be yoking together two different and incompatible ways of representing the past. Here Mary Ann Doane's distinction between the past of historiography and the past of psychoanalysis is suggestive: 'In psychoanalysis, the past is aggressive – it returns, it haunts, it sometimes dominates the present. In historiography, the past is static, inert – qualities which make it, in effect, more knowable.'[13]

The past of the Gothic is closer to that of psychoanalysis: aggres-sively mobile, prone to return, to irruptions into the present. The past in the Gothic never quite stays dead, and is therefore never fully knowable. This is why Gothic fiction so often seems to demand psychoanalytic interpretations as a way of disinterring the repressed secrets of the past. In contrast, critics of the historical novel have traditionally turned to Marxist approaches, aligning the genre with the nineteenth-century realist novel by excluding texts which use fantastic elements.

There is also a problem of nomenclature. Should we talk about the 'Gothic historical novel', or about what Montague Summers and Devendra P. Varma called respectively the 'historical Gothic' or 'historical-Gothic' novel?[14] As with many hybrids, it's not obvious which term should take priority, or if they should be hyphenated. Summers and Varma were primarily interested in the Gothic, and the 'historical' as a subcategory within that mode. My own decision to use the term 'Gothic historical fiction' reflects the fact that my interest is in historical fiction which uses the Gothic as a way of symbolising questions about history and gender which cannot be formulated in other kinds of language. My project here is to take female historical novelists seriously as historians, to listen carefully to what they are saying about the relationship between women and history. Even more improperly, I want to take seriously the *Gothic* historical fiction written by women in order to explore what their use of Gothic conventions tells us about women's position within history.

While literary criticism has tended to focus on ways of separating the two genres, the origins of the Gothic novel and the historical novel are intimately entwined. As David Punter has argued of the early novels which constitute the origins of the Gothic: 'the reason why it is so difficult to draw a line between Gothic fiction and historical fiction is that Gothic itself seems to have *been* a mode of history, a way of perceiving an obscure past and interpreting it.'[15]

One of the obstacles to recognising this has been the neglect, until recently, of a body of work by women writers who produced historical novels before Sir Walter Scott published *Waverley; or, 'Tis Sixty Years Since* (1814). While the majority of critics still, erroneously, trace the development of the historical novel as a genre back through what Virginia Woolf called 'the male line' to Scott, I want to trace an alternative female genealogy which starts with Sophia Lee's extraordinary Gothic historical novel, *The Recess; or, A Tale of Other Times* (1783–5), published over thirty years earlier. This genealogy moves through the short fictions of Elizabeth Gaskell and Vernon Lee, and then the novels of Daphne du Maurier and Victoria Holt, to those of Sarah Waters.

My argument is that the Gothic works as a 'mode of history' which has had particular attractions and importance for women writers. Women writers have used Gothic historical fiction with its obsession with inheritance, lost heirs and illegitimate offspring, to explore the way in which the 'female line' has been erased in 'History'. The very literariness of the Gothic, its repetition of, and play with, obviously stylised generic conventions, draws attention to its own constructedness, makes it, indeed, a kind of metafiction.[16] 'The fantastic', as Rosemary Jackson argues, 'traces the unsaid and the unseen of culture: that which has been silenced, made invisible, covered over and made absent.'[17] Gothic historical novels harness that potential, but root it within the material specificity of history. Here fiction has a close relationship with historiography: the metaphors women historians often use to figure women's relationship with history – of women being 'outside', 'underneath' or 'hidden from' history[18] – are Gothic images of a past which is obscure, dark, buried, needing to be unearthed. The use of such metaphors by historians, as well as writers of fiction, suggests the importance of the Gothic to the ways in which we think about women and history.

Theorising historical fiction

In his 'Introductory' to *Waverley*, Walter Scott set out a manifesto for what he presented as a new mode of fiction:

> Had I, for example, announced in my frontispiece, 'Waverley, a Tale of other Days', must not every novel-reader have anticipated a castle scarce less than that of Udolpho, of which the eastern wing had long been uninhabited, and the keys either lost or consigned to the care of some aged butler or housekeeper, whose trembling steps, about the middle of the second volume, were doomed to guide the hero, or heroine, to the ruinous precincts? Would not the owl have shrieked and the cricket cried in my very title page?[19]

Scott draws what appears to be a firm, clear line between the kinds of novel he is *not* going to write – Gothic, Romance, sentimental, the modern novel of manners – and the less clearly delineated new kind he is going to write, which is 'more a description of men than manners'.[20] The line he draws is between what he presents as a proto-realism (reading from the 'great book of Nature'[21]) and the now clichéd literary conventions of the Gothic novel. In place of the gloomy obscurity of 'other Days', Scott's chosen subtitle, *'Tis Sixty Years Since*, appears to have the rational daylight clarity of historical specificity. To produce this neatly rounded figure, of course, involved Scott in a complex sleight of hand: his 'Introductory' is 'fix[ed]' 'at this present 1st November, 1805', despite the actual publication date some nine years later.[22] To account for this delay, the 'Postscript' to the novel famously (and, indeed, rather Gothically) explains that the unfinished MS was laid aside and 'only found . . . again by mere accident among other waste papers, after it had been mislaid for several years'.[23]

Neverthless, Scott's self-branding of himself as the progenitor of a new genre was remarkably successful. 'Sir Walter Scott, as all the world knows, was the inventor of the historical romance,' an anonymous reviewer remarked in 1845.[24]. This assumption cast a long and deforming shadow over criticism of historical fiction until very recently. *Waverley* became the standard by which other historical fictions, particularly those by women, were judged and, usually, found wanting. A seminal influence here has been Georg Lukács's Marxist *The Historical Novel* (1937), which positioned *Waverley* as the exemplary 'classical historical novel' and argued that it used 'typical' characters to depict history as a progressive process of Hegelian dialectical conflict.[25] Lukács derogates the 'fashion to quote a long list of second- and third-rate writers (Radcliffe, etc.) who were supposed to be important literary forerunners of [Scott]'.[26] For him Scott stands alone as the inventor of the 'classical historical novel', from which springs the realist novel of the nineteenth century.

Lukács's influence can be seen in, for instance, Avrom Fleishman's *The English Historical Novel: Walter Scott to Virginia Woolf* (1971), for many years the defining critical work in this area.[27] For Fleishman, a historical novel must be set forty to sixty years in the past; include 'historical' events – 'especially those in the "public" sphere (war, politics, economic change, etc.)'; and at least one '"real" personage'.[28] What makes a historical novel 'historical', he argues, is 'the active presence of history as a shaping force – acting not only on the characters in the novel but on the author and readers outside it'.[29] If, however, like Lukács and Fleishman, we take Scott as the beginning of the tradition of the historical novel, we start from an exemplary model of the genre which, as I argued in *The Woman's Historical Novel*, simply doesn't work for women writers.

As several critics – Peter Garside, Katie Trumpener, Ina Ferris, Fiona Price, Anne H. Stevens and Richard Maxwell – have pointed out over the last couple of decades, there was, in fact, a large body of work before *Waverley* which is recognisably historical fiction, much of it by women. Initially, critical work focused on the 'national tale', as in Katie Trumpener's *Bardic Nationalism* (1997). More recently two important studies have emerged which have widened the picture. In *British Historical Fiction Before Scott* (2010), Anne H. Stevens examines eighty-five such novels, dating the origins of the genre back to Thomas Leland's *Longsword, Earl of Salisbury: An Historical Romance* (1762), closely followed by Horace Walpole's *The Castle of Otranto: A Gothic Story* (1764). In her account of the genre, Clara Reeve, author of *The Champion of Virtue: A Gothic Story* (1777; republished as *The Old English Baron*), is 'the first female historical novelist in this generic cycle'.[30] Stevens is interested primarily in the way in which generic conventions developed in the period before 1813. She notes that the historical novel borrowed elements from earlier genres: the interpolated story from the romance, for instance, and paratextual elements, such as footnotes, from anti-quarianism.[31] Like David Punter, she makes the point that Gothic and historical novels have a common origin and that generic sep-aration only takes place towards the end of the eighteenth century when they diverge, 'one emphasizing historical settings and featur-ing real historical events and figures and the other emphasizing effects of terror and horror'.[32] Taking an even wider view in *The Historical Novel in Europe, 1650–1950* (2009), Richard Maxwell traces the roots of the genre back to seventeenth-century France and the tradition of the 'secret history', taking Madeleine de Scudéry's *Artamène; ou, Le Grand Cyrus* (1649–53) as his starting-point.[33] Two of the most influential texts he discusses are Madame de Lafayette's *La Princesse de Clèves* (1678) and Antoine Prévost's *Le Philosophe anglois ou histoire de Monsieur Cleveland* (1731–9). Both were import-ant intertexts for Sophia Lee's *The Recess*, and *Cleveland* is an early example of the 'pretender in sanctuary' plot Maxwell sees as central to the genre.[34]

Despite this welcome broadening of the genealogy of the his-torical novel, Scott still appears as the pivot around which discussion of the genre circulates. While Stevens takes Scott as the end point of her study, devoting her Epilogue to *Ivanhoe* (1819), Maxwell positions Scott as the centre of the tradition, so much so that Part II of his book is entitled 'The Franco-Scottish Model for Historical Fiction'. The myth that Scott was the originator of the historical novel has been very hard to dislodge. Even Jerome de Groot's otherwise thoughtful *The Historical Novel* (2010) presents Scott's novels as originary, arguing that *Waverley* 'introduced a new form, the "historical" novel'.[35] While he mentions the 'shortlived Gothic novel's interest in history' as producing a 'nightmarish type of historical novel', he concludes: 'The incipient historical novel, after the example of Scott, became a rational, realist form, shifting away from the excesses of the Gothic to emphasise process, progress and transcendent human values.'[36] It is the gendering of the putative separation between historical and Gothic fiction which particularly interests me. My argument is not only that this separation is never as complete as critics have suggested, but also that Gothic historical fiction continues to be an important mode of writing for women right through to the twenty-first century.

Scott's 'Introductory' to *Waverley* is an attempt forcibly to separate the terms 'historical' and 'Gothic' in ways which are implicitly gendered. His dismissive account of earlier novels does a particular disservice to women writers, and has helped to erase them from the genealogy of the historical novel. The exemplary Gothic novel Scott directly invokes is, of course, Ann Radcliffe's *The Mysteries of Udolpho* (1794). But the subtitle Scott suggests, 'A Tale of Other Days', evokes that of Lee's *The Recess; or, A Tale of Other Times*. Set in the sixteenth and early seventeenth centuries during the reigns of Elizabeth I and James VI/I, *The Recess* is, as April Alliston has argued, 'the first important and fully developed text for both the "female" Gothic and the historical Gothic strains in English fiction'.[37] Although both Stevens and Maxwell accord it an important place in their accounts of the development of the historical novel, it is only relatively recently that *The Recess* has attracted attention from critics.[38]

When Scott lampooned the conventions of the Gothic – the ruined castles and trappings of terror – he was doing so in order to replace them with another set of conventions which came to constitute literary 'realism', the central mode of writing for the novel in the nineteenth century, but one which is (as feminist and poststructuralist critics have repeatedly pointed out) no less of an artificial construct than the Gothic. His work has been seen as reclaiming the novel for male writers through the introduction of 'masculine' history; it was 'a self-conscious attempt to redeem fiction at once for respectability and masculinity', in Leslie Fiedler's words.[39] It does not seem coincidental that the novel was being 'masculinised' in this way at precisely the point at which, as Bonnie G. Smith points out, history was being professionalised by men who were edging out amateur women historians, characterising their work as superficial and trivial. The line which Scott attempted to draw between the Gothic novel and the historical novel was and is an acutely gendered one, which dismisses the work women had done in order to privilege that of a male writer and his followers.

From the end of the nineteenth century until the closing decades of the twentieth century, historical fiction entered the critical doldrums. The fact that during this period historical fiction was 'a genre dominated by women' may well explain, in Sarah Waters's words, 'why it has received such poor and patchy critical attention.'[40] Denigrated as a popular female form in the middle years of the twentieth century, partly as a result of its association with Jean Plaidy−Victoria Holt (see chapter 5), the historical novel became increasingly accepted as serious literary fiction following the publication of A. S. Byatt's Booker Prize-winning *Possession* in 1990. Sarah Waters's own rapid rise to the status of a best-seller who appeals to both academic critics and a popular audience indicates the way in which historical fiction has moved from the margins to the centre during the last few decades. If anything, this trend intensified in the first decade of the twenty-first century: five of the 2009 Man Booker Prize shortlisted novels were historical, including Waters's own *The Little Stranger*, and it was won by Hilary Mantel's *Wolf Hall*.

This shift in critical and popular attitudes towards historical fiction can be attributed to a variety of factors. One is the development of feminist literary and historical studies within a higher-education sector which began to expand in the 1980s, and which helped to further the concomitant growth of Victorian Studies and Gothic Studies.[41] Our current obsession with the Victorian period can be related to the fact that, as Robin Gilmour has noted, the drift in literary studies towards the twentieth century has meant that Victorian literature is now 'central to an English degree to an extent that it was not in the past'.[42] These factors have produced an expanded readership whose education has prepared them to enjoy the increasingly available paperback reprints of original Victorian novels, as well as neo-Victorian novels.

Critical approaches to historical fiction were invigorated in the late twentieth century by what is often referred to as the 'linguistic turn' or 'postmodern turn' in historical studies brought about by the work of theorists such as Roland Barthes, Michel Foucault, Fredric Jameson, Hayden White, Louis Minke and Keith Jenkins. Hayden White's contention in *Metahistory* (1973) that historical narratives are emplotted like literary texts (that is, that they similarly organise the chronicle of events into a story or plot), has proven especially attractive to literary scholars. Equally important has been Jameson's famous formulation:

> That history – Althusser's 'absent cause', Lacan's 'Real' – is *not* a text, for it is fundamentally non-narrative and nonrepresentational; what can be added, however, is the proviso that history is inaccessible to us except in textual form, or in other words, that it can be approached only by way of prior (re)textualisation.[43]

The understanding that history is, if not 'fiction', then a textual version of the past constructed through literary techniques has re-focused interest on historical fiction itself.

The most influential theorisation of postmodernity's effect on historical fiction has been Linda Hutcheon's *A Poetics of Post-modernism: History, Theory, Fiction* (1988). Hutcheon coined the term 'historiographic metafiction' to describe a group of popular novels, such as *The French Lieutenant's Woman* (1969), 'which are both intensely self-reflexive and yet paradoxically lay claim to historical events and personages'.[44] She argued:

> In most of the critical work on postmodernism, it is narrative – be it in literature, history or theory – that has usually been the major focus of attention. Historiographic metafiction incorporates all three of these domains: that is, its theoretical self-awareness of history and fiction as human constructs (historio*graphic* meta*fiction*) is made the grounds for its rethinking and reworking of the forms and content of the past.[45]

An important subset of historiographic metafiction is what has come to be called the 'neo-Victorian novel'. Alternative terms include 'retro-Victorian novel', used by Sally Shuttleworth, and 'faux-Victorian',[46] but 'neo-Victorian', coined by Dana Shiller, is the term which has most critical currency. Shiller uses it to refer to those novels that adopt a postmodern approach to history and that are set at least partly in the nineteenth century. This capacious umbrella includes texts that revise specific Victorian precursors, texts that imagine new adventures for familiar Victorian characters, and 'new' Victorian fictions that imitate nineteenth-century conventions.[47]

A particularly rich body of critical material has grown up around neo-Victorian fiction, to which I will return in chapter 6. Our current affinity with the 'Victorians' is, however, relatively recent. Post-war writers were attracted by the eighteenth century, for instance, while the seventeenth century was important in the late 1980s.[48] Our equally intense current fascination with the Tudors has attracted far less critical attention. This is partly because neo-Victorianism capitalises on a perceived coherence between the form of the realist novel and the historical period within which it was developed.

It is also in neo-Victorian fiction that the Gothic makes an especially vigorous reappearance in the historical novel, seemingly new minted through postmodern ideas about history and fiction. In *Metahistory* White argued that historians structure their accounts of the past by using the four archetypal genres: Romance, Comedy, Tragedy and Satire. These, he argues, have elective affinities with modes of ideological implication as follows: Romantic – Anarchist; Tragic – Radical; Comic – Conservative; Satirical – Liberal.[49] It's notable that White does not discuss the gendering of these plot structures to consider, for instance, the specific associations of romance with the feminine. My own contention here is that we need to add 'Gothic' to Hayden White's list of the ways in which history can be emplotted, and 'feminism' to his list of ideological implications. The texts I discuss in this study demonstrate repeatedly that the Gothic has been one of the central ways in which women writers have emplotted history and theorised their exclusion from mainstream historiographical accounts.

But what happens to the Gothic historical tradition between the early nineteenth century, when it appears to separate into two distinct genres, and the late twentieth century when it re-emerges in the work of writers like Sarah Waters? Does it simply disappear? The historical novel of the nineteenth century is primarily a realist tradition, and the Gothic in this period is associated with texts with modern settings (such as *Dracula* (1897) or the sensation fiction of Wilkie Collins and Mary Elizabeth Braddon). In fact, the Gothic historical strain can be found at its strongest during these years in short fiction partly as a result of the emergence of mass-market periodicals. Gaskell published many of her stories in the early Victorian magazines, including those edited by Charles Dickens. It was not, however, until the 1880s that the term 'short story' first began to be used. Roger Luckhurst attributes the resurfacing of the Gothic tale in the 1880s to the explosion of new magazines which killed off the three volume novel. There was, he remarks, a 'torrent of Gothic imaginings' in the form of Gothic tales by Arthur Machen, Sir Arthur Conan Doyle, Rudyard Kipling, Oscar Wilde, Henry James and others.[50] Similarly, the editors of *The Oxford Book of Historical Stories* (1995), Michael Cox and Jack Adrian, argue that the advances in printing technology in the 1890s and the development of the illustrated general-interest monthly magazine, particularly *Strand Magazine*, 'heralded the golden age of short historical fiction'.[51]

However, the historical short story has received almost no critical attention as a specific genre. As the relentless repetition of the word in the titles of critical studies suggests – Lukacs's *The Historical Novel*, Fleishman's *The English Historical Novel*, Richard Maxwell's *The Historical Novel in Europe, 1650–1950*, Andrew Rance's *The Historical Novel and Popular Politics in Nineteenth-Century England* (1975), Andrew Sanders's *The Victorian Historical Novel 1840–1880* (1978) and, indeed, my own *The Woman's Historical Novel* – attention to historical fiction has been almost exclusively devoted to the novel. There has been very little attempt to theorise the difference between historical novel and historical story. Indeed, Rafael Sabatini included novel extracts as well as stories in *A Century of Historical Stories* (1936), making no distinction between them. Given that Walter Scott has been credited by Walter Allen with the invention of the 'modern short story',[52] this is an interesting omission but it is partly, as I will argue in chapter 3, to do with assumptions about the short story being a 'minor' form.

As with the historical novel, the focus on the Gothic has tended to be on the 'Gothic novel', with both Gothic poetry and short stories being marginalised. The exception to this critical silence is the ghost story, where the spectral figures the haunting of the present by the past. Again, the ghost story is often presented as the invention of Walter Scott. The editors of *The Oxford Book of English Ghost Stories*, Michael Cox and R. A, Gilbert, credit Scott with writing both 'the genre's earliest masterpiece' in 'Wandering Willie's Tale' (1824), and 'one of the earliest self-contained ghost stories' in 'The Tapestried Chamber' (1829).[53] Julia Briggs's early study, *Night Visitors: The Rise and Fall of the English Ghost Story* (1977), which discusses Gaskell and Vernon Lee, drew attention to the ways in which the ghost story 'could be made to embody symbolically hopes and fears too deep and too important to be expressed more directly'.[54] This has made it an especially important form for women writers. Vanessa Dickerson's *Victorian Ghosts in the Noontide: Women Writers and the Supernatural* (1996) suggests that women were drawn to the form because 'the ghost corresponded more particularly to the Victorian woman's visibility and invisibility, her power and powerlessness, the contradictions and extremes that shaped female culture.'[55] She argues: 'It was finally not men's but women's ghost stories that truly treated the return of the repressed and the dispossessed; ghost stories could provide a fitting medium for eruptions of female libidinal energy, of thwarted ambitions, of cramped egos.'[56]

Within the systems of representation in Western culture, Luce Irigaray argues, women exist in a state of *dereliction* or abandonment: 'women are nowhere, touching everything, but never in touch with each other, lost in the air, like ghosts.'[57] Ghost stories, like the Gothic, provided a way of exploring that 'ghosting' within the social and legal structures which declared women 'civilly dead'. The Gothic historical stories I want to discuss in later chapters are sometimes, but not always, ghost stories, but they continue and develop in fascinating ways the use of the Gothic as a mode of history.

The Female Gothic

Coined by Ellen Moers in 1976, the term 'Female Gothic', as she intended it, referred simply to 'the work that women have done in the literary mode that since the eighteenth century, we have called the Gothic'.[58] Her account of this mode started with Ann Radcliffe's novels, 'in which the central figure is a young women who is simul-taneously persecuted victim and courageous heroine', and then moved on to a powerful reading of Mary Shelley's *Frankenstein* (1818) as a 'birth myth'.[59] Moers's study, together with Sandra M. Gilbert and Susan Gubar's seminal *The Madwoman in the Attic* (1979), which took the Gothic doubling of Jane Eyre and Bertha Rochester as their central metaphor for the predicament of the woman author,[60] made the Female Gothic central to the development of feminist criticism. Indeed, this area has been and still is one of the most vibrant areas of literary criticism, attracting such inspirational critics as Margaret Ann Doody, Claire Kahane, Joanna Russ, Kate Ellis, Tania Modleski, Juliann Fleenor, Eugenia C. Delamotte, E. J. Clery, Anne Williams, and Avril Horner and Sue Zlosnik. Since the 1990s, however, the term 'Female Gothic' has been hotly contested and a variety of alternatives suggested: E. J. Clery, for instance, preferred to call her study *Women's Gothic* (2000).[61]

Part of the problem is the slipperiness of the term 'Gothic' itself. Moers noted that it was not easily defined, 'except that it has to do with fear'.[62] 'Fear' and the inclusion of the supernatural are usually taken as the features which distinguish the Gothic from historical fiction. However, the defining feature of the early Gothic novels of Horace Walpole, Clara Reeve and Sophia Lee, as Punter argues, is 'to do with their relation to history'.[63] Concern with terror and horror becomes the defining convention of the Gothic slightly later. In Walpole's *Castle of Otranto* (1764) usually taken as the founding text of the Gothic, Punter argues, 'the supernatural becomes a symbol of our past rising against us, whether it be the psychological past . . . or the historical past.'[64] The next important text, Reeve's *The Old English Baron: A Gothic Story* (1777), was presented in the author's Preface as 'the literary offspring of the Castle of Otranto, written upon the same plan', uniting both 'ancient Romance and modern Novel', and 'being a picture of Gothic times and man-ners.'[65] Reeve made two important innovations: where Walpole situated his novel fairly vaguely between 1095 and 1243, the dates of the first and last crusades, she set hers specifically during 'the minority of Henry Sixth, King of England'; and she eschewed, in the interests of 'credibility', the more 'violent' 'machinery' of the supernatural used by Walpole.[66] In other words Reeve moved the

'Gothic' further towards historical realism and the development of the historical novel. For Reeve, Punter suggests, the past was not a source of fear or wonder but 'of comfort': 'one feels she is encouraging a constant sense of relief at the comparative normalcy of our ancestors.'[67] Both these novels are key intertexts for Lee's *The Recess* and for Ann Radcliffe. But while Lee retains and develops the elements of historical realism introduced by Reeve, Radcliffe foregrounds the psychological and symbolic mode by using a more vaguely delineated setting in the past which transforms the Gothic into a kind of fantasy space.

I will discuss this genealogy in more detail in chapter 2, but the point I want to make here is that if we start, as Moers does and many subsequent critics have done, from Ann Radcliffe as the beginning of the 'Female Gothic' then we miss crucial elements of the genre's engagement with history. By starting with Lee, rather than Radcliffe (or Scott), we can generate a different account of the development of Gothic historical fiction which pays particular attention to what it has to say about gender and history.

Next, however, I want to outline some critical approaches to the Female Gothic which I have found especially useful in looking at Gothic historical fiction. One of the most helpful formulations of the conventions of the Female Gothic is Norman N. Holland and Leona F. Sherman's identification of the elements which link the Radcliffean mode to the modern Gothic of the 1960s: 'The image of woman-plus-habitation and the plot of mysterious sexual and supernatural threats in an atmosphere of dynastic mysteries within the habitation has changed little since the eighteenth century.'[68] Within that dynastic plot feminist critics have drawn attention to the importance of the mother and the related symbolic meanings of the habitation. Claire Kahane borrows from Leslie Fiedler to offer an influential articulation:

[as Fiedler points out] 'beneath the haunted castle lies the dungeon keep: the womb from whose darkness the ego first emerged, the tomb to which it knows it must return at last. Beneath the crumbling shell of paternal authority, lies the maternal blackness, imagined by the gothic writer as a prison, a torture chamber' . . . What I see repeatedly locked into the forbidden centre of the Gothic which draws me

---

16

inward is the spectral presence of the dead-undead mother, archaic and all-encompassing, a ghost signifying the problematics of femininity which the heroine must confront.[69]

In her article Kahane traces a historical shift as the spectral mother of earlier texts becomes an embodied figure in modern Gothic texts.[70] The tension between early critical emphases in the 1970s and early 1980s on the Female Gothic as expressing a fear of being devoured by the all-powerful mother, and later more positive and complex readings, which often focus on the daughter's desire to rescue the victimised/murdered mother, can be seen in the essays collected in Juliann Fleenor's important collection, *The Female Gothic* (1983).[71] Margaret Atwood's novel *Lady Oracle* (1976) offers an extraordinary fictional meditation on these issues through her depiction of Joan Foster, a writer of popular 'costume Gothics'. The so-called 'modern Gothic' of the 1960s has a fascinating place in the tradition I am tracing (see chapter 5), not least in provoking some insightful feminist criticism.

The focus in the 1990s on the distinction between 'Female' and 'Male' Gothic, and the subsequent breaking down of Moers's common-sense correlation of the plot with the gender of the writer, led to another rich body of criticism. Here I have found Anne Williams's formulation of the differing conventions employed by 'Male' and 'Female' traditions in *Art of Darkness: A Poetics of Gothic* (1995) especially useful. She argues that they differ in relation to narrative technique, assumptions about the supernatural, and plot. First, whereas the Female Gothic centralises the female point of view, and generates suspense through its limitation, the Male Gothic uses multiple points of view to generate dramatic irony. Second, whereas the Female Gothic explains the ghosts, the male formula accepts the supernatural as part of the 'reality' of its world. Third, 'the Male Gothic has a tragic plot. The female formula demands a happy ending, the conventional marriage of Western comedy.' Finally, while the Female Gothic is organised around terror provoked by an imagined threat, the Male Gothic 'specialises in horror' and focuses 'on female suffering'.[72]

Williams's formulation is highly suggestive but, as Avril Horner and Sue Zlosnik argue, while it may be appropriate for 'eighteenth-century Gothic novels by women' or the 'popular Gothic novels', it does not work for many 'Female Gothic' texts by women, including those by Daphne du Maurier, their own interest.[73] Part of the problem is that Williams bases her 'Female Gothic' formula on the work of Ann Radcliffe. If we go back beyond Radcliffe to Lee's *The Recess* as the founding text (as I do in chapter 2), we find that many of Williams's assumptions do not work: *The Recess* uses multiple points of view, is tragedy not comedy, and, it could be argued, depicts actual, rather than imagined, female suffering.

Williams's use of psychoanalysis has led to her being singled out for stringent (and unfair) criticism by Chris Baldick and Robert Mighall. They criticise what they see as a misguided tendency in 'Gothic criticism' to privilege psychoanalytic interpretations above historical ones. And they identify criticism of the Female Gothic as particularly guilty of 'the collapse of history into universal psychology':[74]

> the construction since the 1970s of the predominantly universalising category of the 'Female Gothic', as an embodiment of some invariable female 'experience' or of the archetypal 'female principle', leads straight out of history into the timeless melodrama in which (wicked) 'male Gothic' texts always express terror of the eternal '[M]other' while (good) female Gothic texts are revealed to be – as Anne Williams claims – not just 'empowering' but 'revolutionary'.[75]

While I would strongly support the call for historically aware criticism, what Baldick and Mighall miss is the politics behind such *feminist* criticism. As Jane Austen so eloquently demonstrated in *Northanger Abbey* (1818), there is a gendered value system behind the long tradition of valuing 'real history' above the fantasies of the female Gothic. Gothic-loving Catherine Morland famously remarks:

> history, real solemn history I cannot be interested in . . . I read it a little as a duty but it tells me nothing that does not either vex or weary me. The quarrels of popes, and kings, with wars and pestilences in every page; the men all so good and hardly any women at all . . . yet I often think it odd it should be so dull, for a great deal of it must be invention.[76]

Catherine's seemingly artless comments offer a proto-feminist critique, as well as destabilising the boundary between 'fiction 'and 'history'.

Indeed, the Female Gothic novel can be seen as a harbinger of feminist politics, the 'novel of feminine radical protest' in Margaret Anne Doody's phrase:

> It is in the Gothic novel that women writers could first accuse the 'real world' of falsehood and deep disorder. Or perhaps, they rather asked whether masculine control is not just another delusion in the nightmare of absurd historical reality in which we are all involved.[77]

The major peaks within the Female Gothic tradition are closely connected with the waves of the feminism: *The Recess* and some of Radcliffe's novels precede and influenced Mary Wollstonecraft's *Vindication of the Rights of Woman* (1792); the Gothic-realism of Charlotte and Emily Brontë, and the stories of Elizabeth Gaskell prefigure what we call the 'first wave' of feminism in the late nineteenth century, leading to the suffragette movement; the sudden huge popularity of the 'modern Gothics' in the early 1960s just predates the upsurge of second-wave feminism in 1968; finally, it is too early to tell precisely how but the rise of Gothic criticism and the popularity of Sarah Waters's Gothic historical novels may well relate closely to what is now being called 'Third Wave' feminism.

Nevertheless, Baldick and Mighall's comment is useful because it articulates a central conundrum at the heart of Gothic criticism over the comparative merits of psychoanalytic and historical-materialist or historicist approaches.

History, psychoanalysis and myth

Psychoanalysis and history are often seen as antithetical in the same way that history and fiction are seen as oppositional. Gothic texts with their dreamlike imagery seem to cry out for psychoanalytic analysis, yet critics have quite rightly drawn attention to the value of materialist and historical readings. Problems around this are exacerbated in relation to the Female Gothic, where psychoanalytic interpretations have been especially useful in teasing out what Gothic texts have to say about the position of women. As April Alliston comments, 'The language of the female Gothic . . . *literalises the dead metaphor of patriline naming* as an actual death that puts a dead end to all plots, masculine or feminine.'[78] Yet psychoanalytic explanation, she continues, 'leaves out the *historical specificity* of women's legal "orphanage" within patrilineage, which was being emphasised in the official discourses of the later eighteenth century'.[79] Furthermore, E. J. Clery's decision to refer to 'women's Gothic' rather than 'Female Gothic' reflects her criticism of the tendency to reduce texts to 'parables of patriarchy' in a way which obscures the successful status of women as professional writers.[80] Such issues become even more complex in relation to Gothic historical novels which demand that the reader be alert to the intricate tension between two historical periods, the writer's present and the past she is depicting. How, then, can we bring together the psychoanalytic and the historical to interpret the female Gothic historical novel?

In a broader context, this brings us up against historians' traditional distrust of psychoanalysis as a mode of historical analysis on the grounds of its ahistoricism. Discussing this resistance to psychoanalysis, Peter Gay argues that the professional historian, whether 'he' (*sic*) admits it or not, has always been 'an amateur psychologist' in that he 'operates with a theory of human nature' in order to attribute motives, discover causes and so on.[81] History and psychoanalysis are both 'sciences of memory', he suggests, but the latter 'does not merely analyse what people choose to remember, but uncovers what they have been compelled to distort, or forget'.[82] The psychoanalytic historian, he suggests, 'may attend to the metaphors that color cultural discourse . . . Beyond that he may analyse society's reverberating and revealing silences.'[83] While there are problems with Gay's positioning of both disciplines as 'sciences of memory', his analysis is suggestive. Equally useful is Kathleen Woodward's argument that 'Psychoanalysis gives us both a theory and a method for an archaeology of the past.'[84]

Gendering Gay's arguments, Sally Alexander draws attention to the preoccupations shared by psychoanalysis and feminist history:

The first wish of feminist history – to fill the gaps and silences of written history, to uncover new meanings for femininity and women, to propel sexuality to the forefront of the political mind – shares some of the intentions and scope of psychoanalysis . . . what is central to both feminism and psychoanalysis is the discovery of a subjective history through image, symbol and language.[85]

Instead of excluding the unconscious from historical analysis, she calls (like Gay) for a history which includes an awareness of 'repetition, fantasy, and the resistances which constitute psychic life'.[86] More recently, the work of Lyndall Roper and Diane Purkiss on witches, and Alex Owen on women and spiritualism,[87] have all shown how psychoanalysis can be used to elucidate issues around gender, power and the unconscious which may prove recalcitrant to other methods. Their emphasis on silences, memory, repetition, and fantasy, as well as their attention to the subjective meanings of metaphor, image and symbol, chimes with the motifs and conventions of the Gothic, and suggests ways in which we can use psychoanalytic and historical approaches to read Gothic historical fictions.

It is above all, the work of Luce Irigaray which I have found useful in this study. Freud, of course, used Greek myth, specifically the myth of Oedipus, to symbolise what he saw as universal patterns of human development. Yet, as Irigaray points out, 'Contrary to what people say, myths are neither univocal nor timeless.'[88] Furthermore, she suggests:

The theories of Marx and Freud are not adequate, because they remain bound to a patriarchal mythology which hardly ever questions itself as such. Patriarchy, like the phallocracy that goes with it, are in part myths which, because they don't stand back to question themselves, take themselves to be the only order possible.[89]

Such unquestioning acceptance explains why 'patriarchy is mistaken for the only History possible', instead of being merely, perhaps, 'a necessary stage in history'.[90] Myth, Irigaray argues, should be thought of as 'one of the principal expressions of what orders society at any given time'.[91] Thus, rather than being antithetical to history, it offers an alternative way of thinking: 'For myth is not a story independent of History, but rather expresses History in colourful accounts that illustrate the major trends of an era . . . History as expressed in myth is more closely related to female, matrilineal traditions.'[92] Irigaray's work allows us to shift the theoretical lens away from Freud's Oedipal myth and consider other ways in which mythic structures – such as the story of Clytemnestra, murdered by her son – can offer us a metahistorical theorisation of women's exclusion from history.

If we read myth, not as expressing universal trends, but as symbolic of specific but possibly long-term historical trends then what unifies the period from around 1780 to the beginning of the twenty-first century is the persistence of the form of society we have come to call, for want of a better word, 'patriarchy'.[93] As Juliann Fleenor put it in 1983, 'The thread of continuity established in all Gothics is that they all represent an androcentric world.'[94] Although the forms of this shift, what persists throughout this period is a set of societal-cultural structures which subordinate women to men, which confine women to the private, domestic world of childbearing and rearing (whether or not they have children) and deprive them of property rights (often through primogeniture), while men dominate the public sphere. There is, however, a second thread of continuity through this period and that is women's questioning of and rebellion against such structures. Women writers look to history to understand their place within such structures and their contingent differences and similarities. Sophia Lee, for instance, looks back to the Elizabethan period as a time when female power was more visible in the high profiles of two very different queens, and yet women were also less powerful in many ways, more at risk from forced marriage and exclusion from their rightful inheritances. More recently writers have looked back to the Victorian period, similarly identified with a female monarch, to understand the ways in which the structures of that era have defined us.

Like Irigaray, Anne Williams questions Freud's privileging of the myth of Oedipus. She turns instead to the myth of Psyche and Cupid as an interpretive key to the Female Gothic, arguing that Ann Radcliffe's 'romance conventions, which generate the Female Gothic, embody the myth of Psyche'.[95] She also explores the use of the folktale of Bluebeard, a story which is a key intertext for Female Gothic fictions from *Jane Eyre* (1847) to Angela Carter's *The Bloody Chamber* (1979), and which she suggests can be seen as expressing the ways in which the patriarchal family is integral to the 'nightmare' of history. The contents of Bluebeard's forbidden chamber, she argues, symbolise 'patriarchy's secret, founding "truth" about the female: women as mortal, expendable matter/*mater*'.[96] Emily in Radcliffe's *Mysteries of Udolpho*, Williams argues, is both Psyche and Bluebeard's wife, confronting 'the heart of patriarchal darkness'[97] and re-emerging into light and happiness.

This is not the unhistoricised approach that Baldick and Mighall suggest. Drawing attention to the affinities between the story of Henry VIII and his six wives and Walpole's *Otranto*, Williams suggests that Henry 'was simply a public version of Bluebeard, working within the system'.[98] She goes on to argue, in post-structuralist terms, that:

> Since 'history' is a form of narrative, certain episodes of it may seem to invite the categories we use to talk about literature, including 'Gothic' and 'tragedy'. To some extent the use of these terms is metaphorical: a form of 'seeing as', or using literary categories to frame or order the chaos of perception that in fact constitutes 'history'. If the history of Tudor England has a Gothic flavour, however, it is not a 'Gothic novel' but a 'Gothic drama'.[99]

While Williams's approach seems to me extraordinarily suggestive, her account of the Female Gothic is based on the assumption that Radcliffe's novels supply the urtext for the genre. As I have already argued, Sophia Lee's *The Recess* offers a rather different model, one that is both more historicised and more pessimistic about the possibility of a happy ending for women within history. To theorise this I am going to turn, not to the myth of Cupid and Psyche, but to the far darker myth of Clytemnestra as symbolic of the repressed maternal which, Irigaray argues, underlies Western culture. Clytemnestra, Irigaray reminds us, killed her husband Agamemnon, because he sacrificed their daughter Iphigenia, in order to go to the Trojan War. In revenge their son, Orestes, killed Clytemnestra. 'Orestes kills his mother', Irigaray argues, 'because the rule of the God-

Father and his appropriation of the archaic powers of mother-earth require it.'[100] Thus the murder of Clytemnestra symbolises the fact that 'the whole of our western culture is based upon the murder of the mother.'[101] As I will argue, an Irigarayan psychoanalytic approach to Gothic historical fiction can uncover what has been repressed within history – the maternal and matrilineal genealogies - and expose the ways in which our own contemporary fears and desires shape the narratives we impose upon history.

2

The Murder of the Mother: Sophia Lee's The Recess *(1783–5)*

ᔐ

What is now becoming apparent in the most everyday things and in the whole of our society and our culture is that, at a primal level, they function on the basis of a matricide . . . The murder of the mother results, then in the non-punishment of the son, the burial of the madness of women – and the burial of women in madness – and the advent of the image of the virgin goddess, born of the father and obedient to his law in forsaking the mother.

Luce Irigaray, 'The bodily encounter with the mother'[1]

'What would history be if seen through the eyes of women?' asks Gerda Lerner.[2] The answer given in Sophia Lee's extraordinary novel, *The Recess; or, A Tale of Other Times* (1783–5), is that it would be a nightmare cycle of violence, madness and death, culminating in the erasure of the maternal line. *The Recess* retells the history of the Elizabethan and early Jacobean periods from the point of view of the imagined twin daughters of Mary Queen of Scots, Matilda and Ellinor, two marginalised and illegitimate figures who are ultimately, as one of them puts it, 'all an illusion'.[3] Concealed in the eponymous 'recess' to protect them from Elizabeth I, they are, to borrow Sheila Rowbotham's apposite phrase, 'hidden from history'. Presented as letter-narratives written by the two sisters in the first person, one embedded within the other, *The Recess* thus offers a multiply subjective view of history which throws into question our assumptions about the supposed objectivity of main-stream historical accounts. This is not about valorising women as victims but rather a political analysis of the realities of their situation within history. The novel offers a radical reinterpretation of history from a female perspective which both dramatises what Luce Irigaray calls 'the forgetting of female ancestries'[4] and, by its very existence, re-establishes the matrilineal within the narrative of history.

Given the lack of symbolisation of the feminine in Western culture, the fact that it is premised on what she calls 'the murder of the mother',[5] Irigaray argues that the central question which should exercise us is: 'what of the imaginary and symbolic relationship with the mother, with the woman–mother?'[6] Lee's novel addresses pre-cisely this question and shows how the maternal line is repeatedly erased in the dynastic struggles of the sixteenth and early seventeenth centuries, an erasure figured at its most extreme in the execution of the twins' mother, Mary Queen of Scots. A period of British history which is unusually rich in powerful female figures, it was also well known to Lee's readers through the standard histories of the day. Lee's achievement in writing what Margaret Anne Doody describes as 'the first fully developed English Gothic novel', and also 'one of the first recognisable historical novels',[7] is to develop a mode of writing which can combine a symbolic or mythic level with 'real' (documented) history. Thus she can both offer a critique of patriarchal systems of representation and symbolise the matricidal nature of Western society.

Hugely popular in its day, *The Recess* was also influential in estab-lishing a model with which other writers had to negotiate, either to follow or deviate from, and thus in developing generic conventions. Anne H. Stevens quotes a 1787 review which refers to *The Recess* as 'the parent of the modern historic novels'[8] – a genealogy which has, of course, been lost in the focus on Walter Scott. Lee develops two key symbolic motifs – the 'recess' (both womb and tomb, prison and refuge), and the 'murder of the mother' – which become central to the Female Gothic. Both motifs are reworked in sub-sequent texts in a kind of tradition which can be traced through to the twenty-first century. These motifs might appear to invite an ahistorical psychoanalytical interpretation but through its setting in a carefully chosen and detailed historical period Lee's novel always keeps the specificity of history in view. Read through Irigaray's work, Lee's use of a symbolic level can be recognised as a complex and proto-feminist theorisation of women's relationship with history. Reading Ann Radcliffe's work as a direct response to Lee's novel, as I do below, places them both in a matrilineal literary genealogy which reaches back to Madame de La Fayette's *The Princess of Clèves* (1678). Acknowledging this shifts the way in which we think of both the Female Gothic and the historical novel.

'One of the most complex novels of the eighteenth century' in the words of Jayne Elizabeth Lewis,[9] *The Recess* has nevertheless been oddly neglected until very recently. It is only in the last decades that work by, for instance, April Alliston (who made *The Recess* available in a scholarly edition), Jayne Elizabeth Lewis, E. J. Clery, Heather Lobban-Viravong, Megan Lynn Isaac, Anne H. Stevens and Richard Maxwell[10] has made it possible to appreciate the full complexity of Lee's work. The central place of *The Recess* in the development of the historical and Gothic novels, and its significance to the wider writing of history during the period, are still emerging.

As a summary of the intricate plot demonstrates, Lee's twin heroines exist in the interstices of established written history, their imagined lives touching the 'real' world of known facts at key points. The offspring of Mary Queen of Scots' secret marriage to the Duke of Norfolk (contracted when she believed her husband Bothwell dead), Matilda and Ellinor are hidden by their foster-mother, Mrs Marlow, in the 'recess'. A series of underground chambers, this was once part of a convent and rebuilt to conceal priests during the Reformation. Herself illegitimate, Mrs Marlow has retreated from the world after inadvertently marrying her brother. Brought up in hiding until Mrs Marlow reveals their origins and then dies, the sisters enter the dangerous world of Elizabeth's I's court when Matilda falls in love with, and then secretly marries, the Earl of Leicester, the Queen's favourite. As potential heirs to the throne, their identities are kept secret to protect them from Elizabeth's jealousy, both political and sexual. When Leicester's part in the Babington plot is discovered, he and the pregnant Matilda flee first to the recess and then to France, leaving Ellinor to face the wrath of the Queen. Elizabeth discovers the secret of the twins' birth from documents carried by Ellinor. Imprisoned once again in the recess,

Ellinor is forced to sign a forged document denying that Mary is their mother. Following the execution of Mary and Leicester's murder, Matilda flees to the West Indies. There she and her daughter Mary are imprisoned for eight years in Jamaica.

In the meantime, Ellinor, who is in love with Elizabeth's other favourite, the Earl of Essex, is forced by Elizabeth to marry Lord Arlington. When her husband dies, Ellinor fakes her own death and has herself buried in effigy to escape imprisonment as a madwoman. Dressed as a youth, she follows Essex to Ireland where he has gone allegedly to subdue the Irish but, in fact, to further his own plan to marry Ellinor and put her on the throne. The rebel Earl of Tyrone falls in love with Ellinor but she escapes and, dressed as a youth and accompanied by Lady Southampton, is shipwrecked on the coast of Scotland and held prisoner again. Finally returning to England, she visits Essex in prison before his execution for treason, and afterwards descends into madness. When Matilda and her daughter return to England, they retreat with Ellinor to the country where Ellinor dies in front of a portrait of Essex. Matilda brings up her daughter Mary in the seclusion of Richmond hoping to marry her to Prince Henry, eldest son of Matilda's half-brother, now James I, so that Mary may through marriage obtain her royal rights. But Henry dies and Matilda is suspected of poisoning him. Granted an audience with James I, Matilda shows him the testimonials that prove her birth, but he has Matilda and her daughter imprisoned by his favourite, Robert Carr (Earl of Somerset). Mary has, unknown to Matilda, fallen in love with Somerset, and is fatally poisoned by his wife, Frances Howard. Matilda retires to France where she is taken ill and succoured by the daughter of the ambassador to England, Adelaide Marie de Montmorenci. It is to Adelaide that Matilda addresses the narrative-letter which, with numerous other embedded narratives, makes up the novel.

What such a summary does not convey is the ways in which the subjective and constructed nature of historical representation is foregrounded by Lee through her engagement with narrative at two levels. Firstly, the novel engages with and rewrites a host of other texts, including earlier novels and the major histories of Lee's period by David Hume, William Robertson and Oliver Goldsmith. Secondly, Lee deploys conflicting first-person narrative voices within the novel itself. The main body of the novel is Matilda's letter-narrative, but embedded within this is Ellinor's narrative, whose opening sentence addresses it to Matilda as 'you! much loved, but little trusted, dear sister of my heart' (155). Ellinor's narrative explicitly contradicts Matilda's account of events. Furthermore, embedded narratives, mainly by women – Mrs Marlow, Lady Pembroke, Lady Arundel, Rose Cecil, Matilda's daughter, Mary – but also by two key male characters, the Earls of Leicester and Essex, repeatedly destabilise the reader's sense of the reliability of historical narratives by undermining previous accounts. This complex play with subjective voice and form suggests an understanding of a fluid interrelationship between history and fiction which predates twentieth-century postmodern theories of history as narrative. Given that the majority of these letters are from one woman to another, the novel also privileges the dialogue and bonds between women. 'Constructed almost solely round female relationships', as Megan Lynn Isaac has argued, *The Recess* is one of the first novels 'to present and critique the problems and potential of female community within the English patriarchal society'.[11] Left out of mainstream historical accounts, such female narratives have to be re-imagined but, since women and their experience, fears and desires are not 'proper history', this can only be done through fiction – and Gothic historical fiction at that.

While *The Recess* appeared in accounts of the early development of the Gothic it has, thanks to the Lukácsian emphasis on Scott, barely featured at all in the critical material on historical fiction until the recent work of Richard Maxwell and Anne H. Stevens. One of the reasons for this has been a critical obsession with the question of whether this hybrid novel is *really* a 'Gothic' or a 'historical novel'. As Stevens has shown, this confusion is partly because the genre was still in the process of splitting into the 'Gothic', defined by the inclusion of terror and the supernatural, and the 'historical novel', characterised by depictions of historical settings and personages.[12] David Punter, for instance, concludes that *The Recess* is 'not a Gothic but a historical novel . . . in so far as such a line can be drawn'. [13] While *The Recess* uses the language and imagery of the supernatural to figure the marginal status of its two heroines, it does not include any actual supernatural elements, but it does include historical settings and personages. In this sense, therefore, it looks more like a 'historical novel'.

If *The Recess* is considered as a historical rather than a Gothic novel, however, we come up against vexed debates around historical accuracy. On these questions Lee has tended to score badly. There is a general sense that, to be taken seriously, historical novels should not 'falsify' history by altering the details of known events or people. J. M. S. Tompkins was particularly scathing about what she saw as Lee's historical inaccuracy:

> when, in short, the headmistress of a well-known girls' school could publish a novel in which the Armada preceded the execution of the Queen of Scots, and escape censure, then we may conclude that 'historical novel' and 'romance' spell the same sort of entertainment.[14]

In this period, since 'the historic sense was too little developed', she argues, 'Private loves and vengeances replace political motives.'[15] Tompkins's comments are echoed several decades later by David H. Richter:

> *The Recess* carries the burden of a romantic version of history in one obvious sense – history is turned into a romance, or even a soap-opera – but it is also a parodic version, *avant de la lettre*, of Hegel's idea of the World-Historical Individual whose will shapes the world. In *The Recess*, it is desire that reshapes the world. According to Lee . . . history is one hundred per cent personal.[16]

For both Richter and Tompkins, the inclusion of the personal ('desire') marks a text out as 'romance' rather than history. While Hayden White's work suggests that all history can be 'emplotted' as either Romance, Comedy, Tragedy or Satire, each of which correlates with a specific ideology, [17] as I have noted, he does not address the gendering of these genres, and more specifically the association of romance with the feminine. He defines 'Romance' as 'a drama of self-identification symbolised by the hero's [*sic*] transcendence of a world of experience, his victory over it and his final liberation from it'.[18] By contrast, to emplot history as 'romance', both Tompkins and Richter suggest, is actively to distort it by feminising it.

Part of the problem here is a historical (and gendered) shift in meaning, from 'Romance', meaning a quest narrative, to 'romance', meaning a love story. Originally referring to the medieval romantic epic with a male hero, the term increasingly came to mean a love story centered on a female heroine and, in the twentieth century, became even more narrowly associated with popular romantic fiction (including the costume Gothic discussed in chapter 5) and a female readership. Romance, Juliet Mitchell argues, 'has shifted from being the poetic utterance of a free aspiring subject to being an opiate of a trapped sexual subject'.[19] Furthermore, 'romance' is regarded as a debased form, partly because of its association with a female readership.

As Anne Stevens points out, during Lee's period the terms 'romance' and 'novel' were used interchangeably in subtitles.[20] Clara Reeve's *The Progress of Romance* (1785) suggests an attempt to separate the two genres:

> The word *Novel* in all languages signifies something new . . . The Romance is an heroic fable, which treats of fabulous persons and things. – The Novel is a picture of real life and manners, and of the times in which it is written. The Romance in lofty and elevated language, describes what never happened nor is likely to happen.[21]

The 'novel' is associated with what is 'new', contemporary and 'real', the 'romance' with what is fantastic, imaginary and, not the past exactly, but 'what never happened'. In addition to a shift from 'Romance' to 'romance', then, there is a shift in the genre which is considered most appropriate for depicting the past, from 'Romance' to 'Novel'.[22]

In her more positive reading of *The Recess*, Jane Spencer concurs that Lee 'interprets history as a series of love entanglements', but argues that Lee reinstates women into history precisely by 'turning history into romance'.[23] She sees this as part of Lee's assertion that 'the "truth" of history is a lie, based on denying women their rightful place.'[24] The real truth is that 'the form of romance allowed to women – that is, romantic love – is an illusion standing in the way of women's access to the romance of mother–daughter reconciliation and female power.'[25] Spencer's reading is a valuable one but amid this quagmire of shifting (and gendered) generic definitions it is no wonder that critics have had difficulty categorizing *The Recess*. Rather than focusing on Lee's emplotment of history as 'romance' or 'Romance', I want to suggest that she develops the Gothic as a mode of history which can 'interpret' the 'forgetting of female ancestries'. In White's terms, it's worth noting that *The Recess* is not a 'Romance' at all but a 'Tragedy', involving the 'fall of the protagonist' and what we can see as a politically radical '*revelation* of the nature of the forces opposing [wo]man'.[26] In the next two sections, therefore, I want to look firstly at Lee's engagement with her literary predecessors, and secondly at her use of mainstream histories by Hume, Robertson and Goldsmith. Finally, I will offer a detailed reading of *The Recess* through the work of Irigaray.

The Recess *as fiction: texts and intertexts*

Lee's representation of the events of history is structured by a self-conscious engagement with fiction. *The Recess* reworks themes and motifs from several earlier novels, notably Madame de La Fayette's *La Princesse de Clèves* (1678), Prévost's *Le Philosophe anglois ou Histoire de Monsieur Cleveland . . .*(1731–9), Walpole's *The Castle of Otranto* (1764), and Clara Reeve's *The Old English Baron* (1777). These inspire the plot and motifs which make up what we might see as the symbolic level of Lee's text, but she uses them to structure a representation of the historical period she is writing about which closely follows the historians of her day. Her representation of history, then, is a literary one which foregrounds the textual and subjective nature of historiography.

What Richard Maxwell calls Lee's 'free imitation of and commentary upon' Prévost's *Cleveland*,[27] was recognised at the time. Her sister, Harriet Lee, called *The Recess*, 'The first English romance that blended interesting fiction with historical events and characters, embellishing both by picturesque description', noting that '"Cleveland", written, as I believe, by the Abbé Prévót [*sic*], had precedence of all.'[28] As Maxwell, shows, Prévost's story of the imagined illegitimate son of Oliver Cromwell, brought up in a cave by his mother, and then interacting with historical characters of the period, is an obvious precursor. Reworking this novel situates Lee at the beginning of what Maxwell calls the 'pretender in sanctuary' tradition of historical fiction, of which *Waverley* is a later example.[29] On the one hand, the pretender figure can be read, Maxwell argues, as 'a metaphor embodying, even justifying, history-fiction combinations'.[30] On the other hand, the ghost-like status of the pretender allows the historical novel, which emerges with the decline of the absolute monarch, to function as 'an instrument for investigating the phantomlike aura that persists even in the most substantial modern states'.[31] If the nation-state is a kind of phantom state and the pretender is, as Maxwell argues in Lukácsian terms, 'the most equivocal and ghostly of all possible world-historical individuals'[32] where does this leave women who, when married, were legally defined under the concept of *coverture* as 'civilly dead'?

In *The Recess* Lee takes the pretender motif from *Cleveland* and genders it, using it to symbolise women's 'illegitimate' position within a patriarchal society which denies women their rightful (maternal) inheritance. The most 'ghostly' figures of all, she shows, are those female 'pretenders' who are 'seen without being known . . . all an illusion' (157). To symbolise this, she deploys the ghostly language and imagery of the emerging Gothic novel, re-using elements from *Otranto* and *The Old English Baron*. Like the pretender novels, these texts are also concerned with the disruption of lines of inheritance. But while *Cleveland* and the other pretender novels centralise an illegitimate or otherwise doubtful figure (Perkin Warbeck, for instance), the focus of Gothic novels is on the usurpation of a *rightful* line of inheritance. They culminate in the restoration of property to the proper line of inheritance. In *Otranto*, where Theodore is finally recognised as the rightful heir to the castle usurped by Manfred, Walpole, Punter argues, evolved 'a primitive symbolic structure in which to represent uncertainties about the past', within which 'the supernatural itself becomes a symbol of our own past rising against us.'[33] Past wrongs must be righted if order and balance are to be reinstated. The spectral helmet which crushes Manfred's son in *Otranto* fulfils the ancient prophecy which warns that Manfred is not the 'real owner' of the castle,[34] and sets in motion a plot of restoration.

Otranto's plot of usurpation in a haunted castle is rewritten in Reeve's *The Old English Baron* in ways which made it more available to Lee. If Walpole's depiction of history is largely a 'general sense of past-ness',[35] then Reeve's innovation is to shift his plot to a particular moment in British history, a move which makes possible the detailed historical setting of Lee's novel. History is still a background rather than 'a shaping force'[36] but it is more specific. Whereas Walpole's sense of the 'Gothic' past is of a superstitious 'dark age'[37] which haunts and destablises the present, Reeve looks to the past for a model of potential stability. *The Old English Baron*, James Watt noted, 'recovers the past so as . . . to confirm the legitimacy of its hero, in the process restoring a benign and "natural" hierarchy'.[38] Nevertheless, both novels focus on the *male* line, disrupted by a usurper who has to be removed for order to be restored. Both culminate in the restoration of a lost male heir to his rightful position and property, and his marriage to the woman he loves (although Walpole's 'happy' ending is complicated by Theodore's choice of Isabella as a wife with whom he can indulge his melancholy over the loss of Matilda).

What of the place of women in these novels? While Walpole includes what was to become the typical Gothic motif of the persecuted woman in flight from a forced marriage through a haunted castle, his female characters are peripheral to the central confrontation between usurper and rightful male heir. The same is true of *The Old English Baron*, where Emma plays no part in the action other than as a symbolic means of 'ingraft[ing]'[39] the lost heir, Edmund, into Sir Philip Harclay's family. She functions, that is, as an object of exchange between men, cementing political and familial bonds.

Lee's radical move is to use this Gothic plot to explore the disinheritance of women within history. *The Recess* is, in Kate Ferguson Ellis's apt phrase, 'Otranto feminised'.[40] The female characters who play bit-parts in Walpole's and Reeve's novels are moved to centre-stage, and the focus is on the matrilineal and the impossibility, rather than mere disruption, of female inheritance and thus of status as full subjects. By combining a detailed historical background with (imagined) heroines who have a claim to the throne of England itself, Lee foregrounds women's ongoing historical vulnerability as objects of exchange within dynastic struggles.

The seeds of the motif of the lost/murdered mother, developed by Lee, can be seen in Reeve's treatment of Edmund's mother, Lady Lovel. Said to have gone mad and died after the death of her husband, she is seen on the night of her supposed death by a servant who is afterwards persuaded that he saw her ghost.[41] In fact, the funeral is fictitious and the pregnant Lady Lovel has left the house to avoid having to marry her husband's murderer. Having given birth in a field, she is drowned, leaving Edmund to be brought up by two peasants. Edmund's legitimacy is confirmed by supernatural means as the doors of the castle fly open of their own accord to receive him. Played out off-stage in Reeve's novel, the motif of the lost or murdered mother who can neither protect her child nor attest his/her legitimacy is centralised by Lee. 'She lives, but not for you' (11, 12), Mrs Marlow tells the twins before she reveals the identity of their mother. This powerlessness is repeated when the imprisoned Matilda is unable to protect her daughter.

By reworking the convention of the discovered manuscript used by Walpole and Reeve, Lee foregrounds the textual nature of our access to the past. Focalising the novel through her protagonists' consciousnesses allows her to present conflicting interpretations of events which throw into question the reliability of historical documents. The mysteriously acquired manuscript which is the text of the novel is 'authenticate[d]' only by its 'simplicity', although Lee admits to altering the language since 'the obsolete stile of the author would be frequently unintelligible' (5). She also reworks the convention, introduced by Reeve, of including gaps in the text where the manuscript is allegedly illegible, obliterated, or defaced: 'The depredations of time have left chasms in the story, which sometimes only heightens the pathos. An inviolable respect for truth would not permit me to attempt connecting these, even where they appeared faulty' (5). Such gaps not only symbolise the 'chasms' in recorded history but also dramatise Ellinor's descent into madness through the literal fragmentation of the narrative.

While Walpole's and Reeve's characters are cardboard cut-outs moved around flimsy stage sets, Lee turned to a much earlier historical novel to introduce psychological realism. As Alliston has shown,[42] *The Recess* closely resembles Madame de La Fayette's *The Princess of Clèves* (1678), often referred to as the first 'psychological novel'.

Both use Mary Queen of Scots as a central figure. Even earlier than Prévost, La Fayette meshes together fictitious and real characters and events, but she does so to explore the parts played by women in history. Set in the glittering, cultured court of Henri II in sixteenth-century France when Mary was queen-dauphine, the novel plays out the imaginary love story of the married Madame de Clèves against a background of political intrigues. For women novelists, the attraction of this historical period is not only that it includes two regnant queens – Mary Queen of Scots and Elizabeth I – whose lives have been well documented, but also that, partly because of this, desire (*pace* Richter) *does* 'reshape the world'. In the French court, with a king who 'loved the company of women',[43] and where his mistress Diane de Poiters and his wife Catherine de Médicis are ambitious schemers, both marriage and love affairs have political significance. As La Fayette writes,

> Ambition and gallantry were the soul of the court and consumed alike the energies of both men and women. There were so many intrigues, so many different cliques, and the women were so involved in them, that love was often mixed with politics and politics with love.[44]

Love and politics, desire and history, are not, then, as antithetical as Richter assumes in his denigrating of *The Recess* as 'romance', but potentially interwoven.

Under the reign of a female monarch, indeed, the discourse of romantic love could be manipulated for political means, and it seems to be partly that which Lee is suggesting in her comment that 'the reign of Elizabeth was that of romance' (5). Elizabeth I encouraged a cult of courtly writing (as in Spenser's *The Faerie Queene*) which used the tradition of chivalry within the (male) romance to construct her as an idealised love object. The artificiality of this discourse was commented on by David Hume, who quotes a particularly fulsome letter to the Queen from Sir Walter Raleigh as an example of the way in which Elizabeth's courtiers 'feigned love and desire towards her', adding sardonically, 'It is to be remarked that this nymph, Venus, goddess, angel, was then about sixty.'[45] Clearly, there are complex assumptions about gender, age and beauty at work in

Hume's distaste for pre-Enlightenment conventions. Lee, however, follows La Fayette in exploring the psychological predicament of women negotiating the tortuous intricacies of court politics, and the tension between their status as objects of exchange within dynastic struggles and their existence as desiring subjects.

A kind of amateur oral historian herself, La Fayette's queen-dauphine tells the stories of her mother (Mary of Guise), her aunt (Anne Boleyn) and her cousin (Elizabeth I) in the novel, offering these matrilineal genealogies as a warning to other women. 'They say I am like my mother,' she comments, in a resonantly tragic aside, 'but I fear that I shall resemble her only in her ill-fated lot.'[46] This mother–daughter doubling becomes a central motif in Lee's novel: 'have I', bemoans Matilda who closely resembles Mary Queen of Scots, 'then inherited my mother's fate with her features?' (55). Later in an embedded narrative inspired by a portrait of Elizabeth I, the queen-dauphine tells the story of the 'romance'[47] between Elizabeth's parents, Henry VIII and Anne Boleyn. In her version, (male) desire is the motivating factor for historical process, as Henry breaks with the Catholic Church to marry Anne, but then, becoming jealous, has Anne executed. As the queen-dauphine concludes: 'Later, he had several more wives, whom he discarded or had murdered, among them Catherine Howard.'[48] In this proto-Gothic narrative, Henry VIII is a Bluebeard figure disposing of wives with gay abandon.

Lee, then, combines the historical Gothic plots of Walpole and Reeve with La Fayette's focus on female history and psychological motivation. Using first-person narratives allows Lee to deepen her exploration of the place of desire in history and its relation to dynastic inheritance. The 'literariness' of Lee's novel, its intertextual use of fictional texts, is a crucial part of its dialogue with and use of 'real' history. While we tend to think of the recognition that both history and fiction are narrative constructs as a very recent understanding, born of postmodernism, the dividing line between the two modes at this point had not yet crystallised. As an examination of Lee's use of historical sources will show, Lee's complex meshing of what we have come to see as two separate genres – history and fiction – cannot simply be dismissed as the result of a lack of understanding of what history *should* be.

The Recess *as history: 'rival queens'*

Although it is plotted through the emergent Gothic conventions, Lee's representation of the past in *The Recess*, as she states in the 'Advertisment', 'agree[s] in the outline with history' (5). That is, although she changes some details for narrative purposes (the date of the Armada and details of Leicester's first marriage), for the most part she follows fairly closely the accounts in David Hume's multi-volume *History of England* (1759–62), William Robertson's *History of Scotland* (1759) and Oliver Goldsmith's *History of England* (1771).[49] Hume himself, as Stevens reminds us, famously called his 'the historical age' and these works were part of the new interest in the past and ways of understanding it.[50] During the period 1776–1832, however, as James Chandler has argued, the evidence for this 'new historical outlook' is to be found not in works of historiography (although important works like Catherine Macaulay's *History of England* (1763–83) were published) but in 'historically self-conscious works of journalism, criticism, poetry, drama, and, *above all, fiction*'.[51] Fiction was particularly important for women writers because (notwithstanding the example of Catherine Macaulay) it offered them a more hospitable arena for their talents than mainstream historiography.

This is not to say that women were not encouraged to *read* history. In 'Of the study of history' (1741) Hume himself recommended the study of history as 'an occupation, of all others, the best suited both to [women's] sex and education'.[52] Women, he suggested, might learn from it, '*That* Love is not the only passion, which governs the male-world, but is often overcome by avarice, ambition, vanity, and a thousand other passions.'[53] (Lee's *The Recess* might be said to offer a perfect illustration of this point.) However, Hume starts from the supposition that women have an 'aversion to matter of fact' which leads them to prefer novels, romances and 'secret history[ies]' which, he argues, do not contain 'that truth, which is the basis of history'.[54] His insistence on the educational importance of history, particularly that of 'their own country', for all 'persons of whatever sex or condition',[55] might have had especial appeal for Lee who, with her sisters, ran a girls' school in Bath. On the other hand what Hume terms his 'raillery against the ladies'[56] must have been rather irritating. Not only Austen's *Northanger Abbey* but her juvenile *The History of England*, written by 'a partial, prejudiced and ignorant Historian' whose principal reason for writing is to 'prove the innocence' of Mary Queen of Scots ,[57] suggests that Lee's gendered revision of Hume's *History* in *The Recess* articulated a more widespread female dissatisfaction with 'real solomn history'.

Hume, Robertson and Goldsmith were all concerned to write history in a lively narrative style which would engage the reader's interest. Indeed, as Stevens points out, parts of Robertson's *History*, such as the killing of Rizzio, read like passages from a Gothic novel, employing clichéd generic markers and language which has supernatural connotations.[58] Both Hume and Robertson aim at an objective and even magisterial impartiality, while Goldsmith is more obviously partisan. All three focus on character and motivation, and Robertson emphasizes the importance of the personal:

> In judging the conduct of Princes, we are apt to ascribe too much to political motives, and too little to the passions which they feel in common with the rest of mankind. In order to account for Elizabeth's . . . conduct towards Mary, we must not always consider her as a Queen, we must sometimes regard her merely as a woman.[59]

This sentiment is echoed in Lee's Advertisement: 'too often the best and worst actions of princes proceed from partialities and prejudices, which live in their hearts, and are buried with them' (5). Her emphasis on personal motivation, then, is not at odds with the historiography of the time.

However, Lee's novel both replicates and throws into question the sexual stereotyping in the accounts of Hume and Robertson where 'mere' women, even if queens, are presented as more driven by personal motivations than men. Both historians construct their accounts of what they repeatedly call the 'rivalry' of Elizabeth I and Mary Queen of Scots in terms of personal motivations, such as sexual jealousy, as much as politics. From the moment Mary assumed the title of Queen of England, Goldsmith writes, 'a determined personal enmity began to prevail between the rival queens.'[60] While political interests initiated the rupture between Elizabeth and Mary, according to Robertson, 'rivalship of another kind contributed to widen the breach, and female jealousy increased the violence of their political hatred.'[61] History is depicted here in gendered terms as a narrative of personal female rivalry. While stereotyped, this does at least move women and the personal to centre-stage in a way that makes this period of history particularly available to the female novelist. While Lee follows these histories in her depiction of Elizabeth, she also shows men such as Leicester, Essex, Tyrone and Sidney as driven by personal desire: almost every male character falls in love with one of the heroines. This counters the assumption that only women are driven by the personal. At the same time, Lee's deployment of two conflicting narratives allows for an alternative interpretation: that such love is feigned for political ends, motivated by the heroines' status as potential heirs to England's throne. Lee's novel thus draws attention to the gendering of historical interpretation.

Moreover, Lee's changes to recorded history are not the result of ignorance or of a lack of proper respect for historical fact. The most important indication of this is what looks like Lee's 'invention' of the twin daughters of Mary Queen of Scots. This must almost certainly have been inspired by the fact that Mary appears to have miscarried twins while imprisoned in Lochleven in 1567. Mary's pregnancy at this time is well documented, although there has been much debate over exact details. Robertson includes as an appendix a letter from Sir Nicholas Throkmorton to Queen Elizabeth, dated 18 July 1567, describing his negotiations with Mary. Throkmorton writes:

> I have also persuaded her to conform herself to renounce Bothell [*sic*] for her husband, and to be contented to suffer a divorce to pass betwixt them; she hath sent me word that she will in no ways consent unto that, but rather die; grounding herself upon this reason, taking herself to be seven weeks gone with child, by renouncing Bothell, she should acknowledge herself to be with child of a bastard, and to have forfeited her honour, which she will not do to die for it.[62]

The issue of legitimacy – the Queen's understandable refusal to bastardise her child – is taken up by Lee in important ways, and I will return to this point. By 24 July Mary had suffered a miscarriage, and it was during the illness following this that she was induced to sign the abdication papers.[63] The fact that she miscarried twins – '*deux enfants*' - was later recorded by her French secretary, Claude Nau, who joined her service in 1575 and published his *Memorials* in 1578.[64] Antonia Fraser suggests that conception occurred the previous April, when Bothwell abducted the Queen and probably raped her at his castle in Dunbar. Uncertainty over her possible pregnancy could have hastened their wedding. If the pregnancy was of three months' duration, Fraser suggests, the recognition of twins would have been possible.[65]

This documenting of the miscarriage of twins is too much of a coincidence for Lee not to have known of it. The key issue here, however, is not the accuracy of the documentary evidence but the use Lee made of it for her fiction. On the one hand what looks the most purely fictional element of the novel, its counter-historical element, actually takes off from historically documented fact: the Queen of Scots was at one point pregnant, potentially with twins. On the other hand, the alternative history Lee weaves from this fact is so blatantly untrue as to encourage the reader to look for an alternative, possibly symbolic reading.

This question of the twins' legitimacy is central to the themes and form of this hybrid novel. Matilda and Ellinor are, Stevens suggests,

> both legitimate and illegitimate, born within marriage, but a secret and bigamous one [since Mary discovers after marrying Norfolk that Bothwell is still alive], just as they are both fictitious and historical, invented characters who interact with the major historical figures of the day.[66]

Thus Lee's 'illegitimate history' 'subtly questions the authority of historiography, suggesting that reading a novel may be a superior means to understand the past'.[67] Lee's novel, Stevens suggests, is 'both legitimate (because it is dealing with major public events and claiming to provide the "real truth" behind them) and illegitimate (because a popular and debased form, the sentimental novel)'.[68]

The power of writing to legitimise identity within history is figured by the testimonials of their lineage that Matilda and Ellinor repeatedly struggle to preserve. Discovering Ellinor's, Elizabeth tears them into 'atoms, she never thought small enough' (171), while James VI/I retains Matilda's. Lacking written evidence of their identity, the twins are ghost-like traces haunting the edges of mainstream written history. Their own letter-narratives attempt to substitute for these testimonials but, addressed to women, they form a circular feedback loop which remains outside mainstream history. Ellinor's narrative itself disintegrates into fragments which mimic the 'chasms' Lee tells us are left by 'the depredations of time' (5).

Moreover, the 'voluntary confession' (178) denying her birthright which Ellinor is forced into signing indicates how easily written documents (such as the famous casket letters used to incriminate Mary Stuart in the murder of her husband) can be forged. Ellinor signs it because she is confronted by yet another written document, 'an order for the execution of the Queen of Scots, signed, dated, authentic, complete in every form' (179). Repeating Elizabeth's earlier action, Ellinor tears the document into 'a thousand atoms' (179) but cannot halt the execution. It is Ellinor's forged confession which James VI/I later uses as his pretext for imprisoning Matilda and her daughter. Lacking pen and paper, Matilda is then reduced to sewing together fragments torn from books to form a message asking for help. These fragments or 'atoms' symbolise Matilda's final attempt to reconstruct the identity which is denied to her and her daughter. Her attempt, that is, to write herself out of the recess and into 'legitimacy' and history. The documents historians depend upon as evidence, Lee reminds us, can be copied, forged, fragmentary or duplicitous, and their power to assert the 'truth' depends on who wields them and the pattern into which such fragments are 'stitched'.

These issues also connect to questions Hume, Robertson and Goldsmith raise around the 'legitimacy' of female rulers. 'Illegitimate' has two connected meanings: (1) 'not authorized by law, improper' and (2) 'not recognized as lawful offspring, bastard' (*OED*). Elizabeth may or may not have been legally a 'bastard', but as a female monarch she was always at risk of being seen as 'improper'. Doubts over her legitimacy, as Hume notes, were at the root of her insecurity on the throne and made Mary, the next heir and supported by the power of France, 'a formidable rival'.[69]

What Hume depicts as Elizabeth's 'jealousy against the Queen of Scots' can be read as a defence against Mary's potentially more 'plausible' claim to the throne.[70] But in one sense neither woman is a 'legitimate' or 'plausible' monarch because of their gender. Thus Lee's emphasis on the illegitimacy of Matilda and Ellinor reflects the ambiguous position of Elizabeth as well as that of Mary (as the initial letters of their names suggest). Like Matilda and Ellinor, Elizabeth is the daughter of a murdered mother, Anne Boleyn. Even worse, Elizabeth's mother was killed by her father, Henry VIII, who then declared Elizabeth illegitimate. Thus Elizabeth is haunted by the spectre of illegitimacy which destabilises her claim to the throne. In addition, Lee's heroines' names recall two earlier Queens of England: the Empress Matilda (or Maud), only legitimate child of Henry I, who conducted an unsuccessful war to claim her inheritance, and her daughter-in-law Eleanor of Aquitaine, consort of Henry II and one of the most powerful women in Europe, who spent much of her later years imprisoned. The former is invoked by Ellinor when she fakes her own death and is 'boldly conveyed like the Empress Maud through the midst of my enemies' in a coffin (218). The history of female rulers, Lee suggests, has been chequered indeed.

The narrative of rival Queens constructed by Hume and Robertson is also a debate over who is the 'proper' woman. For Hume, Mary was 'a woman of great accomplishments both of body and mind, natural as well as acquired; but unfortunate in her life, and during one period very unhappy in her conduct'.[71] 'She seemed', Hume suggests, 'only to partake of so much of the male virtues as to render her estimable, without relinquishing those soft graces which compose the proper ornament of her sex.'[72] Robertson echoes this: 'Formed with the qualities we love, not the talents that we admire, she was an agreeable woman rather than an illustrious queen.'[73] In contrast, Elizabeth is represented by Hume as having an 'ambitious and masculine character', being conceited, hypocritical, vain, and mean, and (quoting Bess of Hardwick), 'not made like other women'. [74] Hume's concluding comments are telling: 'We may find it difficult to reconcile our fancy to her as a wife or mistress; but her qualities as a sovereign, though with some considerable exceptions, are the object of indisputed applause and approbation.'[75] If Elizabeth is the more successful Queen, Mary, despite her possible status as adulteress and accessory to the murder of her husband, is the more 'proper' woman.

In her depiction of the two Queens as opposing types, Lee follows the accepted 'outline' of history. Her Elizabeth is also a vain, jealous woman 'with a heart more full of policy than feeling' (26), making a 'barbarous, unfeminine use of power' (82). In contrast, Mary is defined by loss – of love and power. Her portrait shows 'a lady in the flower of youth, drest in mourning, and seeming in every feature to be marked with sorrow; a black veil half shaded a coronet she wept over' (10). She weeps over rather than wears the crown. Seen only once in the flesh by her daughters and then at a distance through a grated window, Mary is an idealised, sentimental figure, fragile from her eighteen years of captivity, yet still matchlessly beautiful: 'Her beads and cross were her only ornaments, but her unaffected piety, and patient sufferance, mingled the Saint with the Queen'(75).

Above all, Mary seems sanctified by her maternity – at least in the eyes of her daughters for whom the unknown woman in the portrait calls forth 'a thousand melting sensations' (10) which hint at their connection, confirmed by Matilda's striking and uncanny resemblance to her. This valorisation of maternity is repeated by other characters. 'There is something so tender in the name, the idea of a mother, although unknown,' (21) says the twins' foster-mother, Mrs Marlow, recalling her separation from her own mother at birth. The maternal has a symbolic meaning beyond mere presence. While Lee's historical sources present women as inevitably rivals, *The Recess* consistently validates female relationships of all kinds, but particularly those based on maternal genealogies. Elizabeth's greatest sin is her treatment of her cousin and sister-sovereign, Mary Queen of Scots: 'What did we not think that faithless woman deserved, who thus treated her equal, her relation, her friend!' (75).

The need to take sides in this narrative of rival queens throws into relief the subjective nature of historiography in ways which Lee exploits. Historical accounts, Robertson points out, particularly in assessments of character, depend very much on where you happen to be standing. 'The picture the English draw of this great Queen [Elizabeth]', he points out, is as a monarch whose memory is 'still adored in England' despite her flaws.[76] The view from Scotland is very different:

> Whoever undertakes to write a history of Scotland finds himself obliged, frequently, to view [Elizabeth] in a very different and less amiable light . . . her craft and intrigues, effecting what the valour of her ancestors could not accomplish, reduced that kingdom to a state of dependence on England [and in her behaviour to Queen Mary] we must allow that she not only laid aside the magnanimity which became a Queen, but the feelings natural to a woman.[77]

This is the insight Lee illustrates in *The Recess*, but her concern is with the way in which gender, rather than nationality, might shape historiography.

The use of conflicting narrative points of view in *The Recess* allows Lee to expose the contingent nature of historical narratives. It also seems to ask the reader to take sides with either Matilda or Ellinor. Presented through the eyes of love, Leicester and Essex initially appear as romantic heroes. Matilda, like Miranda in *The Tempest*, falls in love with the first man she sees, the Earl of Leicester, then in his fifties and the acknowledged favourite of Queen Elizabeth. To Matilda's eyes, Leicester has 'a noble height and perfect symmetry', a complexion of 'clear and polished brown' and 'large, dark and brilliant eyes' (39). In love, Matilda, for the first time, sees her sister as a rival whose 'superior charms' make Matilda 'meanly cheat her of an opportunity of making a first impression' by sending her on an errand (41). Repeating the pattern, Ellinor falls in love with the Earl of Essex, Queen Elizabeth's other favourite, before she even sees him. Having read his letters, she has already decided he is 'born to decide my destiny' (159). When she sees him, he has the 'height and majesty of Lord Leicester united with a countenance no less perfect' (159), circumstances which should alert the reader to trouble.

The move from Matilda to Ellinor as narrator involves a radical shift of perspective. We now see Leicester through Ellinor's eyes as a callous adventurer whose 'apparent passion' (156) for Matilda is motivated by her status as potential heir to the throne. To Ellinor what is striking is, 'how diametrically opposite . . . the impressions each [sister] took of his character!' on first meeting him (155). To her, Leicester, despite his physical attractions, is cold, callous, 'tyrannic in his pursuits' (156), ambitious, proud and vain. In fact, Ellinor's view of Leicester accords with the portrait drawn by Hume. Possessing 'all those exterior qualities which are naturally alluring to the fair sex', Hume says, Leicester managed to 'blind even the penetration of Elizabeth, and conceal from her the great defects, or rather odious vices, which attended his character', namely the fact that he was 'proud, insolent, interested, ambitious; without honour, without generosity, without humanity'.[78]

Similarly, the narrative of Lady Pembroke casts doubt on Essex's love for Ellinor in the light of his plan to marry her and put her on the throne: 'I cannot agree with this fair visionary, who so easily adopts the romance of her lover,' comments Lady Pembroke (220). Reading Ellinor's narrative, Lady Pembroke adds, 'the sweet mistress of Essex had a very partial knowledge of his character or information of his actions' (256). Ellinor's knowledge is 'partial' in being both incomplete and biased. Love (or desire) is the deluding element which prevents a true assessment of character: 'Oh love! Exquisite delusion! Captivating error!'(158), as Elinor puts it, recognising what she is unable to escape. Reading Ellinor's narrative shakes Matilda's confidence in her own judgement. 'If *she* was indeed more clear sighted than myself – But why do I enter on so vain a discussion' (271), Matilda questions, but her refusal to confront the issue bodes badly for her daughter's future. The sisters replicate Elizabeth's blindness towards her favourites' shortcomings according to Hume. But they also repeat their mother's failure to judge wisely in her marriage choices: first Darnley, then Bothwell, and, in Lee's version, Norfolk. As Mrs Marlow reports, 'ambition had raised a flame in [Norfolk's] heart, he mistook for love' (27). In the third generation Matilda's daughter repeats this when she falls in love with Somerset. Thus the embedded narratives continually throw into question the interpretations we are given and repeatedly expose women deluded by male declarations of love which are motivated by ambition. The discourse of 'romance', Lee suggests, is merely a cover obscuring women's real historical position as objects of exchange within political and dynastic machinations.

The centrality of the controversial figure of Mary Queen of Scots to the development of the historical novel suggests that the position of this 'captive queen' (a phrase repeatedly used of her by Hume and Robertson) symbolises something important for women writers and readers. While she has continued to obsess the English, whose ancestors cut off her head, Mary's symbolic meaning shifts across the centuries as Jayne Lewis shows in *Mary Queen of Scots: Romance and Nation* (1998). She is less a historical figure than an enigmatic symbol capable of endless reinterpretation. For Lewis, her most enduring role is 'that of the mother in a family romance of epic proportions'.[79] Perhaps each generation gets the Mary they deserve. 'One of Mary's most important modern roles', Julian Goodare argues, is 'as a popular image in women's fantasy'.[80] Lee's choice of Norfolk (whose proposed marriage to Mary never happened) rather than Bothwell (probably the father of the miscarried twins) as a paternal figure is especially interesting. In the post-Freudian fiction of the twentieth century, such as Margaret Irwin's *The Gay Galliard* (1941) or Jean Plaidy's *The Captive Queen of Scots* (1963), Bothwell plays the role of the rough-but-sexy hero, who awakens the Queen's desire. In contrast, Norfolk seems more in accord with late eighteenth-century sentiments: he is described by Hume as 'Beneficent, affable, generous . . . prudent, moderate, obsequious', and by Robertson as 'the most powerful, and popular man in England'.[81]

In English history Mary is, of course, another failed 'pretender', as Hume's comments illustrate: 'The queen of Scots, [Elizabeth's] antagonist and rival, and *the pretender to her throne*, was a prisoner in her hands.'[82] Mary's fictive daughters and granddaughter repeat that failure. *The Recess*, like pretender novels such as Mary Shelley's *The Fortunes of Perkin Warbeck* (1830) or failed-hero novels such as Jane Porter's *The Scottish Chiefs* (1810), is another version of what I have called 'histories of the defeated'.[83] Part of their attraction for women writers lies in their capacity to unpick notions of history as progress, to show that narratives of progress tend to elide or ignore the position of women. While Hume, Robertson and Goldsmith all represent history as progressive, moving towards liberty (in Hume and Goldsmith's case), or union between Scotland and England (in Robertson's case), Lee presents women's history as a matrilineal cycle of repeated defeats. The Gothic narrative form of the text with its doublings and echoes, and its repeated returns to the womb–tomb recess, reinforces this to an almost over-determined extent that signals the need to read it on a symbolic or mythic level.

The Recess *as myth: an Irigarayan reading*

The central historical image which haunts *The Recess*, although it happens off-stage, is the beheading of Mary Queen of Scots. The news of her mother's execution, and the brutal severing of the maternal tie it symbolises, is relayed to Matilda in a letter which produces extreme emotion:

> I saw in the first lines the decided fate of the royal Mary – I seemed to behold the savage hand of Elizabeth, dipt in the blood of an anointed sister sovereign. – I felt she was my mother, my fond, my helpless mother, and my heart floated in tears which were hours working their way up to my burning eyes. The furies of Orestes surrounded me, and thundered parricide, nothing but parricide, in my ear. (117)

Here Lee invokes the myth of Clytemnestra, murdered by her son, Orestes, who is then pursued by the Furies in revenge. In this section I want to explore how the myth of Clytemnestra from the *Oresteia*, central to Irigaray's 'The bodily encounter with the mother', provides the mythic structure which underpins *The Recess*'s rereading of history.

Acknowledging that 'our imaginary still functions in accordance with the schema established through Greek mythologies and tragedies', Irigaray takes issue with Freud's description in *Totem and Taboo* of 'the murder of the father as founding the primal horde'.[84] Freud forgets, Irigaray contends, 'a more archaic murder, that of the mother'.[85] In Lacanian terms, the primacy of the phallus as the ultimate signifier in Western phallogocentric culture, Irigarary suggests, obscures an earlier connection to the mother symbolised by the umbilical cord:

[The phallus] becomes the organiser of the world of and through the man-father, in the place where the umbilical cord, the first bond with the mother, gave birth to the body of both man and woman. That took place in a primal womb, our first nourishing earth, first waters, first envelopes, where the child was *whole*, the mother *whole* through the mediation of her blood.[86]

To counter Freud's Oedipal theory, Irigaray offers a reading of the murder of Clytemnestra as a symbolic representation of the suppression of the matrilineal by a new patriarchal order. Such mythic structures symbolise psychic structures which are nevertheless historically specific. This narrative of the suppression of one order by another itself suggests a chronological movement, and the possibility that patriarchy is not, in Irigaray's words, 'the only History possible', but merely 'a necessary stage in history'.[87]

A passionate lover rather than a virgin-mother, Clytemnestra kills her husband, Irigaray reminds us, 'because he sacrificed their daughter to conflicts between men, a motive which is often forgotten by the tragedians'.[88] Iphigenia was sacrificed to the gods to ensure a wind to take Agamemnon to the Trojan War, that battle over ownership of Helen which is perhaps 'the forgotten prototype for war between men'.[89] Orestes, encouraged by his sister Electra, kills his mother in revenge because 'the rule of the God-Father and his appropriation of the archaic powers of mother-earth require it.'[90] Both Orestes and Electra go mad, a madness represented by the Furies (the Eumenides or Erinyes) who haunt Orestes, 'like the ghosts of his mother'.[91] It is Apollo, 'lover of men rather than women',[92] and his sister, Athena, the goddess born not of woman but from the head of her father, Zeus, who save Orestes from the Furies. Orestes thus represents and establishes 'the new patriarchal order', an order where 'regulation Athenas' in the 'pay of men in power' 'bury beneath their sanctuary women in struggle so that they will no longer disturb the new order of the home, the order of the polis, now the only order'.[93] As Irigaray summarises it:

The murder of the mother results, then, in the non-punishment of the son, the burial of the madness of women – and the burial of women in madness – and the advent of the image of the virgin goddess, born of the father and obedient to his law in forsaking the mother.[94]

For Irigaray, this myth powerfully represents the 'matricide' which is at the heart of our culture; that is, the erasure and denial of the maternal creative function and the desire for the mother's body which is 'forbidden by the law of the father'.[95]

This mythic representation of the 'murder of the mother' maps onto *The Recess* in fascinatingly suggestive ways. If Mary, identified with sexual passion, and possibly adulterously implicated in the murder of her husband Darnley, plays the part of Clytemnestra in this psychic drama then Lee's version of Elizabeth, 'Virgin Queen' and daughter of the wife-murdering Henry VIII, can be identified with Athena. She is, in Irigaray's words, the 'image of the virgin goddess, born of the father and obedient to his law in forsaking the mother'.[96] Elizabeth's manipulation of male desire through the discourses of courtly love fits too with Irigaray's description of such 'regulation Athenas' as 'extra-ordinarily seductive . . . but [not] in fact interested in making love'.[97] The madness of Ellinor, as her name suggests, echoes that of Electra. The 'unpunished son' here might at first glance seem to be James VI/I, the man 'who could tamely submit to the murder of his mother' (214) in Matilda's words, and who then locks up his half-sister and niece.

Initially, however, Matilda identifies herself with the parricidal Orestes. Believing that her sudden flight from England led to the discovery of the Babington plot, she feels complicit in her mother's murder: 'Perhaps even at the moment she laid that beauteous head . . . on the block, every agony of death was doubled, by the knowledge her daughter brought her there' (118). Yet just a page later Matilda reads Lady Arundel's account of Elizabeth's discovery of the testimonials to their birth carried by Ellinor and decides Ellinor was to blame: 'Lovely, ill-fated sister, it was you then who accelerated our hapless mother's death!' (120). In contrast, Ellinor's own narrative emphasises her sense of betrayal as Matilda and Leicester leave her to face Elizabeth's wrath: 'Betrayed, delivered up by Lord Leicester, – neglected, forgotten by my sister' (171). Forced to sign the documents denying her own birthright, Ellinor is sent spiralling into madness by what she sees as her part in her mother's murder:

'It was surely', she writes, 'at this tremendous crisis in my life, my fermented blood first adopted and cherished those exuberances of passion' (178). It is the sight of Fotheringay Castle, place of her mother's execution, which tips her into the 'total insanity' (263) from which she never recovers. Lee's narrative suggests both sisters are what Irigaray calls 'accomplices in the murder of the mother'.[98] In putting their romantic love for men – Leicester and Essex – before their love for each other, or their mother, they remain, in Irigaray's words, 'objects to be used and exchanged between men, rival objects on the market'.[99] Their failure to support each other repeats Elizabeth's failure to support the 'sister sovereign' whose blood stains her hands.

The title symbol of the novel, the recess itself, is an almost over-determined figure of the maternal body, as both womb and tomb, which is open to several layers of closely connected interpretation. When the twins first come to consciousness in the recess, 'whatever was necessary for subsistence or improvement' is supplied, 'as it seemed by some invisible hand' (7). This can be read as an image of what Irigaray calls 'a primal womb, our first nourishing earth, first waters, first envelopes, where the child was *whole*, the mother *whole* through the mediation of her blood'.[100] Their existence is centred on a symbiotic union with their supposed mother: '*She* was our world' (8). Yet already the twins differ in their attitudes, Matilda seeing the recess as a 'hallowed circle'(9) protecting them from the outside world, while Ellinor sees it as a prison presided over by a giant or magician who will one day devour them. The doubling of the twins allows Lee to dramatise ambivalence towards the maternal body. This already-ambivalent wholeness is fractured further by the discovery that Mrs Marlow is not their mother, and that their mother 'lives, but not for you' (12). By using the recess as a symbolic representation of the maternal, Lee is able both to depict ambiva-lence and deflect it from the historical figure of Mary Stuart herself, or indeed from Mrs Marlow, who is in many ways the twins' 'real' mother. This double loss of the maternal bond, echoed in their simultaneous expulsion from the recess, signals the fact that in a patriarchal culture their mother is always already dead to them.

The single scene where Matilda and Ellinor see their mother, from a distance through a grated window, emphasises this already fractured maternal bond. The description of Mary Stuart with 'her charming arms thrown round the necks of two maids, without whose assistance she could not move' (75), as Alliston has noted (344), reworks the account of the Queen being supported to her execution by two attendants given by Hume, Robertson and Goldsmith. It would in any case be a reader unusually ignorant of history who did not know that Mary Stuart was/is to be executed. This vignette is the verbal equivalent of Roland Barthes's famous commentary on the photograph of a murderer awaiting execution in *Camera Lucida*: 'He is dead and he is going to die . . .'[101] Similarly for the reader of *The Recess*, the Mary Stuart depicted by Lee 'is dead and is going to die'. History here is 'separation', in Barthes's phrase, specifically a separation from the maternal which has always already taken place.[102]

The reference to the decapitation of Mary Stuart in Matilda's narrative – 'the moment she laid that beauteous head . . . on the block' – could be read as a Freudian image of castration, a destruction of the powerful phallic mother. But read in Irigarayan terms, it suggests perhaps even more powerfully the tearing apart of the mother's body, the severing of the umbilical cord which links mother and child, which Irigaray posits as the founding moment of patriarchy. The failure to represent the mother and the maternal bond in Western culture, Irigaray argues, leaves women always in 'danger of going back to the primal womb, seeking refuge in any open body, constantly living and nesting in the bodies of other women'.[103] The mother herself, 'as an inverted effect of the blind consumption of the mother', becomes 'a devouring monster'.[104] The twins' repeated returns to the recess – sometimes as refuge, sometimes as prison – signify the danger of 'going back to the primal womb'. But the twins also repeatedly form relationships with other women – Mrs Marlow, the sisters Lady Pembroke and Lady Arundel, Rose Cecil, their aunt Lady Mortimer, Lady Southampton, the slave woman Anana, Adelaide Montmorenci – which suggest the seeking of refuge in other women as surrogate mothers.

The recess also symbolises the twins' existence 'outside' or 'hidden from' history, both as illegitimate women and as invented characters. Here it connects very closely to the Gothic language of the text. Lee deploys Gothic language and imagery – live burial or entombment, spectrality, death-in-life – extensively to symbolise the erasure of the feminine within history. The recess is repeatedly described as not just as a 'prison' but as a 'tomb'. Its entrance is hidden by 'a high raised tomb' topped with four gigantic statues of armoured men, two headless (37), which recall *Otranto*. 'Can I who have voluntarily passed my youth in a tomb', asks Mrs Marlow, 'dread to bury my dust in it?' (15), thus making the womb-like recess also (literally) the tomb of the twins' 'mother'. Both Matilda and Ellinor are repeatedly represented as 'buried' or 'entombed': brought up in the recess they are 'entombed alive, in such a narrow boundary' (10); after Leicester's death Matilda finds herself 'entombed alive' (125) in a convent cell which, with its 'obscure casement of painted glass' (124), recalls the recess; after her marriage to Lord Arlington, Ellinor retreats to 'that Abbey destined alike to entomb me in playful childhood, and in blasted youth' (207); confined to the Scottish castle by order of James VI, she reflects 'Ah, how easy it is to be unknown! To be entombed alive' (239); finally, Matilda and Mary are 'entombed' (306) in prison on the orders of James VI/I.

This image of live entombment figures what Irigaray calls women's state of '*dereliction*' or abandonment within a patriarchal system which fails to offer women adequate symbolisation,[105] Women are, Irigaray says, 'nowhere, touching everything, but never in touch with each other, lost in the air like ghosts'.[106] Matilda and Ellinor repeatedly fail to 'be in touch with each other', and experience themselves as 'like ghosts'. Facing the prospect of being 'buried in a cloister', Matilda describes herself as 'more like a spectre than myself' (60). In the most powerfully dramatic and Gothic moment in the novel, Ellinor, driven mad by the death of her mother and Essex, confronts Elizabeth I in a scene which vividly recalls both *Macbeth* and *Hamlet*. Believing Ellinor dead, the queen mistakes her for a ghost, imploring Lady Pembroke to 'save me from this ghastly spectre!' (266). Even Lady Pembroke who knows that this 'beauteous phantom' is Ellinor, comments that 'surely never mortal looked so like an inhabitant of another world' (266). The spectral here is, like the sisters themselves, a visual illusion 'seen without being known' (157). Tellingly, Ellinor's identification with the murder of her mother emphasises the forced separation of women: "'I do not mind how you have me murdered, but let me be buried in Fotheringay; and be sure I have *women* to attend me . . . you know the reason'" (267). The 'reason', of course, being the fact noted by Hume, Robertson and Goldsmith, that Mary Stuart was initially denied female attendants at her execution. In a moment which recalls Lady Macbeth's ravings, Ellinor then catches Elizabeth's hand and 'survey[s] it with inexpressible horror. "Oh, you have dipt mine in blood!" exclaimed she, "a mother's blood! I am all contaminated – it runs cold to my very heart."' (267). Ellinor's exclamation thus repeats Matilda's earlier image of 'the savage hand of Elizabeth, dipt in the blood of an anointed sister sovereign' (117).

It is this ghostly intimation of her own guilt which tips Elizabeth into a kind of madness where she 'complains of an ideal [ghostly] visitor' (268), and then into death. Hume, Robertson and Goldsmith all have Elizabeth die of melancholy and depression caused by the discovery that the Countess of Nottingham had kept from her a ring sent by Essex before his execution. This story, Hume comments, is one which 'has long been rejected by historians as romantic, but which late discoveries seem to have confirmed'.[107] Lee retains the 'romantic' notion of haunting guilt but rewrites the cause. While the murders of Essex, Mary Stuart and, indeed, that of Matilda whom Ellinor believes dead at this point, are merged here, it is Elizabeth's guilt over the murder of her 'sister sovereign' which is embodied most forcefully in the spectral figure of Ellinor. In its eschewing of the actual supernatural, then, the novel is a 'realistic' portrayal of history, but it is nevertheless shot through with the language of the supernatural, deployed to figure women's illegitimate and powerless status within history, as well as their failure to support each other when they do have power.

Unhappy endings: 'the forgetting of female ancestries'

Matilda's letter-narrative opens with an image of 'the grave on the verge of which I hover' (7). It ends with her bequest of a casket to Adelaide Montmorenci, and her request that Adelaide visit the 'nameless grave' (326) where Matilda's 'ashes' will have been interred (326). This image of the grave, nameless so that 'no trace of [Matilda's] ever having existing would remain' (7), is another version of the recess. Circular in its form, Matilda's narrative provides the 'memorial' which Adelaide's 'partial affection demands' (7). Only female affection, it seems, can ensure that some trace remains as a memorial to Matilda's existence. The survival of the discovered manuscript, which Lee in the guise of editor presents to us, however, suggests the power of that affection, since Adelaide (or her descendants) have preserved it, however partial it may be (in either sense of the word) and passed it on to us.

We have come to associate the Female Gothic, as in the formulae Anne Williams describes (see the Introduction), with a happy ending, almost always a marriage ending. This is, of course, both a Comedy and a Romance ending and it structures two of Lee's other key intertexts, Shakespeare's *As You Like It* (another tale of usurpation which provides her epigraph) and *The Tempest*. Like the restoration of the rightful heir in *Otranto* and *The Old English Baron*, it suggests the reinstatement of a proper order. *The Recess* does not give us this ending. Indeed, Lee's novel more closely resembles a Jacobean tragedy where all the main characters end up dead. In White's terms, as I have argued, *The Recess* does not emplot history as Romance at all, but as Tragedy, a structure which White would link with radical ideologies, among which we might place feminism.

In many ways *The Recess* is closer to Willams's Male Gothic formula. In addition to the tragic plot of the Male Gothic, it uses multiple points of view. While it does not include the 'real' supernatural of the Male Gothic, it uses the language of the spectral rather than the explained supernatural of the Female Gothic. And Lee's evocation of the dead and dying bodies of women that litter history – the decapitated Mary Queen of Scots, mad Ellinor, Mary dying of poison – aligns her more with the horror of the Male Gothic, with its 'focus on female suffering' than with the Female Gothic's organisation around 'an imagined threat and the process by which that threat is dispelled'.[108] We need therefore a different set of paradigms to theorise *The Recess*. We also need to be aware that Ann Radcliffe's version of what we have come to call the 'Female Gothic' is not the originary plot but a secondary reworking of an earlier version.

In contrast with the reinstatement of the legitimate male heir in *Otranto* and *The Old English Baron*, matrilineal inheritance in *The Recess* is repeatedly blocked and erased. April Alliston has pointed out that *The Recess* is unusual in extending the story of its heroine into motherhood, so that it includes the history of Matilda's daughter, Mary.[109] Lee's novel is perhaps even more unusual in that it also includes the daughter's death, before that of the mother. The deaths of Mary Queen of Scots, Ellinor and Mary leave Matilda the sole survivor of a female line which will end with her. For women, Lee's novel suggests, history has been cycles of violence and loss, repeated through the generations. The fictional Matilda, Ellinor and Mary remain illegitimate, spectral and for ever excluded from history. The novel thus symbolises what Irigaray calls the 'forgetting of female ancestries' within history.

More than that, however, the novel is also an act of what Irigaray calls the 'interpretation' of that forgetting. Lee uses fiction to trace and re-imagine forgotten female genealogies, to piece together the fragments of documentary evidence about historical women's lives (inspired by that suggestively elusive record that Mary Stuart miscarried twins) and to reinsert them into 'History'. While she grounds this in a historical narrative which 'agree[s] in the outline with history' (5), she uses myth to provide a symbolic theorisation (or 'interpretation') of the ways in which the matrilineal has been excluded from 'History'. Written history, Lee's novel suggests, offers evidence (albeit fragmentary and incomplete) of the victimisation, suppression and erasure of women in the past, but precisely because of that erasure of the female, traditional history can never, *pace* Hume, tell the whole truth. Perhaps only fiction, with its ability to use the figurative language of the Gothic, can do that.

Coda: the daughter's story: Ann Radcliffe and the Female Gothic

There is a certain irony in the fact that the 'forgetting of female ancestries' has been replicated in literary criticism. Critics have 'forgotten' Lee's status as a 'parent' of both the Gothic and historical novels. Instead, Walpole and Scott have been positioned as the 'fathers' (the 'sole creators' in Irigaray's terms) of these genres.

Moreover, the creation of the Female Gothic has been attributed almost solely to 'Mother Radcliffe' (in Keats's telling phrase). Both Ellen Moers and Anne Williams based their influential accounts on the Radcliffean model. E. J Clery's more historicised study gives more attention to Lee but her understandable lauding of Radcliffe as 'a great original' has the effect of yet again erasing Lee's achievement.[110] Yet Radcliffe's own status as an originator has also been downgraded: 'Considering that she virtually invented a whole new class of fiction, "the supernatural romance" or what we today call the Gothic novel,' Rictor Norton writes, 'it is astonishing that she has been relegated to merely a footnote in literary history.'[111] More recently in the face of controversy around the term 'Female Gothic', Robert Miles has re-asserted Radcliffe as its 'proper matrix', and argued that if the term still works as a critical category, it is 'because of Radcliffe's aesthetic legacy'.[112] This positioning of Radcliffe alone as the 'mother' of the Female Gothic makes it easier to ignore women's contribution to the development of the historical novel.

In this section I am going to discuss Radcliffe, not as the 'mother' of a new genre, but as a 'daughter' of Sophia Lee, and as a writer who is closely concerned with the symbolic representation of matrilineal genealogies. Radcliffe's second novel, *A Sicilian Romance* (1790), is a systematic and self-conscious reworking of *The Recess*. As Clery and Alison Millbank have acknowledged, its plot closely resembles that of *The Recess*. Clery goes as far as suggesting that this resemblance, and that of Radcliffe's first novel *The Castles of Athlin and Dunbayne* (1789) to *The Old English Baron*, suggest that Radcliffe was paying 'conscious homage to her two most illustrious forebears in the terror mode'.[113] I would go further than this and argue that the plots of Radcliffe's first five novels all engage with *The Recess* in some way. *The Romance of the Forest* (1791), for instance, establishes its heroine, Adeline, in a ruined abbey where, in a chamber which closely resembles Lee's recess, she discovers the ancient manuscript which reveals her parentage. It is as if Radcliffe were almost obsessively attempting to rewrite the tragic ending of Lee's novel (or of 'History'), and recover her heroines' lost lineages, usually through recovering the 'murdered mother'. But the ways in which Radcliffe rewrites Lee's novel have important implications for our understanding of the development of the Gothic novel, the historical novel, and (despite Lukács's dismissal of the 'second and third-rate writers (Radcliffe etc.)' before Scott[114]) what has come to be seen as the main literary tradition of the novel in the nineteenth century.

Each of Radcliffe's mature novels opens with an indication of its setting in a precise historical moment. *A Sicilian Romance* is set in the same period as *The Recess*, 'Towards the close of the sixteenth century'.[115] *The Romance of the Forest* is set in the seventeenth century, while *The Mysteries of Udolpho* (1794) opens in 1584. In *The Italian* (1797) the action opens in 1758 although the framing narrative is set in 1764 (the year of Radcliffe's birth). *Gaston de Blondeville* (1826), a very different kind of novel, is set in the reign of Henry III. Despite this, Radcliffe's historical backgrounds have been regarded as little more than window dressing. She is, Frederick Garber remarks, 'cheerfully anachronistic' in her characterisation of her heroines.[116] Her sense of history was 'superficial, perfunctory and unreliable', Norton concedes, 'certainly not the kind of know-ledge one would expect from someone who had been taught by Sophia Lee, the creator of the historical novel'.[117] In fact, he con-cludes that there is no real evidence for the common assumption that Radcliffe attended Lee's school in Bath.[118] Like other critics, Norton suggests that Radcliffe compensated for her lack of the classical education by including references to English and Italian literature, particularly Shakespeare, but also a few contemporaneous women writers (mainly feminists).[119] The use of Shakespeare, of course, connects Radcliffe with Lee, particularly her deployment of *Hamlet* and *The Tempest* in *A Sicilian Romance*.

While Lee provides a detailed and in the main accurate historical background, Radcliffe moves from her specific opening date into a far more vaguely delineated historical setting. As their titles sug-gest, Radcliffe frames her novels as 'Romance': *A Sicilian Romance*; *The Romance of the Forest*; *The Mysteries of Udolpho: A Romance*; *The Italian;, or, The Confessional of the Black Penitants: A Romance*. Indeed, Ian Duncan has importantly argued that Radcliffe was responsible for 'a powerful revaluation' of the term romance at this point, 'replenishing romance with sensibility, emphatically reclaimed for a feminine identity', a gendering which was not reversed until the work of Scott.[120]

In teasing out the relation between history and romance in Radcliffe's novels, the distinction made by Clara Reeve is useful: 'History represents human nature as it is in real life; alas, too often a melancholy retrospect! Romance displays only the amiable side of the picture, it shews the pleasing features, and throws a veil over the blemishes.'[121] Radcliffe's historical settings, Jane Spencer has suggested, are distancing devices used 'to create a fantasy world' where 'fantasies of power [are combined with] with expressions of fear about women's vulnerability in the real world'.[122] Spencer reads Radcliffe as a conservative writer, whose novel can be seen as 'criticising the status quo of male authority but not ultimately challenging it'.[123] In contrast, both Norton and Robert Miles emphasise Radcliffe's radical Unitarian background. She was, Norton argues, 'fully aware of the radical politics of her time and sympathized with them'.[124] Radcliffe, he writes, 'avoided overt political statement by setting most of her works outside of England and in an exotic past, but they all illustrate the Dissenting valorization of merit over station'. [125] There, is however, more to be said about Radcliffe's use of history.

It is *A Sicilian Romance*, rather than the better-known *Udolpho*, that is the ur-novel of the Female Gothic. As Robert Miles points out, the novels we now regard as Female Gothic are all in some ways 'variations' on the basic plot of *A Sicilian Romance*: 'a heroine caught between a pastoral haven and a threatening castle, sometimes in flight from a sinister patriarchal figure, sometimes in search of an absent mother, and, often, both together'.[126] While Austen's *Northanger Abbey* (1818) names *Udolpho* as an exemplary Gothic text, for instance, it must be the plot of *A Sicilian Romance* which leads Catherine to conclude that General Tilney has murdered or imprisoned his wife.

In *A Sicilian Romance,* two sisters, Julia and Emilia Mazzini, having lost their mother early, are brought up by a surrogate mother, Madame de Menon, sequestered in their father's castle in Sicily. Their father is remarried to Maria de Vellorno, a woman who (like Lee's Elizabeth I), regards the two young sisters as sexual rivals. When Julia finds a portrait of a lady with 'an air of dignified resignation' (27), which recalls that of Mary Stuart in *The Recess*, it similarly affects her. Madame de Menon reveals that it is the sisters' mother, telling the story of her own tragic marriage intertwined with that of Louisa. As in *The Recess*, it is love which precipitates Julia into a 'new world' (20), when she falls in love with Hippolytus, the friend of her brother Ferdinand (there are clear echoes of *The Tempest* here). Like Lee's Matilda, Julia finds that 'Love taught her disguise' (21), and she no longer shares every thought with her sister. Fleeing from her father's attempts to force her into marriage with the Duke de Luovo, Julia (again, like Matilda) leaves her sister to face the consequent wrath.

After repeated flights across the landscape of Sicily — including encounters with *banditti*, taking refuge in a convent, and a shipwreck (recalling both *The Recess* and *The Tempest*) — Julia finds herself in a cavern. Fleeing into its 'innermost recesses' (172), she enters on her knees 'a low and deep recess' (172), which leads through a door to a 'highly-vaulted cavern' (172), then via a dark passage to a small room. There she finds 'the pale and emaciated figure of a woman' (174), who exclaims, 'My daughter!' (174), before fainting. She is, of course, Julia's mother, Louisa Mazzini, as her 'resemblance to Emilia' confirms (174). She has been imprisoned by the Marquis in a subterranean dungeon — this 'recess of horror' (176) — located under the southern buildings of the castle of Mazzini. The Marquis has had her 'buried in effigy' (177), as Ellinor 'buried' herself in *The Recess*, so that he could remarry. Here it is the mother, rather than her daughters, who is confined to the 'recess'. In a reversal of the twins' sighting of Mary Stuart through a grating in *The Recess*, Radcliffe has Louisa recounting how on one occasion she was allowed to look through a window at her daughters walking in a wood, '[Julia] leaning on the arm of your sister' (178). Although we see through the eyes of the imprisoned mother here, both scenes illustrate the importance of the mother's gaze in constituting the identities of her daughters.

As the epigraph — 'I could a tale unfold . . .' — suggests, *A Sicilian Romance* is a feminised version of *Hamlet* where it is the 'ghost' of the mother who reveals the wrongs done to her by the father and encourages her (female) child to right them. The existence of the imprisoned marchioness provides an explanation for the allegedly 'supernatural' events in the novel: lights in the uninhabited southern buildings and 'hollow' groans from beneath. As Alison Millbank suggests, Louisa's live burial represents the Irigarayan 'murder of the mother' in Western culture. In Julia's symbolic return to the 'womb' through those endless subterranean passages, Radcliffe 'moves towards a testing out of what it might mean to acknowledge the mother, and to establish social networks built upon this Utopian project'.[127] Moreover, Julia chooses to share her mother's imprisonment, a move which Millbank sees as 'precipitating her maturation and sexual union'.[128] Millbank's persuasive reading accords with my own Irigarayan reading of *The Recess* in many ways, but I want to focus more precisely on how Radcliffe rewrites her intertext.

While Radcliffe provides, like Lee, a framing narrative which introduces a discovered manuscript, Radcliffe uses an impersonal or third-person omniscient narrative voice for the main narrative. She then, like Lee, interposes embedded first-person narratives, several of which resemble those from *The Recess*: Madame de Menon's account of her own and Louisa's intertwined early lives (28–34), which echoes that of Mrs Marlow; the Marquis's story of the murder of Henry Della Campo and the alleged 'haunting' of the castle (532–3); Cornelia's story of how she ended up in the 'obscure recesses of St Augustin'(116), which echoes both Lee's Mrs Marlow and Matilda's escape from the French convent; Julia's account of her escape from the castle of Mazzini (105–8); and Louisa Mazzini's own narrative, which reworks the stories of Matilda and Mary Stuart (175–80). With the exception of the Marquis's spurious ghost story, these narratives do not contradict each other as Lee's do. Instead, they offer back-stories which explain the mysteries of the novel or, as Miles points out, amplify its main themes, specifically 'the readiness of Sicilian fathers to sacrifice their daughters to the needs of primogeniture, to the dynastic demands of the "house"'.[129] Radcliffe is not interested in the subjective and indeterminate nature of historiography exposed by Lee's conflicting and fragmented narratives, but in the grievances of the past and the possibility of a Utopian narrative of female progress.

Compared with *The Recess*, Radcliffe's focus on one sister sometimes leaves readers wondering why she includes Emilia at all. In fact, Radcliffe reminds the reader familiar with *The Recess* of the narrative of competing sisters (and rival queens), but swerves aside from it. Ellinor's address to her 'much loved, but little trusted, dear sister of my heart' (155), for instance, is revised by Julia, who writes, 'Dear Emilia, adieu! You will always be the sister of my heart – may you never be the partner of my misfortunes' (72). By centralising a single figure Radcliffe creates what Clery calls 'the persona of the heroine as artist and as author-surrogate' which became her 'trademark'.[130] This 'heroine-as-original-genius'[131] provides a coherent female point of view which distinguishes Radcliffe's fiction from the Gothic of Walpole's *Castle of Otranto*. By centralising this female point of view, Radcliffe foregrounds the father figure of Walpole's Gothic plot as the villain and indicts him for the abuses of patriarchal power. Unlike Manfred, Mazzini is not a usurper according to standard laws of inheritance. Thus Radcliffe suggests the ways in which female powers and rights have been usurped wholesale by a legal system (primogeniture) which privileges the male. As the second sister and, indeed, the villainess Maria De Vellorno, recede into the background, the gendered confrontation between the powerful father and the daughter who resists him is thrown into relief.

Overall, Radcliffe moves Lee's plot out of what we have come to think of as the mode of the historical novel and into a more exclusively 'Gothic' mode. In addition to simplifying Lee's plot to the narrative of one sister, she also transfers it from England (although *The Recess* also encompasses Ireland, Scotland, Jamaica and France) to Sicily. Her motive for this seems to be that it allows her to portray Mazzini as having 'unlimited power of life and death in his own territories' (69, 180),[132] thus foregrounding patriarchal powers. This move shifts the novel further from the realm of the 'real' occupied by *The Recess* into the realm of the fantastic and the symbolic. Otherwise, Radcliffe includes no actual historical events or personages, and her novels offer little sense of 'history as a shaping force'.[133] Neither are her anachronistic characters the representative socio-historical types demanded by Lukács.

However, as Miles has pointed out, Radcliffe situates her novel very specifically in what was regarded during her time as 'a "Gothic cusp" . . . a transitional phase when the Gothic epoch came to an end, and the modern one began'.[134] This 'historical myth', Miles reminds us, took on new meanings for the radicals of Radcliffe's period, including Mary Wollstonecraft, who regarded 1790 as the breaking of another new dawn of egalitarian modernity over an old corrupt 'Gothic' order. Like Wollstonecraft, Radcliffe genders this understanding in her novels, where the system of primogeniture which supports the power of the old 'Gothic' male order is repeatedly attacked. As Miles notes, 'The temporal setting [of *A Sicilian Romance*] links a Gothic feudal past, with repressive, patriarchal institutions.'[135] Fathers, not only the Marquis, but also the Duke and the Abate, represent the Gothic, feudal past, while their daughters stand not so much for the present, I would suggest, but for a Utopian future.

Radcliffe's sense of this historical shift is articulated first in the framing narrative where an unnamed (and ungendered) traveller encounters the ruins of the castle of Mazzini which inspire him/her to read the manuscript recording their history in the convent library. The friar who produces this interprets the decaying ruins in moral terms as 'a singular instance of the retribution of Heaven' (1). This moral, borrowed from *The Old English Baron* – 'a striking lesson to posterity, of the over-ruling hand of Providence, and the certainty of RETRIBUTION'[136] – is repeated at the close of the manuscript. The narrator concludes:

> In reviewing this story, we perceive a singular and striking instance of moral retribution. We learn, also, that those who do only THAT WHICH IS RIGHT, endure nothing in misfortune but a trial of their virtue, and from trials well endured derive the surest claim to the protection of heaven. (199)

In contrast to *The Old English Baron*, the final image of *A Sicilian Romance* offers an ideal of harmonious female community: Louisa surrounded by her daughters and grandchildren. The ending thus ratifies the rebellion against the all-powerful father and suggests that 'heaven' is on the side of the women.

Another building, the ominously Gothic abbey of St Augustin, 'a proud monument of barbarous monkish superstition and princely magnificence' (117), is the trigger for Radcliffe's clearest articulation of historical shifts. Like the castle, the abbey stands for the institutionalised male power which, at best, offers women only the choice between marriage to a man they cannot love or immurement in a convent. The abbey, the narrator comments, calls to mind 'the memory of past ages' and their 'contrast to the modes of his own times':

> The rude manners, the boisterous passions, the daring ambition, and the gross indulgences which formerly characterized the priest, the nobleman, and the sovereign, had now begun to yield to learning – the charms of refined conversations – political intrigue and private artifices. Thus do the scenes of life vary with the predominant passions of mankind, and with the progress of civilization. The dark clouds of prejudice break away before the sun of science, and gradually dissolving, leave the brightening hemisphere to the influence of his beams. (116)

The Gothic darkness produced by male bastions of power – Church, aristocracy and monarchy – is here dispersed by the sunlight of 'civilisation' brought by historical 'progress'. And progress, Radcliffe's ending suggests, requires the release of women from the bondage they have suffered in the past.

This, then, is the major difference between Sophia Lee and Ann Radcliffe. In her novels, Radcliffe deploys a notion of history as progress which is very far removed from Lee's tragic vision of endlessly repeated cycles of violence against women. But Radcliffe is only able to sustain this vision of history as progress which will, eventually, release women from their 'imprisonment' in male institutions, by framing her mature novels as 'Romances'. In Hayden White's terms, her novels not only emplot history as Romance, but their marriage endings suggest the reconciliation he associates with Comedy (which he regards as a 'qualification' of the Romantic apprehension of the world).[137] Both Romance and Comedy, White suggests, stress 'the emergence of new forces or conditions' out of processes that appear at first glance to be changeless.[138] Radcliffe's use of a distanced but strangely dreamlike and obviously un-English past (rather than the historical accuracy of Lee's novel) helps to conceal a strong indictment of the immoral and, indeed, unchristian nature of male power, which nevertheless culminates in a reconciliatory marriage ending. This technique both encodes Radcliffe's political critique and foregrounds its symbolic nature as the 'murder of the mother' is replayed in novel after novel.

The structures of romance allow Radcliffe symbolically to enact a Utopian recovery of the murdered mother and write a happy ending to Lee's plot. In *The Recess*, Matilda dreams of relieving her mother's imprisonment: 'I would have sought her prison; I would have been the companion of it' (35). Instead, she is imprisoned herself, 'a sad inheritor of my mother's misfortune' (144). Her daughter, 'Beloved Mary – dear inheritor of misfortune' (293), is her companion in this cycle of victimisation. Mary's filial response to this imprisonment contains the seeds of Radcliffe's ending: 'Alas the order of nature is inverted, and I am obliged to become the monitor,' Mary tells her distraught mother, concluding, 'I shall never think that place a prison which contains you, nor that fate a misfortune I owe to your fondness' (306). More positively, in *A Sicilian Romance* Julia suggests that providence has 'conducted me through a labyrinth of misfortunes to this spot, for the purpose of delivering you!' (181). Radcliffe's repeated play on the word 'deliver' – Julia later declares that 'heaven can bless me with no greater good than by making me the deliverer of my mother' (182) – foregrounds the symbolic imagery of rebirth inherent in Julia's lengthy passage to the womb/tomb cave which holds her mother but also her determination to effect her mother's release.

Radcliffe's rewriting of history as romance allows the daughter to 'deliver' her mother, and offers a Utopian happy ending to which we can aspire while we recognise its symbolic meaning. If *A Sicilian Romance* feminises the plot of *Hamlet*, it also gives it a happy ending, transforming it into a version of Shakespeare's last Romance play, *The Tempest*, but one where it is the 'usurped' mother who is re-instated and reunited with her lost daughter. Louisa and Julia are rescued through the intervention of Hippolytus, and they are re-united with Ferdinand under a symbolic lighthouse, which counters the dark Gothic structures of castle, abbey and recess-cave. Women can and must make the effort to assert their maternal genealogy, Radcliffe seems to suggest here, but it will be easier for them to release themselves if they are joined in this project by the men of their own generation who have much to gain from this rebellion against the 'Gothic' forces of their elders. While Lee's heroines are trapped in a history which cannot be altered and which, as Reeve reminds us, often offers a 'melancholy retrospect', Radcliffe uses romance to look to the possibility of a different future coming out of the past.

It could be argued that Radcliffe's framing of history as romance comes at the expense of dehistoricising the specificity of women's past. Certainly, in relation to Scott, and partly as a result of his 'Introductory', she has been repeatedly positioned as unhistorical. Ian Duncan argues that what he calls 'Scott's recovery of romance for the representation of a public, national life' involves 'at once its thoroughgoing historicisation and its redefinition as masculine'.[139] Read in relation to Lee's novel, however, rather than as a sole originator of the Female Gothic or as a 'second or third- rate . . . forerunner' of Scott's 'classical historical novel',[140] Radcliffe can be seen as a 'daughter' as well as a 'mother' in a matrilineal genealogy which helps us to re-write literary history, giving due recognition to all the women writers who originate and innovate genres.

3

Be-witched and Ghosted: Elizabeth Gaskell's Gothic Historical Tales

ର

I did feel that I had something to say about it that I *must* say and you know I can tell stories better than any other way of expressing myself.

Elizabeth Gaskell, letter to Mary Green[1]

I have so longed for some little thing that had once been [my mother's] or been touched by her. I think that no one but one who has been so unfortunate as to be early motherless can enter into the craving one has after the lost mother.

Elizabeth Gaskell, letter to George Hope[2]

Fiction – 'telling stories', that childhood euphemism for 'lies' – is, as Elizabeth Gaskell understood, one way of telling the truths that cannot be expressed in other ways. From early in her writing career Gaskell understood the potential of the Gothic, as developed by Sophia Lee and Ann Radcliffe, as both a mode of history and a symbolic language of the psychological which could convey the female experience repressed in other modes of writing. However, as the novel became increasingly associated with realism in the nineteenth century, it was to the short story that Gaskell turned as a mode which offered greater freedoms. Her powerful stories use Gothic motifs and conventions – particularly the haunting figures of the lost mother and the dead or dying child – to figure repressed anxieties and desires and to symbolise and explore the psychologies of oppression. They offer a searing proto-feminist indictment of the vulnerability of women and children within structures which support and even encourage male power and violence. This analysis is, however, always very carefully located within history. Her work, like Sophia Lee's, combines the symbolic power of the Gothic with a sophisticated understanding of the gendering of historical narratives but it does this within the so-called 'minor' form of the short story. If Ann Radcliffe, as I argued, partially de-historicised the Gothic in her swerve to the Utopian, then Gaskell re-historicises it. Equally, however, she reintroduces into historical fiction the symbolic language of the Gothic Walter Scott had attempted to banish.

The range and sophistication of Gaskell's historical fiction has been obscured, partly because much of it is in the form of short fiction, and partly because of its Gothic elements. She wrote, of course, one major historical novel, *Sylvia's Lovers* (1863), which has earned her a place in some, but not all, of the traditional accounts of the historical novel.[3] But the vast bulk of her historical fiction was either short stories or novellas. Furthermore, her use of the Gothic, a mode of writing which, post-Scott, was seen as antithetical to 'real' history, has been a problem. As Patsy Stoneman remarked,

> Irritation changes to embarrassment when critics deal with Gaskell's minor works, many of which have subjects – ghosts, bandits, witches, murders, madmen, imprisonment, tortures, mutilations – which fit neither her earnest social image nor her cosy feminine one.[4]

Although Jenny Uglow's 1987 biography drew attention to Gaskell's use of Gothic conventions to 'link the cruel repression of wives and daughters to the pressure of history and the patriarchal power of the aristocracy',[5] it is only in the last decade that the publication of her *Gothic Tales* (2000), edited by Laura Kranzler, has enabled this to be fully acknowledged. Essays by Marion Shaw and Shirley Foster have also given more serious attention to her short fictions in general.[6] It is, in fact, in these short fictions that we can see most clearly Gaskell's exploration of the permeable boundaries between fact and fiction, and the depth of her thinking about history as a representation of the past.

Like that of Lee and Radcliffe, Gaskell's work is haunted by the figure of the lost mother. On the surface this seems easily accounted for by Gaskell's own circumstances: left motherless at thirteen months, she was brought up by her aunt while her father married again. Similarly the dead or dying children that recur in text after text reflect her own losses: while four daughters survived, her first daughter was stillborn, and her beloved son Willie died from scarlet fever aged nine months. The much-repeated story that she began *Mary Barton* (1848) on the suggestion of her husband to take her mind off the loss of Willie encourages a reading of her fiction as sublimated therapy. Such biographical explanations, however, only partly explain her obsession with these figures and may, in fact, help to obscure their political implications. Like Radcliffe, Gaskell was a Unitarian whose radicalism is often overlooked. Furthermore, this emphasis on the personal and on an artless, almost intuitive mode of writing obscures the self-consciousness of Gaskell's experimentation with form and her engagement with the gendering of history.

Most of Gaskell's Gothic tales are not-quite-ghost-stories which deploy the language of the supernatural but, with the notable exceptions of 'The Old Nurse's Tale' (1852) and 'The Poor Clare' (1856), include no actual supernatural. Since, as I argued in the Introduction, there has been almost no attempt to theorise the historical short story as opposed to the historical novel, Gothic novel or ghost story, it is useful to explore some of the issues involved before discussing these hybrid stories.

While the novel maps change over time, the short story tends to focus on a single moment in time. The novel, Jean Pickering argues, is about process and causation, 'gradual discovery rather than instantaneous perception', while the short story highlights an 'instant of revelation [which] is a metaphor for a whole life'.[7] If the novel is about 'evolution', she suggests (in appropriately Darwinians terms), the short story is about 'revelation.'[8] As Nadine Gordimer put it:

> Short-story writers see by the light of the flash; theirs is the art of the only thing one can be sure of – the present moment. Ideally, they have learned to do without explanation of what went before, and what happens beyond this point . . . A discrete moment of truth is aimed at – not *the* moment of truth, because the short story doesn't deal in cumulatives.[9]

Seen in this light, the short story seems by its very nature to be anti-historical and anti-rational. The novel seems the eminently natural and obvious form in which to write historical fiction since it can best express the cause and effect of change over time. The unfolding of history as a cumulative process of dialectical conflict between opposing forces, certainly as Lukács conceptualises it, appears to need the baggy length of the novel to encompass it. In this context, the historical short story looks like an anomaly, almost an impossibility. Yet Scott, as I have already noted, has been lauded as the founder of the modern short story with 'The Two Drovers' (1827) which figures dialectical and national conflict in the symbolic fight between the Scottish Robin Oig and English Harry Wakefield. Moreover, it includes a certain element of the supernatural in the (fulfilled) prophecy of Robin's foster-mother.[10]

The relationship between the supernatural and the novel, particularly the nineteenth-century realist novel, is a fraught one. The realist novel as it developed out of Scott's historical fiction in the nineteenth century explicitly defined itself against the 'unrealistic' Gothic novel, partly by eschewing the supernatural, which seeks refuge in this period in short fiction. As Scott noted, 'The supernatural [. . .] is peculiarly subject to be exhausted by coarse handling and repeated pressure. It is also of a character which is extremely difficult to sustain and of which a very small proportion may be said to be better than the whole.'[11] This explains, as Julia Briggs notes, why true ghost stories are short, although the Gothic novel often uses the explained supernatural, as Radcliffe does, to create suspense and manipulate reader expectations. Briggs suggests that the ghost story's advantage over the historical novel is that it offers 'a direct rather than vicarious encounter [with the past], occurring within a contemporary setting which increased its immediacy'.[12] However, the very appearance of a ghost sets the genre at odds with accepted definitions of the historical novel. Scott's sentiments are echoed by Gordimer: 'Fantasy in the hands of the short-story writers is so much more successful than when in the hands of novelists because it is necessary for it to hold good only for the brief illumination of the situation it dominates.'[13]

Elizabeth Bowen put it even more strongly when she commented that she felt it was 'unethical – for some reason? – to allow the supernatural into a novel'.[14] If the realist novel defines itself by its 'ethical' refusal to admit the supernatural, then the historical novel with its claims to represent what 'really' happened in the past, the 'factual' rather than the 'fictional', would seem to be under even more pressure to exclude the supernatural.

These issues may explain the 'embarrassment' Stoneman detected in critics faced by Gaskell's deployment not only of Gothic conventions but also, on occasion, of the supernatural. It may also explain the failure to recognise Gaskell's sustained engagement with history in her short fictions. If we concentrate not on what historical fiction 'ought to be' (i.e. long, 'realistic', set 'sixty years' in the past) but on what Gaskell actually does with the historical, then we can recognise the sophistication of her use of the Gothic historical tale. She uses this form both to symbolise women's exclusion from mainstream history and to formulate different kinds of historical narrative which might be more open to women's experience and female historians.

While it might be argued that the scale of the short story leads to tighter control than in the novel, the opposite seems true, in Gaskell's hands at least. The short story offers an open form which allows Gaskell to evade some of the ideologically inflected conventions of the realist novel, particularly its insistence on forms of closure which reflect moral judgements on women. Death is the appropriate ending for the 'fallen woman' in *Ruth* (1853), just as the 'happy ending' of marriage closes off Margaret Hale's possibilities in *North and South* (1854–5). The 'realism' of the realist novel, as feminist critics have repeatedly noted, is just as much a matter of ideologically driven literary conventions as the fantasy of the Gothic novel. In contrast, as Clare Hanson has noted, the short story has appealed to a range of marginalised groups, 'losers and loners, exiles, women, blacks', who are not part of the 'ruling "narrative" or epistemological/experiential framework of their society'.[15] As she argues:

> The short story is a vehicle for different kinds of knowledge, knowledge which may be in some way at odds with the 'story' of dominant culture. The formal properties of the short story – disjunction, inconclusiveness, obliquity – connect with its ideological marginality

and with the fact that the form may be used to express something suppressed/repressed in mainstream literature.[16]

The short story as a form, and particularly the ghost story, thus allows Gaskell to articulate what Carol A. Martin in an early feminist reading of her 'two major ghost stories', 'The Old Nurse's Tale' and 'The Poor Clare', calls 'her profound discontent with the position of women in a patriarchal society.'[17] Similarly, Maureen T. Reddy draws attention to the 'feminist rage' in Gaskell's short fiction, and argues that Gothic tales like 'The Grey Woman' (1861) 'gave Gaskell a means of dealing with the tension between her life as a woman and the central myths of womanhood she found in her culture, a task for which realism and, to a lesser extent, romance, were inadequate.'[18] While my reading of Gaskell's feminist analysis of women's position accords with that of Martin and Reddy, I want to focus specifically on her use of history.

Furthermore, Clare Hanson suggests that rather than being a poor relation to the novel (as the term 'minor' suggests), the short story is actually a more 'literary' form in 'its orientation towards the power words hold, or release and create, over and above their mimetic or explicatory function.'[19] In its 'connection with the unknown and with fantasy', she argues, 'the short story is a form which is close to the unconscious.'[20] More readily than the novel, it is a 'channel for the expression of repressed or unconscious desire', but because of this orientation towards desire it also 'refuses to give us a world of law and order'.[21]

This suggestive theorisation is helpful in thinking about why Gaskell turns to short fiction to tell 'stories' which are repressed by the grand narratives of the dominant culture. It allows us to read the supernatural and Gothic elements as symbolic expressions of unconscious desires and fears within history. Gaskell's Gothic tales are carefully and specifically located: 'The Poor Clare', for instance, opens with a date, 'December 12th, 1747', as does 'Lois the Witch', which begins 'In the year 1691', while the main action of 'The Grey Woman' takes place 'in '89, just when every one was full of the events taking place at Paris'.[22] As Marion Shaw puts it, 'Gaskell's fiction is everywhere obsessed by history',[23] by the ways in which the present is shaped by the past, and by the difference between 'then' and 'now'. This is not just a vague sense of 'the past' but an informed interest in the specifics of particular historical periods, whether it be the Civil War or seventeenth-century America. Moreover, Gaskell is fascinated not just by material differences – the increase in female literacy, the decline of the whaling industry, the rise of the trading middle classes – but by psychological difference, changes in the ways people think. Such shifts are much more difficult to document and to articulate, and traditional forms and language may be inadequate to the task. As Gaskell said in relation to her novel *Mary Barton*, 'There are many such whose lives are tragic poems which *cannot take formal language.*'[24] The Gothic gave Gaskell a different kind of language from that which dominates her realist novels, a language which drew on a coherent and established set of motifs or metaphors. It enabled her to develop a sophisticated proto-feminist critique of what we would now call the power structures of patriarchy and its psychological effects on women.

Writing before the development of a Freudian language of the unconscious and the fictional techniques (stream of consciousness, dream sequences, disrupted chronology) we associate with it, Gaskell refined and, above all, historicised the language and symbolism of the Female Gothic to express psychological truths. As Jill Matus has shown, Gaskell used Gothic vocabulary and Gothicised imagery in *Mary Barton* and *North and South* to convey the 'effect of very powerful feelings on psychic functioning and the haunting aftermath of intense emotional experience'.[25] Gaskell was, Matus suggests, in advance of medico-psychological discourse in her interest in the effect of shock on psychic states:'Without using the term "subconscious" or "unconscious", Gaskell is nevertheless drawing close to the idea they convey of a part of the mind that is not conscious, but is able to influence actions and behaviour.'[26]

In her Gothic tales, where she does in fact use the term 'unconscious', Gaskell developed this further. In using Gothic language, she was able to draw on what Eve Kosofsky Sedgwick has called the 'coherence of Gothic conventions',[27] where even the ostensibly casual use of a word like 'buried' or 'unspeakable' will bring with it particular associations. But Gaskell was also able, thanks to the work of Lee and Radcliffe, to exploit the gendering of these conventions. As a kind of metafiction, as I have suggested, the Gothic by its very nature draws attention to the mechanics of its conventions. Further-more, as a mode of history and a kind of metahistory, it is always already recognisably and self-consciously gendered.

Uncanny histories and female historians: 'Clopton Hall' and 'Morton Hall'

Gaskell's first piece of published prose, 'Clopton Hall', included in William Howitt's *Visits to Remarkable Places* (1840), shows the obvious influence of Radcliffe. But it also suggests a careful reading of Jane Austen's *Northanger Abbey* (1818), not just as a parody of the Gothic novel, but as a critique of male history and an exploration of what the Gothic has to offer the female historian. An account of visiting Clopton Hall near Stratford-on-Avon when she was a school-girl, it is an embryonic attempt at writing Gothic history as a way of symbolising women's experience in the past. Opening with an account of the approach to the house through the surrounding land-scape, it moves through a grass-filled court with 'broken down' walls and 'massy pillars surmounted with two grim monsters', towards a brick house of 'that deep, dead red almost approaching purple'.[28] The description recalls both the thorn-enclosed palace of *Sleeping Beauty* and the half-ruined castles of Radcliffe's novels. In a bedroom 'said to be haunted' is the portrait of Charlotte Clopton (39). The 'fearful' legend Gaskell retells is that Charlotte had died during an epidemic and been buried in haste. A few days later the tomb was opened to bury another Clopton:

> but as they descended the gloomy stairs, they saw by torchlight, Charlotte Clopton in her grave-clothes leaning against the wall; and when they looked nearer, she was indeed dead, but not before, in the agonies of despair and hunger, she had bitten a piece from her white round shoulder! Of course, she had *walked* ever since. (40)

Being buried alive by mistake is, Freud suggests, to some people 'the most uncanny thing of all'.[29] But this is, he argues, only a trans-formation of the phantasy 'of intra-uterine existence'.[30] We are back, then, to the womb-tomb of Sophia Lee's recess.

One of the major sources of the uncanny Freud identifies is, of course, repetition:'The constant recurrence of the same thing – the repetition of the same features or character traits or vicissitudes, of the same crimes, or even the same names through several consecutive generations'.[31] This uncanny recurrence is the central motif of Gaskell's piece. Wandering the corridors, the narrator finds 'a curious carved old chest': 'And when it was opened,' she writes, 'what do you think we saw? BONES! – but whether human, whether the remains of the lost bride, we did not stay to see, but ran off in partly feigned, and partly real terror' (40). The 'lost bride' comes from Samuel Rogers's poem 'Ginevra'.[32] On her wedding day Ginevra concealed herself in an old oaken chest for a prank. She was not found until fifty years later when the chest was opened:

> And lo, a skeleton,
> With here and there a pearl, an emerald-stone,
> A golden-clasp, clasping a shred of gold.
> All else had perished – save a nuptial ring,
> And a small seal, her mother's legacy,
> Engraven with a name, the name of both,
> 'Ginevra.'
> There then had she found a grave![33]

The young bride's live burial implicitly suggests the deathly consequences of marriage for women: Ginevra's mother, whose name she shares, died giving birth to her. This recurrence is tripled by a reference to 'a well called Margaret's Well, for there had a maiden of the house . . . drowned herself' (40).

The uncanny, then, is central to Gaskell's handling of female history in 'Clopton Hall'. The vault, the chest, the well and the house itself are all recurring versions of the tomb-like womb Freud associates with the uncanny. As Nickianne Moody puts it, 'The concept of the *Unheimlich* provides a fictional space which can recover the past.'[34] For Gaskell it provides a space within which the unrecorded history of women can be recovered, and a way of symbolising the 'constant recurrence' of certain elements of women's experience through the generations.

Gaskell is feeling her way in 'Clopton Hall', through a recovery of the despised Gothic, towards a very different kind of history from that associated with the great nineteenth-century historians, Thomas Babington Macaulay and Thomas Carlyle, or their much-admired Walter Scott. Despite some shifts away from political history, nineteenth-century historiography remained overwhelmingly male in conception and subject matter. As Carlyle famously wrote in *Heroes and Hero-Worship* (1841): 'Universal History, the history of what *man* has accomplished in this world, is at bottom the History of the *Great Men* who have worked here.'[35] Among his heroes he includes 'The Man of Letters'. His review of Lockhart's biography of Scott argues explicitly for the benefits of a vigorously masculinised history to an emasculated nation. Scott is an 'old fighting Borderer of prior centuries' who rescues literature in 'this sickliest of recorded ages, when British Literature lay all puking and sprawling in Werterism, Byronism, and other Sentimentalism tearful or spasmodic'.[36] Writing is equated with fighting: 'In the saddle, with the foray-spear, [Scott] would have acquitted himself as he did at the desk with his pen.'[37] In Scott's writing the 'old life of men' is resuscitated:

> Not as dead tradition, but as a palpable presence, the past stood before us. There they were, the rugged old fighting men; in their doughty simplicity and strength, with their heartiness, their healthiness, their stout self-help, in their iron basnets, leather jerkins, jack-boots, in their quaintness of manner and costume; there as they looked and lived: it was like a new-discovered continent in Literature.[38]

History here is exclusively male. Like all writers of her age, Gaskell knew Scott's work well and she learnt from him. But she learnt about *women's* history from *Northanger Abbey* and the Female Gothic fictions Scott had rejected. Nineteenth-century readers, J. R. Watson notes, would have recognised the way her fiction, as in 'The Sexton's Tale' and *Sylvia's Lovers*, redefines Carlyle's notions of heroism.[39] As Suzanne Lewis has pointed out, Gaskell's heroes are 'usually women', while her male characters manifest their heroism in ways which are gendered female: 'suffering, endurance, silence'.[40] Gaskell's Gothic historical fictions repeatedly depict women rescuing other women or children, as Amante in 'The Grey Woman' heroically rescues her mistress from her husband and is murdered for it.

Gaskell's eschewing of what Austen's Catherine Morland calls 'real solemn history', the 'quarrels of popes and kings. With wars or pestilences in every page',[41] that Carlylean history of 'Great Men', is precisely the point of 'Clopton Hall' and her later historical fictions. Gaskell's narrator, like Austen's Catherine, gets her history from literature, including Gothic novels, because in 'real history' there are 'hardly any women at all.'[42] The only title the narrator can recall from the books in Clopton Hall is that of Dryden's *All for Love, or the World Well Lost*, a retelling of the last hours of Cleopatra and Antony. Moreover, given the setting near Stratford-on-Avon, Charlotte's fate inevitably recalls Juliet's live burial.[43] Cleopatra's monument and Juliet's tomb are both versions of the uncanny recess. If the fighting man is the archetypal historical figure in Scott's fiction, the woman buried alive is the central figure in Gaskell's. Though 'stories' – fiction, poetry and drama, fairy tales, legend and anecdote – Gaskell writes a female Gothic history which can (re)-create the unrecorded history of women and symbolises their repeated repression through depicting the 'live burial' of women in the past.

'In a certain sense all men are historians,' Carlyle asserted in 'On History'.[44] Gaskell's Gothic historical fictions explore the ways in which all *women* are historians too, taking as her examples some of the most marginalised members of the sex, a schoolgirl in 'Clopton Hall', a spinster in 'Morton Hall', a servant in 'The Old Nurse's Tale', a dowager aristocrat and a disabled girl in 'My Lady Ludlow'.[45] If these are not '[Wo]men of Letters' to counter Carlyle's heroic 'Man of Letters' this is partly because Gaskell's fictions privilege oral tale-telling over written history. As the title of her collection of short stories *Round the Sofa* (1859) indicates, her historical fictions are often situated in informal domestic spaces, as tales told between women. Moreover, she privileges an emotional, often familial, connection between the female historian and her subject. In 'Clopton Hall', when Gaskell's narrator and her schoolgirl companions open the chest they find (in contrast to the laundry list found by Austen's Catherine), 'BONES!' While their 'partly feigned, and partly real terror' suggests the *frisson* Catherine seeks in her Gothic reading, the actuality of the bones, however qualified, suggests the historical reality of women's 'burial' within history.

In 'Morton Hall' (1853) Gaskell returns to and further explores the possibilities of the Gothic as a way of writing women's history. Again the story centres on a 'haunted' house and uses a tripartite structure, telling the stories of three generations of women through a first-person narrator. The tripartite structure itself loosens the form of the short story, shifting it away from the 'discrete moment of truth' Gordimer refers to. Rather than the 'past' of legend, 'Morton Hall' is located within historical period and process, as characters' lives are related to the sweep of British history. The narrator is Bridget Sidebotham, whose family have been followers of the Mortons for generations, and who writes down the history of Morton Hall because it is about to be pulled down. Bridget begins with a reference to 'real solemn history'– the repeal of the Corn Laws and the Gunpowder Plot,[46] but swiftly moves to her real interest in the women of the house. As Shirley Foster notes, the story traces women's changing roles through the centuries and 'describes the gradual shift from a hierarchical, restrictive society to one in which women are no longer constrained by subservience to male tyranny'.[47] That Bridget, like the narrator of 'Clopton Hall', turns to the Gothic as a way of writing the women's history is indicated through a reference to a Gothic novel, Jemima Luke's anti-Catholic *The Female Jesuit; or, The Spy in the Family* (1851).[48] The conventions of the Gothic, with its focus on the 'secret private history' (167), give Bridget a framework which can explain the misfortunes which have befallen her family. These 'mysterious dispensations', she writes, can be 'accounted for at once, if we were objects of the deadly hatred of such a powerful order as the Jesuits, of whom we had lived in dread ever since we had read the *Female Jesuit*' (167). Bridget is looking for a 'story' that explains the repeated oppression of women and, like Catherine Morland, finds the Gothic is the only narrative which foregrounds women's concerns. Like Austen, however, Gaskell is interrogating the usefulness of such stories if they are taken too literally.

The first section, told by the housekeeper Mrs Dawson, is the most obviously Gothic. It is the story of the Puritan Alice Carr, who comes into possession of the Hall when it is taken from the Royalist Sir John Morton and given to her father by Oliver Cromwell. After the Restoration, Sir John Morton marries Alice, this beautiful 'stern, hard woman' (169), partly because it is the easiest way to regain his property and partly because 'he fancied her [in] a man's way': 'she was a beautiful woman to be tamed' (172). Unbending in her Puritan ways which drive Sir John to hate her, Alice still loves him with 'a terrible love' (172). Finally, Sir John pretends that Alice is mad, dresses her 'in her riding things all awry' (176) and carries her off to shut her up, according to local gossip, either in London or in a convent abroad. Returning to the house after Sir John is killed at the battle of the Boyne, she curses the Mortons to 'die out of their land, and their house to be razed to the ground', while 'pedlars and huxters' live there (177).

The curse provides a Gothic framework for reading the decline of the family through the next two sections, which recount events Bridget and her sister witness themselves. In the middle section, when the family is reduced to penury, Phyllis Morton heroically dies of starvation attempting to protect her nephew, Sir John, who has gambled away his money. In the final section, three spinster sisters of the cousin who has inherited the Hall come to live there, and the narrative focuses on their conflicting attempts to educate their niece, Cordelia. Miss Morton, the eldest, who is writing a book to be entitled *The Female Chesterfield*, ties Cordelia to a chair to listen to her letters, while the youngest, Miss Annabella, has her read Gothic novels aloud. Bridget herself attempts to educate Cordelia into patient female self-sacrifice by telling her the story of Miss Phyllis's 'love and endurance' (200). The Gothic here is just one of a range of outmoded narratives which are eventually rejected. Cordelia grows up to marry the mill-owner Marmaduke Carr, a distant descendent of Alice Carr's family, and they name their baby Phyllis. Bridget sees this marriage between Carr and Morton as fulfilling Alice's prophecy, but through a move towards a happier future.

In some ways, 'Morton Hall' reads like a gendered version of Scott's depiction of history as dialectical conflict moving towards synthesis. In *Waverley* and *Ivanhoe* (1819) a marriage symbolically uniting England and Scotland or Norman and Saxon signals the birth of a new unified Britain. Similarly, Gaskell depicts two opposing forces, here Cavaliers and Puritans, fighting over property (Morton Hall). But she also uses the Gothic to depict earlier forms of marriage as a war between the sexes. The marriage of Marmaduke Carr and Cordelia Morton represents not only a reconciliation of different religions and classes, but also the possibility of a new equality between the sexes. However, Gaskell destabilises this kind of interpretation through her use of Bridget as a potentially unreliable narrator. Moreover, while she uses a similarly symbolic marriage to end *North and South*, she does not repeat this. Her later short fictions increasingly problematise marriage and eschew this kind of happy ending.

Suzanne Lewis suggests that the subject matter of 'Morton Hall' 'sits oddly' with the *Cranford*-like narrator whose 'forte is not the broad sweep of history, the decline and restoration of aristocratic fortunes, but observation of the small details of human behaviour'.[49] But this is, I think, part of Gaskell's point, in that it is in these 'small details', preserved in oral narratives told between women, that women's history is to be found. 'Morton Hall' offers a nuanced exploration of the role of women story-tellers as the recorders of female genealogy and the modes of history open to them, including the Gothic. As in *Cranford*, humour conceals serious commentary. Ethelinda, for instance, refers to those 'long chapters in the Bible which were all names' as 'geography' (193). While Bridget cannot remember the 'right word' (193), her story is a mapping of female 'genealogies' which uses the Gothic to keep women's stories in living memory. While 'Morton Hall' interrogates the pitfalls of the Gothic it also acknowledges its possibilities for women. Gaskell's subsequent stories return to the Gothic and exploit its possibilities as a mode of history in increasingly sophisticated ways.

The spectre of sexuality: 'The Poor Clare'

Gaskell's two ghost stories proper, 'The Old Nurse's Story' (1852) and 'The Poor Clare' (1856), are, not coincidentally, also the most Brontëesque. Both are matrilineal stories which use the Gothic to explore the repressed spectre of female sexuality and the yearning for the lost mother or child. 'The Old Nurse's Story', which again uses an unconventional female 'historian' to retell women's secret, private histories, is only loosely located in historical period. 'The

Poor Clare', however, is carefully shaped through its relation to recorded history. The first words of the story – 'December 12th, 1747' (49) – draw attention to the date of the written narrative, when the narrator, a lawyer, is an old man. A further date places his own part in the action from 1718 (61–2). These dates place the story in relation to the two Jacobite rebellions of 1715 and 1745, and it begins with the return of Squire Starkey and his Irish wife from exile in St Germains and Antwerp where he has been, following his part in James II's attempt to regain his throne in 1690. Starkey returns to his ancestral home in the Trough of 'Bolland' (Bowland) with his wife, her old nurse Bridget Fitzgerald and her daughter Mary, a girl of 'dazzling beauty'(51), the result of an unhappy marriage.

As with Bridget Sidebotham, it is 'the deep secrets of family history' (83) which interest the narrator and his uncle, but here it is in their capacities as lawyers. Questions of inheritance and legitimacy are as intrinsic to these as they are to the dynastic struggles of the Stuarts. The tracing of genealogy is central to the cases of disputed property inheritance on which they work and the narrator is asked to inquire into 'the existence of any descendants of the younger branch of a family [the Fitzgeralds of Kildoon] to whom some valuable estates had descended in the *female line'* (62, emphasis added). This is a story, then, which is concerned with tracing lost female genealogies and inheritance. The lost heir the narrator is seeking turns out to be the woman he is already in love with, Lucy, so he is, despite his profession as a lawyer, emotionally connected to the history he tells. Lucy is the possibly illegitimate child of Bridget Fitzgerald's daughter Mary, and a man named Gisborne, who probably deluded Mary into believing she was married to him.

The emotional core of the story is the grief felt by Bridget when Mary leaves home on bad terms with her mother. Like Demeter, Bridget travels in search of her daughter, returning looking as though she has been 'scorched in the flames of hell' (57), to live alone in the woods, shunned by the community as a witch. Left with only a little dog to remind her of her lost daughter, Bridget is devastated when it is wantonly shot by Mr Gisborne and she unknowingly curses him: '"You shall live to see the creature you love best, and who alone loves you . . . become a terror and a loathing to all"'

(59). The Gothic curse here, as in 'Morton Hall', figures the psychological consequences of trauma through the generations. The excess of Bridget's mother-love, frustrated and corrupted by Gisborne's destruction of her daughter (symbolised in the shooting of the little dog), manifests itself in spectral form. An uncanny double comes to haunt Bridget's granddaughter, Lucy. It is 'a ghastly resemblance, complete in likeness, so far as form and feature and minutest touch of dress could go, but with a loathsome demon soul looking out of the grey eyes, that were in turns mocking and voluptuous' (78).

The spectral double can only be exorcised by Bridget's transformation from witch into nun, a metamorphosis described thus by the Catholic Father Bernard: 'her former self must be buried, − yea, *buried quick*, if need be' (94, emphasis added). Metaphorical burial alive as a Poor Clare allows Bridget to redeem 'the sin of witchcraft' (91) by succouring the wounded Gisborne and starving to death in his place.

'The Poor Clare' was written while Gaskell was working on *The Life of Charlotte Brontë* (1857), and there are clear intertextual links: the spectral double in the mirror recalls *Jane Eyre* (1847), while Lucy's name and the figure of the nun recall *Villette* (1853). Conversely, the biography reads like a Gothic novel with Brontë as a motherless heroine, oppressed by a monstrously eccentric father, and buried in a Gothic landscape haunted by her dead siblings. Branwell's excesses are presented as the 'secret' of Charlotte's life, that she was forced 'to touch pitch as it were' and be 'defiled' by it.[50] Yet Gaskell knew about and, as Jenny Uglow points out, in the biography suppressed her knowledge of Brontë's love for Monsieur Heger. Uglow's account of the genesis of 'The Poor Clare' (in a tale Gaskell heard in Paris) suggests its unconscious resonances with what Gaskell felt she had to repress in the 'factual' biography: 'Uncannily [the story] seized on something hidden in the life Elizabeth was planning to write.'[51] Read in this way, the 'voluptuous' nature of Lucy's double figures the spectre of sexuality, the secret of Brontë's sexual desires, which must be 'buried quick'. Equally central to the biography, however, is Gaskell's presentation of Brontë as divided between two potentially irreconcilable identities: 'her life as Currer Bell, the author; and her life as Charlotte Brontë, the woman'.[52] Gaskell's assertion that a woman must not 'hide her gift in a napkin'[53] uses a deceptively domestic image to refute the notion that women must 'bury' their literary gifts 'alive'.

'The Poor Clare' also rewrites elements of Walter Scott's collection of historical short stories, *Chronicles of the Canongate* (1827), the frame narrative of which is written by a lawyer, Chrystal Croftangry, who records oral histories, often told to him by women. One of these, 'The Highland Widow',[54] is the story of Elspat MacTavish, who has obvious affinities with the witch-like Bridget Fitzgerald. Both women are tall and striking, even queenly, live alone in isolated cottages, are marginalised by their Jacobite sympathies and Catholicism, and both doom their descendents through misdirected mother-love. Whereas Scott depicts Elspat as animal-like in her inability to understand the historical circumstances in which she is caught, however, Gaskell allows Bridget actively to redeem herself through self-sacrifice, thus giving her some autonomy within history.

Equally importantly, Gaskell casts doubt upon the reliability of her lawyer-narrator in ways which ask us to look more carefully at male historians' attitudes, particularly in relation to the gendering of witchcraft. Her hypochondriac, even hysterical, lawyer-narrator is given his genealogical task to distract him from illness brought on by overwork. His ensuing obsession – 'Something resistless seemed to urge my thoughts on' (68) – affects his mental state. While recovering from this second illness in Harrogate he meets Lucy, and sees her demonic double himself. Far from being the rational, sceptical narrator typical of ghost stories, his own narrative bears the traces of hysteria which make it potentially unreliable. Compared with Gaskell's female narrators, it is notable that he privileges written, legal and male-authored documents and that these reveal a history of oppression of women. Among the references cited in the story are Sir Matthew Hale (a judge who presided over the trial of two women for witchcraft in 1661–2), Defoe's 'A True Relation of the Apparition of One Mrs Veal', usually considered the first ghost story, and the Salem witch trials.[55] In the face of his uncle's researches into witchcraft cases and of 'dreadful ways of compelling witches to undo their witchcraft' (83), the narrator represents enlightened attitudes, asserting that 'Bridget was rather a wild and savage woman than a malignant witch' (83). But what links together the older men in the text, despite their different religions, is that they all believe that Bridget is a witch. They differ only in the way she should be treated: the Anglican clergyman asserts: 'it's the law of the land that witches should be burnt! Ay, and of Scripture, too' (87); the narrator's Puritan uncle talks of extracting confessions; and the Catholic Father Bernard wants Bridget's witch self 'buried quick'. In the character of Bridget Gaskell uses the Gothic to open up debates around representations of one of the most iconic and troubling of the rare female figures in mainstream history, a figure she returns to explore in far greater depth in 'Lois the Witch'.

His-story as hysteria: 'Lois the Witch'

Gaskell's finest Gothic historical story, 'Lois the Witch', is a fictionalised account of the Salem witch trials, during which around 200 people were accused of witchcraft, over 150 people were imprisoned, 55 escaped by confessing themselves guilty, 19 were hung, 1 pressed to death, and 4 died in prison. In Gaskell's story a young orphaned English woman, Lois Barclay, goes out to Salem in 1691 to live with Puritan relatives, her Aunt Grace Hickson and cousins Manasseh, Faith and Prudence, and is there falsely accused of witchcraft, put on trial and hanged as a witch.[56] Recent commentary has drawn attention to Gaskell's use of historical sources, as well as the story's relation to Victorian thinking about superstition, to contemporaneous alarm about hysterical female revivalists in Ulster, and to Unitarianism.[57] 'Lois the Witch' anticipates, Deborah Wynne has suggested, the work of Freud and modern feminist historians.[58] What interests me is the way Gaskell uses the language and symbolism of the Gothic to explore the workings of the unconscious in the psychological trauma of real historical events.

While Lois herself is invented, the story is closely based on Charles Upham's *Lectures on Witchcraft, comprising a History of the Delusion in Salem in 1692* (1831), to the extent of quoting passages almost verbatim, including the declaration of regret later signed by the jurors.[59] This technique makes explicit Gaskell's fictionalisation of documented historical material; she quotes, for instance, the 'dire statistics of this time' and refers to 'the minister *I have called* Nolan' (based on George Burroughs) (218, emphasis added). Upham's book had been reviewed by Harriet Martineau, who drew attention to its contemporary relevance: 'The days of witchcraft are past', she argued, but society 'will not be safe till every man ascertains and applies his Christianity for himself' rather than relying on the clergy.[60] Gaskell's story can be read as a response to Martineau's call to 'expose indefatigably the machinery of spiritual delusion'.[61] The days of witchcraft were not quite 'past', however: A. W. Ward notes the deep impression made on Gaskell when she was visiting a country magistrate and he was summoned to 'prevent an attempt to bring to her death an old woman in a neighbouring village who was suspected by the inhabitants of being a witch'.[62] By ending with the real historical document, Gaskell moves out of fiction into 'real' history which offers an implicit warning to her readers: This *really* happened and we must remember it.

Like Upham and Martineau, Gaskell treats the witch craze in Salem as a 'delusion' (219) in 'Lois the Witch', and she follows Upham in emphasising 'rational' explanations for the allegedly supernatural: 'How much of malice, distinct, unmistakable personal malice, was mixed up with these accusations, no one can now tell' (218). The accusations against Lois are motivated by personal malice on the part of her ironically named cousins: Prudence is seeking attention, while Faith is jealous of Pastor Nolan's interest in Lois. Their mother, Grace, supports the accusations to protect her un-stable son Manasseh, who is obsessed with Lois. Moreover, Faith is doubly culpable because she knows that the girls who begin the accusations of witchcraft are acting, and she withholds the infor-mation which would save the life of Hota, the Indian woman they first accused.

As Marion Shaw points out, Gaskell offers a 'modern, positivist analysis of the psychology of belief in witchcraft'.[63] The impersonal, present-day (ungendered) narrative voice repeatedly takes this stance, drawing the reader's attention to historical change in the belief in 'the sin of witchcraft': 'We read about it, we look on it from the outside; but we can barely realise the terror it induced' (185). Witchcraft is used as a marker of historical distance: 'you must remember, you who in the nineteenth century read this account, that witchcraft was a real terrible sin to her, Lois Barclay' (211). Witchcraft cases, as Lyndall Roper points out in *Oedipus and the*

Devil (1994), 'seem to epitomize the bizarre and irrational, exem-
plifying the distance that separates us from the past'.[64] However, the
psychology underlying the behaviour of Manasseh and his sisters is
presented as recognisable to the modern reader: 'If Lois had been a
modern physician she might have traced somewhat of the same
temperament in his sisters as well – in Prudence's lack of natural
feeling and impish delight in mischief, in Faith's vehemence of
unrequited love' (180). Gaskell thus uses the tools of 'modern'
nineteenth-century thinking to expose what Martineau called 'the
machinery of spiritual delusion.'

In this text Gaskell is further in advance of contemporaneous
thinking than even Matus suggests, in that she repeatedly uses the
term 'unconscious' to indicate those buried meanings, desires and
fears of which the subject is not fully aware. The desire 'conscious
or unconscious, of revenge' (186), she suggests, may motivate accusations of witchcraft, particularly where supernatural 'evidence' is
involved. To figure such unconscious motivations, Gaskell turns to
Gothic imagery as well as the language of the body. Caught talking
to Lois by Faith, Pastor Nolan displays a 'crimsoned and disturbed
countenance' as if he 'felt the veil rent off the unconscious secret
of his heart' (198). The image of the 'veil' in this context inevitably
recalls Hawthorne's 'The Minister's Black Veil' (1836), where the
black veil obscurely worn by the minister becomes the outward
symbol of the veil drawn by all over their inward secrets.[65] Gaskell's
earlier punning on the sexual meanings of 'bewitched', when Captain
Holdernesse teases Lois that there is '"one under her charms"' (150),
suggests a part played by unconscious male fears of female sexuality
in the events. Lois herself in prison examines her own 'unconscious'
motivations, using the language of witchcraft: 'Could she indeed
be possessed by a demon and be indeed a witch, and yet till now
have been unconscious of it?'(211); could her 'evil thoughts' 'all
unconsciously to herself, have gone forth as active curses into the
world' (211). It is the material weight of the heavy chains that bind
her which convinces her of 'her own innocence and ignorance of
all supernatural power' (211), and brings her 'strangely round from
the delusions that seemed to be gathering about her' (212). In this
passage, Gaskell shows the dangerous power of the concept – or
'story' – of witchcraft to express fears for which there was no other

acceptable language, particularly when 'panic calls out cowardice, and cowardice cruelty' (212). Even Lois is nearly convinced of her own guilt.

Gaskell uses the allegedly outmoded conventions of the Gothic, particularly the curse, in a way which suggests their continued relevance as a way of symbolising buried issues of gender which explain the victimisation of women in a wider psychological sense. Modern psychology and Gothic superstition sit side by side as possible explanations for the event, and it is the latter which perhaps offers us a more profound understanding of gender. Lois herself, orphaned, sent to live with an unsympathetic aunt in an isolated prison-like village 'surrounded with two circles of stockades' (151) in a strange country inhabited by savage Indians and pirates, in danger of being forced to marry a man she does not love, and finally imprisoned in the recess-like dungeon, is an archetypal Gothic heroine. The Gothic landscape of 'New *England*', the 'dreary, dark wood' hemming in the settlement, 'full of dreaded and mysterious beasts and still more to be dreaded Indians' (160), is an uncanny repetition of the home she has left. Early in the story Lois tells of the ducking of a supposed witch in England as a child:

> 'She caught the sight of me, and cried out, "Parson's wench, parson's wench, yonder, in thy nurse's arms, thy dad hath never tried for to save me, and none shall save thee when thou art brought up for a witch" . . . I used to dream that I was in that pond, all men hating me with their eyes because I was a witch.' (150)

The witch here is a version of the figure of the 'murdered mother' central to the Female Gothic. Four-year-old Lois's gaze is as helpless to offer any succour as that of Matilda and Ellinor in *The Recess* as they watch their mother through the window. Similarly, the witch's fate foreshadows Lois's. At the moment of Lois's own accusation, 'the silver glittering Avon, and the drowning woman she had seen in her childhood at Barford, – at home in England, – were before her, and her eyes fell before her doom' (205). Differences of age, class and country are overridden here by their shared vulnerability as women who will suffer, in that classic Gothic curse, for and through 'the sins of the fathers'.

Gaskell uses Female Gothic conventions to expose the gendering of the witchcraft trials and the issues of maternity which lie beneath them. As she notes, 'it was most frequently a woman or girl that was the supposed subject' of witchcraft (185). This was an issue ignored by both Upham and Martineau, and which still troubles historians: 'No one has ever satisfactorily explained why witches have mostly been women,' writes Frances Hill in *A Delusion of Satan* (1997), pointing out that misogyny is an inadequate explanation, since the accusers have themselves mostly been women.[66] Upham's definition of the word 'witch' is nevertheless profoundly gendered:

> Witch was sometimes specially used to signify a female, while wizard was exclusively applied to a male. The distinction was not often, however, attempted to be made – the former title was prevailingly applied to either sex. A witch was regarded by our fathers, as a person who had made an actual deliberate and formal compact with Satan, by which compact it was agreed that *she* should become his faithful subject . . . A witch was believed to have the power, through *her* compact with the Devil, of afflicting, distressing, and rending whomever *she* would.[67]

Despite the initial suggestion that the term can be applied to either sex, the rest of the passage unequivocally refers to the witch as 'she'.

The vast majority of people accused as witches during the Salem trials were female. The first was Tituba (fictionalised as 'Hota' and 'Nattee' in Gaskell's story), a West Indian slave owned by the minister Samuel Parris (Gaskell's 'Pastor Tappau'), and beaten by him into a confession which implicated two other women. These two were particularly vulnerable to accusation, being 'middle-aged, assertive, awkward and so despised as to be almost outcasts': Sarah Good was a widow with a scandalous past, Sarah Osborne a homeless beggar woman.[68] Of the nineteen people hanged, thirteen were women and six were men (although another man was pressed to death), while of the four who died in jail, only one was male.[69]

Yet the afflicted accusers were also female – starting with the hysterical fits of nine-year-old Betty Parris and her orphaned cousin, eleven-year-old Abigail Williams, and spreading to seven or eight other girls, including twelve-year-old Ann Putnam (a source for

Gaskell's 'Prudence', who is given her recantation at the end), and then several young married women, including Ann Putnam's mother, also Ann. Upham's rationalist analysis details the social factors which contributed to the witch trials, including the isolated and anomalous status of the village, property disputes involving the Putnam family, and the development of factions centred around Parris and the minister he had replaced, George Burroughs. It has been confirmed and elaborated by Paul Boyer and Stephen Nissenbaum.[70] Neither account of these 'rational' origins, however, offers any real explanation of why both accusers and accused should be mainly female. In Boyer and Nissenbaum's account 'rational' explanations involving property disputes account for male motivations, but they turn to cod psychology and fairy tales to explain 'irrational' female elements. They argue, for instance, that the accusation of Martha Cory by Ann Putnam was the result of a 'projection' of the Putnams' hatred for Mary Varen, the second wife of Thomas Putnam, Sr, who had deprived his first family of the property they expected:

> Whatever the reason, it seems clear that the Putnams in 1692 (like Hansel and Gretel in the folk tale) projected their bitterness onto people who were, politically or psychologically, less threatening targets: notably older women of Mary Veren Putman's generation.[71]

Boyer and Nissenbaum's analysis confirms Peter Gay's point that historians, whether they acknowledge it or not, have always been 'amateur psychologist[s]'. Given the troublingly 'irrational' nature of witchcraft, it is not surprising that some of the most suggestive work on the usefulness of psychoanalysis for historical analysis has focused on the witch, particularly that of Diane Purkiss and Lyndall Roper.

The witch has been an important figure for women writers, feminist theorists and historians of gender partly because, as Purkiss points out, 'witches were among the few women given any space whatever in pre-feminist history.'[72] Witches share with queens and nuns the distinction of being among the few women about whom we have much documentary evidence, however partial or subjective. These figures, not surprisingly, carry a huge symbolic weight.

The figure of the witch as a victim of patriarchal misogyny proved especially attractive to feminist theorists such as Mary Daly and in one sense Gaskell's portrayal of Lois fits very neatly into this paradigm of what Purkiss calls the 'utterly innocent victim.'[73] Nevertheless, as Purkiss argues:

> The witch is not solely or simply the creation of patriarchy . . . women also invested heavily in the figure as a fantasy which allowed them to express and manage otherwise unspeakable fears and desires, centring on the question of motherhood and children.[74]

Roper's detailed study of witchcraft in early modern Germany offers evidence which supports this analysis. She found that the majority of women accused of witchcraft were older, post-menopausal women, often lying-in maids accused by the mothers of the infants they were caring for. Witchcraft, she argues, expresses conflicts between women, evoking deep emotions which 'have to be understood in psychic terms', but which are only expressed through witchcraft in particular historical moments.[75] It is this historical specificity of expression which interests Gaskell.

The themes of much witchcraft have their origin 'in deeply conflicted feelings about motherhood', Roper argues, and thus what modern psychoanalysis and seventeenth-century witchcraft have in common is that 'in the end a mother, or a figure in a maternal position, is made responsible for our psychic ills.'[76] Purkiss develops similar ideas, citing Hélène Cixous on the witch as an abject figure who symbolises 'that lost maternal space': 'The more it is desired, the more it is feared.'[77] Both Cixous and Catherine Clément, Purkiss notes, link the witch and the hysteric ('the one who cannot escape the past'), but for Clément the hysteric represents 'not merely the private realm of events, but the repressed past of patriarchy, a past which includes the moment which contained the figure of the witch'.[78] If we return to the idea that witchcraft marks 'utter historical distance', it now appears misleadingly narcissistic: 'The primitivism of the witch', Purkiss warns, 'reinforces historians' view of themselves as rational, scientific, Enlightened.'[79] This signals a major difference between Charles Upham and Gaskell. For Upham, the comparison between past and present brings, although with certain qualifications, 'a grateful and admiring conviction of the wonderful progress that has been made'.[80] Gaskell's story offers no such certainty of progress. She may explain the supernatural but, in contrast to Radcliffe, she does not offer her Gothic heroine a happy ending.

Gaskell's sometimes verbatim use of Upham has obscured important changes she made to her source material which foreground the issues of gender and maternity raised by Roper and Purkiss. Firstly, while Lois is a typical Gothic heroine, she is far from being typical of these accused of witchcraft, who were mainly women between fifty and seventy. While the details of her trial draw on those of Rebecca Nurse and the wife of Jonathan Cary, both these women were much older. Lois is, in fact, much closer in age and status to the girls who made the accusations. Gaskell's change highlights the utter innocence of the alleged 'witch', as her deeply ironic title suggests. But it also collapses the difference between accusers and accused and suggests their shared powerlessness. As Hill points out, of the afflicted girls, the majority were living with families which were not their own, while Ann Putnam, who did live with her parents, had a mother who was 'deeply disturbed'.[81] Lois's own circumstances are most similar to those of Abigail Williams, the orphan living with the Parris family. 'In Salem village', Hill suggests, 'young women were as rigidly controlled, as powerless, and as dissatisfied as perhaps they have ever been anywhere', making them 'as susceptible to hysteria as are the physically weak to disease'.[82]

The conventions of the Gothic are used by Gaskell to suggest the psychological pressures on a community, particularly the women, which is 'all day, and for many days shut up within doors' (172):

> Salem was, as it were, snowed up and left to prey upon itself. The long, dark evenings, the dimly-lighted rooms, the creaking passages . . . the white mist, coming nearer and nearer to the windows every evening in strange shapes, like phantoms . . . the distant fall of mighty trees in the mysterious forests girdling them round, the faint whoop and cry of some Indian seeking his camp . . . these were the things that made winter life in Salem, in the memorable time of 1691–2, seem strange, and haunted, and terrific to many. (172)

If this Gothic landscape makes things 'particularly weird and awful to the English girl' (172), it also imprisons those women and girls who already inhabit it. Gaskell thus shows how Salem produces the ideal conditions under which women were likely to use the witch, in Purkiss's words, 'as a fantasy which allowed them to express and manage otherwise unspeakable fears and desires'.[83] But it is a fantasy which leads them to 'prey upon' each other. While Gaskell's modern, positivist reading of these fears centres on sexual desire, her handling of the issue of motherhood is buried more deeply in the Gothic structures of the text and connects to issues of race as well as gender.

The second major change Gaskell makes to her source material concerns her depiction of the two 'Indian' characters, Hota and Nattee. The historical Tituba, a slave of Caribbean origin, was never hanged, despite being the first woman accused, because she confessed to witchcraft and accused Sarah Good and Sarah Osborne, who were then hanged. Gaskell splits this figure into two Native American characters, Hota and Nattee. While Gaskell may have mis-read the term 'Indian' in Upham's text (taking it to mean 'Native American' rather than 'West Indian'), her doubling of this figure foregrounds the way in which discourses of witchcraft were used by colonists to 'explain' the difference of the Indian (touched on by Upham), but further links this to gender and issues of maternity. Both Indian women (like the lying-in nurses discussed by Roper) are surrogate mothers to the white children they look after, Hota to the Tappau girls (who start the witchcraze) and Nattee to Faith, Prudence and Lois. While Hota's story follows that of Tituba, with the exception of her hanging, Nattee is a more detailed figure. The terrifying stories she tells Faith, Prudence and Lois of 'the wizards of her race' (160), are threaded through with 'a ghastly, unexpressed suggestion of some human sacrifice being needed to complete the success of any incantation to the Evil One' (160). Again, Gaskell delineates the 'unconscious' motives which lie behind Nattee's supernatural stories:

> [Nattee] took a strange, unconscious pleasure in her power over her hearers – young girls of the oppressing race, which had brought her down to a state little differing from slavery, and reduced her people to outcasts on the hunting-grounds which had belonged to her fathers. (160)

Equally disempowered, the white girls and Indian woman turn on each other through the fantasy of witchcraft which is the only language available to them – 'stories' which in this case have a deadly effect.

Although Gaskell acknowledges the 'dire statistics' of those hanged in history, within her fiction only three people are hanged: Hota, Nattee and Lois. She foregrounds further the connections between gender and race as forms of otherness by showing Nattee and Lois imprisoned together in the dungeon awaiting their execution. Unable to help the Barford witch, Lois now 'mothers' Nattee, cradling her in her lap and comforting her with 'the marvellous and sorrowful story' (222) of Christ's death. Lois's own final cry of 'Mother!' (223), however, suggests the inadequacy of the Christian 'story' to compensate for women's unmothered state on earth. This cry to the lost mother signals the community's abandonment of Lois, its profound inability properly to mother this girl at any level. Her own mother was so wrapped up in 'the selfishnesss of conjugal love' while dying that she 'thought little of Lois's desolation' (141). Her aunt Grace sacrifices Lois to the needs of her son. And, as a member of a race demonised as being in league with the devil, Nattee is so profoundly disempowered that she needs to be 'mothered' by Lois herself. Equally unmothered, the Tappau girls, Faith and Prudence all turn to the fantasy of witchcraft to express those otherwise unspeakable fears and desires, projecting them onto figures who are even more vulnerable than themselves.

As Gaskell's story shows, the 'hysteric' and the 'witch' are, if not quite mother and daughter, then very close kin, sharing a profound disempowerment within the dominant narratives of patriarchy, which leaves them only able to generate fantasies – or 'stories' – which project guilt onto each other. Those fantasies are historically specific, but Gaskell's revisioning of Upham's *History* suggests the ways in which Gothic fiction can counter or draw attention to blind-spots and gaps in supposedly modern, rationalist accounts of the past, exposing their own historical contingency.

Ghosted by patriarchy: 'The Grey Woman'

If 'Lois the Witch' uses fictional Gothic conventions to tease out the gendering of documented history, 'The Grey Woman' (1861) uses the techniques of the realist historical novel to rewrite a fairy tale as 'real history'. Possibly Gaskell's most radical use of the Gothic to symbolise women's historical position within a society which renders them mere ghosts of themselves, 'The Grey Woman' re-writes Perrault's 'Bluebeard' (the text Anne Williams places at the centre of the Female Gothic), but also draws on two similar tales from the Brothers Grimm, 'The Robber Bridegroom' and 'Fitcher's Bird'.[84] Gaskell's merging of the similar structures of these stories across French and German cultures suggests the ubiquity of the patriarchal structures which victimise women. As Reddy argues, a feminist reading of the story's 'submerged meanings' reveals it as 'a terrifying fable about female sexuality, marriage and society'.[85] It is also a fable about the forms and uses of women's history.

Published in the year John Stuart Mill finished *The Subjection of Women* (1869), Gaskell's story explores the psychic consequences of what Mill called 'the legal subordination of one sex to the other' in marriage.[86] It was *The Subjection of Women*, the 'first great text book of English feminism', Mary Beard argues, which was respon-sible for making Blackstone's description of women as a 'subject sex' a 'dogma of history', which encompassed not just married women but all women.[87] Beard argues that Mill's theory over-simplified Blackstone's formula and ignored its qualifications in practice. Mill's analysis was indeed swingeing. He argued that, 'Marriage is the only actual bondage known to our law. There remain no legal slaves, except the mistress of every house.'[88] Further-more: 'The vilest malefactor has some wretched woman tied to him, against whom he can commit any atrocity except killing her, and, if tolerably cautious, can do that without much danger of the legal penalty.'[89]

Notwithstanding Beard's contention that women had in actual-ity more agency than Mill allows, Gaskell's story suggests the symbolic – and literal – truth of his analysis. Indeed, the cover of fiction perhaps enabled Gaskell to be more courageous than Mill in publishing her own analysis of the 'ghosting' of women within patriarchy. Who, after all, can object to a fairy tale? In fact, Gaskell's story symbolically exposes the secret which underlies patriarchy, the institutionalised 'murder of the mother' and its psychic effects on the daughter. To do this she returned to the fairy-tale structures

which underlie the female Gothic but locates them within a narrative frame which foregrounds the social and cultural realism of
historical fiction.

Like so many Gothic texts, 'The Grey Woman' is presented as a
found historical manuscript, embedded within a present-day frame
narrative. The frame narrator, on holiday in Heidelberg in the
1840s, takes coffee at a mill where she sees a portrait of a young
woman, Anna Scherer, the great-aunt of the present miller. The
miller's paralysed wife tells her of the tradition that Anna 'lost her
colour so entirely through fright' and became known as the 'Grey
Woman' (289). The miller then produces a manuscript, a letter
written by Anna to her daughter Ursula, which the narrator and
her friend translate and transcribe.

Opening in 1789, the manuscript tells how Anna, the motherless
daughter of a German miller (like the heroine of 'The Robber
Bridegroom'), marries a French aristocrat, M. de la Tourelle. A
beautiful but effeminate young man, his 'blue and silver' clothes
(295) and 'pale blue eyes' (305) hint at his Bluebeard origins. His
name, the feminine French noun for 'turret', suggests both a phallic
identification with the Gothic château, Les Rochers, to which he
takes her, and a disturbing gender instability. Confined to one wing
of his château, Anna becomes 'tame to my apparent imprisonment'
(304). Craving news from her father and brother, she is encouraged
by her maid Amante to enter her husband's room secretly to retrieve
a letter. Concealed under a table, she listens in terror as it is revealed
that her husband is (like the robber bridegroom) chief of the 'Chauffeurs', a group of violent robbers who have killed a neighbouring
landowner, whose chilly dead hand Anna accidentally touches.
Moreover, Tourelle has already killed an earlier wife, Victorine,
because she could not keep her mouth shut. Her terror drives Anna
to bite a piece out of her own hand (310), a moment which recalls
Charlotte Clopton's similar self-devouring.

The account of Anna's courtship suggests how the legal insti-
tution of marriage deprived women of their identity, changing even
their nationality. Initially unsure if she loves a man who frightens
her with the 'excess of his demonstrations of love' (296), Anna
sleepwalks into an engagement: 'I was bewitched – in a dream – a
kind of despair' (298). Her marriage brings 'a more complete and

total separation than [she] had ever imagined' (305) from her father and brother, who tell her that she is 'a Frenchwoman now' (299). Once in the château, she writes, 'It seemed as if I were only now wakening up to a full sense of what marriage was'(299). The château itself, a classic Gothic pile which joins two parts, old and new, 'by means of intricate passages and unexpected doors' (300), symbolises the unhappy joining of the sexes in marriage and the bride's psychological entrapment. Mistress of the house in name only, and increasingly afraid of her husband's possessiveness, she has 'no experience to help me unravel any mysteries' (301). As a description of a young women's experience of the structures of marriage and male sexuality, Gaskell's story is sobering.

In the second section, Anna, aided by Amante disguised as a man, escapes, but the two women find themselves on the run in a landscape shadowed by the violence of the Chauffeurs and littered with the bodies of murdered women. First an old woman at a mill, where they take refuge, is killed, then a German baroness with hair the same gold colour as Anna is killed in mistake for her, and finally Amante herself is fatally stabbed. This is a world where male violence against women is persistently repeated, as in the repetitive symbolic patterning in Gaskell's fairy-tale intertexts: Bluebeard's murdered wives; the two sisters killed and dismembered in 'Fitcher's Bird'; and the murdered girl whose finger is cut off in 'The Robber Bridegroom.

But such violence does not just exist in fairy tales, as Gaskell's framing of the story within documented history indicates. Moreover, another influence on 'The Grey Woman' may have been the seventeenth-century murder case of Madame la Marquise de Gange, which Gaskell retold in 'French Life' (1864).[90] This drew on several of Gaskell's visits to France and, since accounts of the murder trial were available in several sources,[91] she could easily have read it earlier than the piece suggests. A beautiful heiress, Madame de Gange was murdered at the behest of her second husband, the Marquis de Gange, a man 'as beautiful as she was, but of a violent and ferocious character'.[92] The details of this horrific case read like a Gothic novel. Gaskell draws attention to the terrible vulnerability of the wife within her own home, the hideously drawn-out events on 'that long and terrible May afternoon'[93] and the attempts of several other women to save her. Isolated in her husband's lonely château near Avignon, where his two brothers, the Abbé and the Chevalier de Gange, came to live with her, Mme de Gange suspected that she was being poisoned. As Gaskell comments: 'It gives one an awful idea of the state of society in those days (reign of Charles II in England), to think of this helpless young woman, possessed by a too well-founded dread, yet not knowing of any power to which she could appeal for protection.'[94]

After the abortive attempt to poison Madame, the Abbé offered her the choice of 'a pistol, a sword, and a cup of poison'.[95] Taking the poison, she escaped and took refuge with a group of women in the village, one of whom tried to give her an antidote. The Chevalier arrived and, claiming that she was mad, drove the women into the other room and stabbed Madame with his sword. When the other women burst into the room and tried to protect her, the Abbé then beat her on the head with his pistol. It took nineteen days for her to die of the poison, during which time her husband tried to force her to revoke the will she had made leaving her property to her mother. After reading this case in a book borrowed from her landlady, Gaskell describes going with her companions to see a portrait of Mme de Gange at the convent in Ville-Neuve. Dressed in the black and white of a nun's habit, Madame is portrayed holding red and white roses in her hands. Gaskell's comments recall the portrait of Anna in 'The Grey Woman': 'Her face was one of exquisite beauty and great peacefulness of expression – round rather than oval – dark hair, dark eyebrows, and blue eyes; there was very little colour excepting in the lips.'[96] In an ironic comment on the valuation of women's history, Gaskell records that the nuns are surprised that she wants to see the portrait at all, assuming that she really wants to see 'The Last Judgement' painted by King Réné (*sic*).

The uncanny climax of 'The Grey Woman' reworks that of 'Fitcher's Bird'. In Grimms' tale, the bride disguises herself as a bird to escape the house of the wizard husband who has killed her two sisters. As a decoy, she takes 'a skull with grinning teeth, put[s] some ornaments on it and a wreath of flowers' and sets it in a garret window.[97] The returning wizard fails to recognise the disguised bride but seeing the skull in the window, thinks it is her and greets it kindly. Her relatives are then able to rescue her and burn the wizard. In Gaskell's story, after her escape Anna (bigamously) marries a kindly doctor who gives a home to her and her daughter. But her terrifying experiences have transformed her appearance, turning her hair grey and her complexion 'ashen-coloured' (339). Looking out of a window, she sees her husband, 'young, gay, elegant as ever' (339), but when he glances up, 'he saw me, an old grey woman, and he did not recognise me!' (339). 'Yet', Anna says, 'it was not three years since we had parted, and his eyes were keen and dreadful like those of the lynx' (339).

The uncanny image of Anna as 'grey', invisible even to her husband, as dead as the grinning skull in the fairy tale, symbolises the 'ghosting' of women in patriarchy. Women's subjection within marriage, their status as 'civilly dead' as their legal existence was 'suspended [or] incorporated into that of the husband', in Sir William Blackstone's formulation, rendered them invisible, ghost-like.[98] As Vanessa Dickerson has shown, Gaskell was not the only Victorian woman writer to explore the implications of this. Ghost stories frequently expresses the 'otherness' of Victorian woman, their ambiguous legal and social position: 'the Victorian woman was above all the ghost in the noontide, an anomalous spirit on display at the centre of Victorian materialism.'[99] Returning to her former home, Anna finds even her brother does not recognise her. Only by demonstrating the likeness between her daughter and the portrait of her younger self can Anna convince him who she is: 'his sister Anna, *even as though I were risen from the dead*' (291, emphasis added).

The likeness between mother and daughter suggests the potential repetition of such violence in the next generation. Anna's letter narrates her own history in order to explain to her daughter, Ursula, that she cannot marry the man she loves because he is the son of the man Tourelle murdered. Yet it offers a wider warning against marriage itself. The Gothic 'secret' Anna's history reveals is that encapsulated in the Bluebeard stories: 'patriarchy's secret founding "truth" about the female', in Williams's phrasing, 'women as mortal, expendable matter/*mater*'.[100] In the frame narrative, as Reddy notes, the paralysis of the miller's wife 'is symbolic of the position of women in patriarchal marriage.'[101]

Moreover, both parts of the narrative are set at the time of revolutions: the frame narrative is set in the 1840s, a time of revolutions across Europe, and the embedded narrative opens during the French Revolution. Anna meets her husband in "89, just when everyone was full of the events taking place in Paris' (295). Reddy suggests that the former date 'may imply that a revolution among women as a class is possible, but that men's fear of such a change makes it improbable'.[102] However, Anna later refers to 'the unruly time that was overspreading all Europe, overturning all law, and all the protection which law gives' (324). The effect of this combined with the dominating presence of the Chauffeurs – 'there were hundreds of them . . . rich and poor, great gentlemen and peasants, all leagued together' (336) – suggests less the possibility of a revolution for women, than a sense of women's existence within a widespread state of 'terror' during unstable times which make them even more vulnerable than usual.

In the face of both public and private violence towards women, Gaskell's story suggests the importance of women's own accounts of the past in thinking about the ways in which history is constructed. The name of the château in 'The Grey Woman', Les Rochers, was also the name of Madame de Sévigné's château, a visit to which Gaskell describes in 'French Life'. This reference locates Anna's letter within a historical tradition of educational letters from mothers to daughters. Anna, like the unnamed narrator of the frame narrative, and like Bridget Sidebotham, Lady Ludlow and Margaret Dawson and the schoolgirl of 'Clopton Hall', is a female historian. While her narrative recounts the 'ghosting' of women brought about by what Irigaray calls the 'murder of the mother', the key point is that Anna, thanks to Amante, escapes being murdered. Or perhaps, as the phrase 'risen from the dead' (291) suggests, she is reborn, delivered by Amante. The 'murdered' mother thus becomes the mother as historian who tells her story as a warning to the next generation.

Throughout her writing career, Gaskell repeatedly returned to the Gothic historical story, exploring and refining it as an alternative mode of representing the past which could both symbolise and counter women's lack of representation within 'real solemn history'. Her Gothic historical stories record the persistence of patterns of violence towards women throughout history and insist that we remember this. They explore women's vulnerability within patriarchal institutions such as marriage which deny them an identity, 'ghosting' and 'be-witching' them. And they develop the potential of Gothic motifs to convey psychological states, particularly the otherwise unspeakable traumas of the past. But they also analyse the dangers of the 'stories' – or fantasies – which are available to women as ways of dealing with fears and anxieties which cannot be overtly expressed. Where women have appeared in mainstream histories, they have tended to do so in certain roles, and Gaskell is particularly interested in the way representations of women have clustered around certain iconic figures: the nun, the witch, the fairy-tale bride, the hysteric. In contrast to Carlyle's 'Great Men history', her stories interrogate the representations of these female figures, but they also celebrate the untold heroism of women, like Amante, who protect other woman at whatever cost to themselves. Above all, Gaskell emphasises the important role of female historians telling women's stories as a way of acknowledging those women in the past who were 'buried quick'. The non-discursive, unrecorded past cannot be recovered, but it can be re-created in ways which point to the blind-spots and erasures of the dominant narratives we call 'history'.

4

Puzzling over the Past: Vernon Lee's Fantastic Stories

Is not what we think of as the Past – what we discuss, describe, and so often passionately love – a mere creation of our own? Not merely in its details, but in what is far more important, in its essential, emotional, and imaginative quality and value? Perhaps some day psychology may discover that we have a craving, like that which produces music or architecture, for a special state of nerves . . . obtainable by a special human product called the Past – the Past which has never been the Present?

Vernon Lee, 'Puzzles of the Past' (1904)[1]

'What are the relations of the Past and Present?' asked Vernon Lee in 1904. 'Where does the past begin? And, to go further still, what *is* the Past?'[2] These were questions to which she returned repeatedly in a body of work which uses the Gothic to figure the past, and its relation to the present, in a particularly sustained and sophisticated way. In 'Puzzles of the Past' she concludes that what we usually think of as 'the Past' is a 'fiction', 'a mere creation of our own' or a 'special human product', constructed out of our own emotional needs, desires and fears.[3] Both Lee's fiction and her non-fiction (she wrote widely on art, music, history, aesthetics and travel) are informed by this understanding of 'the Past', as constructed and subjective, the product of a particular viewpoint at a particular time and place. In this sense 'the Past' is something that has never actually existed. Indeed, the charm of the past, she writes in 'In Praise of Old Houses', is partly because it is 'the one free place for our imagination'.[4] For Lee this understanding proved profoundly liberating.

This is not the same as arguing, as Fredric Jameson does, that we can only ever access the past through texts. For one thing Lee is perhaps more interested in the ways in which we engage imaginatively with the past through landscape, architecture, ruins, music, sculpture, paintings, legend, myth or even gardens. Her use of 'the Past', rather than 'history', draws our attention to an important distinction between what happened in the past ('past time', *OED*), and the written record, the ways in which we write about the past. The *OED* definition of 'history' is instructive here: 'continuous methodical record of important or public events; study of past events, esp. human affairs; aggregate of past events, course of human affairs; whole train of events connected with nation, person, thing etc.'

'History' is, then, a particular form of discourse, one way (but not, perhaps, the only way) of studying the past, and of constructing a methodical and chronological narrative record of it. And as such, Lee's fiction suggests, it is the product of desire, of a 'craving' for something which answers our needs in the present. It is desire which drives the historian narrator of Lee's 'Amour Dure' (1887) to Italy — 'I had longed, these years and years, to be in Italy, to come face to face with the Past,' he writes[5] — and the ghost he encounters there may be a projection of that desire. It is this understanding of 'the Past' as a space of desire and imagination which allows Lee to use the spectral, often as witnessed by unreliable narrators, to explore the ways in which gender and sexuality always inflect and shape historical narratives.

Lee is best known for a handful of supernatural stories — 'Amour Dure', 'Oke of Okehurst; or The Phantom Lover', 'The Wicked Voice', 'Dionea', all from *Hauntings: Fantastic Stories* (1890), and 'Prince Alberic and the Snake Lady' (1896) — which have now been reprinted.[6] Her novels, in contrast, have received very little attention with the Radcliffean *Penelope Brandling: A Tale of the Welsh Coast in the Eighteenth Century* (1903) being almost completely neglected. Even her biographer Vineta Colby writes: 'Lee's novels — those, that is, that were written in the popular modes of social realism (*Miss Brown*) and neo-gothic thriller (*Penelope Brandling*) deserve the neglect they have received.'[7] Yet Lee herself described *Penelope Brandling* as 'far and away my best work bar *Ariadne*',[8] and a reading of this novel allows us to see an important trajectory in Lee's writing. From an analysis of the ways in which male narratives construct/ repress the feminine in the early tales, she moves towards the construction of an autonomous female voice and the recovery of a maternal history in *Penelope Brandling*. Her fiction is also an important link between the work of Ann Radcliffe and Elizabeth Gaskell and that of Daphne du Maurier.

Above all, Lee is fascinated by what is repressed – the feminine, the maternal, sexual desire. She exploits to the full the capacity of the fantastic to trace 'the unsaid and the unseen of culture: that which has been silenced, made invisible, covered over and made absent'.[9] And she returns repeatedly to the notion of the pagan past, repressed and covered over by the (now nominally) Christian present, but erupting, often in the form of art works – statues, portraits, tapestries – to haunt the present. As she put it in the Preface to *Hauntings*:

> the Past, the more or less remote Past, *of which the prose is clean obliterated by distance* – that is the place to get our ghosts from. Indeed we live ourselves, we educated folk of modern times, on the borderland of the Past, in houses looking down on its troubadours' orchards and Greek folks' pillared courtyards; and a legion of ghosts, very vague and changeful, are perpetually to and fro, fetching and carrying for us between it and the Present. (p. 39, emphasis added)

This is the past of which there is no written record, no 'history'. The borders between past and present are permeable, particularly in places where traces of the past remain visible in the landscape. The 'ghost' is what connects the two. Lee's ghosts are not the kind investigated by 'modern ghost-experts' of the Society for Psychical Research, but 'things of the imagination', 'born of ourselves, of the weird places we have seen, the strange stories we have heard' (38, 39) .

The meaning of the supernatural, Lee rightly argues in her essay 'Faustus and Helena' (1880), is historically contingent. She dates the modern craving for the supernatural, the ghostly, to the destruction of the 'belief in the religious supernatural' through the new sciences of the late eighteenth and early nineteenth centuries.[10] This produced the first flood of writing we now call 'Gothic', as writers such as Goethe began 'to work on ghostly tales and ballads'.[11] Attitudes to the supernatural are culturally produced and historically located: 'To raise a real spectre of the antique is a craving of our own century.'[12] Moreover, central to the modern understanding of the spectral is obscurity: 'We moderns seek in the world of the supernatural a renewal of the delightful semi-obscurity of vision and keenness of fancy of our childhood.'[13] This obscurity is central to her fiction. As Angela Leighton notes, there is often something odd about Lee's stories, 'something which makes any moral or ideological interpretation hard to sustain at all'.[14] While several critics have read her fiction as masking lesbian desire,[15] there is a sense in which it exceeds such readings, just as it exceeds the psychoanalytic analysis it appears to invite.

Nevertheless, Lee's personal history has important bearings on her work. She was born Violet Paget in Boulogne-sur-Mer in 1856 to a mother, Matilda Adams, who had been born and brought up in what Lee refers to as 'a remote district of Wales',[16] actually Middleton Hall, Carmarthenshire. Lee's father, Henry Ferguson Paget, of French and English parentage, had grown up in Poland, and been tutor to Lee's elder half-brother before he married her mother. Lee spent a peripatetic childhood in Europe until her family settled in Florence, where she spent most of her adult life, visiting Britain to establish literary contacts. It was Lee's mother who actively educated her daughter to be a writer: 'my mother', Lee writes, 'had made up her mind that I had to become, at the very least, another De Staël.'[17] Lee adopted the name 'Vernon Lee' (taking part of her brother's name) because, as she put it, 'I am sure that no one reads a woman's writing on art, history or aesthetics with anything but unmitigated contempt.'[18] She published her first book, *Studies of the Eighteenth Century in Italy* (1880) when she was just twenty-five, and went on to publish over forty books. Her writing is difficult to categorise because it so often mixes genres, crossing the boundaries between history and art criticism, travel writing and aesthetics, fiction and history. Christa Zorn suggests that 'Her blending of fact and fiction was most creative and provocative in the area of history writing, a traditionally "masculine" genre.'[19]

However, it may have been precisely that mixing of genres, as well as her inclusion of the supernatural, which pushed Lee towards the short story in the 1880s. 'Amour Dure', for instance, was originally projected as a novel entitled *Medea da Carpi*, but cut into a short story for magazine publication when Blackwood rejected it. Lee noted: 'he thinks it a pity to put the historical facts into a fictitious frame! Isn't that a joke!'[20] The 1880s was, as I noted in the Introduction, a high point for the publication of Gothic tales in the new literary periodicals. Lee's own 'Prince Alberic and the Snake Lady' was first published, for instance, in *The Yellow Book*, a magazine with strong associations with the Decadent movement. Much of this writing is associated with male writers, in whose writings women appear as *femmes fatales*. Certainly, Roger Luckhurst's anthology, *Late Victorian Gothic Tales* (2006), includes only one story by a woman, Vernon Lee's 'Dionea', although that appears to fit the stereotype in having a male narrator and a *femme fatale* in the shape of a (possibly) reincarnated Venus.[21] Bram Dijkstra's *Idols of Perversity: Fantasies of Feminine Evil in Fin-de-Siècle Culture* (1986) offers a compendious survey of such images which include the vampire, the lamia, Lilith, and Salome.[22] While acknowledging the work that feminist critics have done to reveal this display of gynophobia as a reaction to the successes of the New Woman, Martha Vicinus also argues that we need more complex readings of the ways in which women could problematise these stereotypes.[23]

Much of the criticism on Lee has focused on formative male influences and contexts: Henry James, Algernon Charles Swinburne, Oscar Wilde, Walter Pater, John Ruskin. 'Her primary influences were male,' write Catherine Maxwell and Patricia Pulham, suggesting that there is as yet no evidence of any woman, other than her mother, who was equally important.[24] Recent work by Emily Harrington, however, has argued for the importance of her connection with A. Mary F. Robinson, her close companion from 1880 to 1887,[25] and she also collaborated with Kit Anstruther-Thomson, her later companion.

Another as yet unrecognised formative influence was Ann Radcliffe, who interested Lee because of the ways in which her novels had shaped attitudes to Italy. Lee was intensely aware, as Hilary Fraser points out, that things 'signify differently at different historical moments'.[26] In her first book, *Studies of the Eighteenth Century in Italy*, Lee instances Dr Burney crossing the Apennines, 'wholly unconscious of . . . delightful Radcliffian thrills', as an example of the way Romanticism changed attitudes to landscape.[27] In the eighteenth century, she points out, the name 'Italy' 'did not suggest what it suggests to us . . . There had been no Byron, no Sismondi, no Lady Morgan, no Ruskin: the generation of Goethe, of Madame de Staël, of Beckford, nay, even of Ann Radcliffe, had not as yet appeared.'[28]

Our sense of place, of history, is mediated by our reading. Lee makes this point again in *Euphorion* where she notes the effect of the 'grim and ghastly romances of the school of Ann Radcliffe'.[29] But Lee is also paying tribute here to female writers – Lady Morgan, Madame de Staël (her mother's model of a female writer, of course), Ann Radcliffe – and the ways in which they have shaped our sense of history and place.

There is a sense in which the influence of these female writers is buried in Lee's work beneath her more obvious references to male writers. In her fascinating study, Patricia Pulham has explored the way in which Lee's work is 'haunted' by the feminine/maternal, particularly the maternal voice (represented by the castrato voice of the singer in 'The Wicked Voice'), which Lee had to repress/reject in order to be able to be taken seriously as a writer.[30] If the early tales, especially *Hauntings*, act out that repression of the feminine then the neo-Gothic *Penelope Brandling* enacts a recovery of the female and maternal which is also a recovery of the matrilineal literary genealogy represented by Ann Radcliffe.

The hauntings of Hystory: 'Amour Dure' (1887, 1890)

The four stories which make up *Hauntings* offer an extended engagement with the ways in which the feminine has historically been constructed through male eyes. Each uses a first-person male narrator who is at best unreliable and at worst possibly unbalanced. They symbolise the central forms of representation in Western culture: a historian in 'Amour Dure', a writer with an interest in mythology in 'Dionea', a painter in 'Oke of Okehurst', and a composer in 'The Wicked Voice'.[31] While the tales are set in the present, each narrator becomes obsessed with, or haunted by, a feminine figure from the past who is in some sense summoned by his own desire: a Renaissance duchess, Medea da Carpi, who has been responsible for the deaths of at least five men; Dionea, possibly a reincarnation of Venus, who drives a sculptor to sacrifice his wife and kill himself; the wife of a country squire, Alice Oke, whose obsession with her seventeenth-century predecessor and namesake drives her husband to shoot her; and an eighteenth-century castrato, Zaffirino, whose voice has killed a woman. In précis, these stories seem to be versions of the Male Gothic – male over-reachers, tempted and, like Lewis's Monk, dragged down to hell by *femmes fatales*. But Lee's deployment of potentially hysterical first-person narrators suggests we read these stories as a critique of such narratives.

With its historian narrator, 'Amour Dure' offers the most sustained account of the gendering of historical narratives and the ways in which they are unconsciously constructed by desire. The story is in the form of a diary written by Spiridion Trepka, a Polish historian, alienated by the 'modern scientific vandalism' and pedantry (41) of contemporary German historians such as Grimm and Mommsen, and come to Urbania in search of 'the Past' (41) he identifies with Italy. This eludes him until he becomes obsessed by the figure of a Renaissance duchess, Medea da Carpi, who, after causing the deaths of at least five men including two husbands, was executed by two female infanticides on the orders of an ex-cardinal, Duke Robert II. Increasingly distracted from his intended research by his hunt for information about her and alienated from contemporary society, Trepka declares that he is 'wedded to history, to the Past, to women like Lucrezia Borgia, Vittoria Accoramboni, or that Medea da Carpi' (54). Confessing that 'she haunts me' (55), he turns to re-imagining her history and asks himself, 'Am I turning novelist instead of historian' (55).

Trepka's act of imaginative empathy with Medea (and it was Lee who introduced the word 'empathy' into English thinking[32]) goes beyond the 'facts' to produce what is an almost textbook 'feminist' version of Medea. Her actions are understandable if she is recognised as an intelligent, educated woman, abducted against her will by one man, and by another 'treated like a chattel, made roughly to understand that her business is to give the Duke an heir, not advice' (56). Trepka defends a notion of historical difference, asserting that 'we must put aside all pedantic modern notions of right and wrong' (56). However, he then moves from this empathy with her to an obsession which appears to raise her ghost. There are several indications that this ghost is a projection of his own desire. The portrait of her he discovers is first seen in a mirror, where he 'expect[s]' to see a 'ghost' (61), and he appears to summon her by singing 'Vieni, Medea, mia dea' (come, Medea, my goddess) (64). She subsequently entices him to attack the statue of her killer Duke Robert, and after this frenzied attack, a note to the diary informs us, the body of Trepka is discovered 'dead of a stab in the region of the heart, given by an unknown hand' (76).

In 'Amour Dure', the *femme fatale* who is the symbolic embodiment of 'the Past' is revealed as a construction of the male subject who is himself historically constructed. 'Amour Dure' is, Christa Zorn argues, a 'key text' in Lee's rethinking of the relationship between 'history and historian, writer and text'.[33] By representing the ghostly Medea as the production of male hysteria, Lee exposes the subjective nature of both history and historian. Medea is associated in the story with a litany of historical *femmes fatales* including her namesake in Greek myth, Lucrezia Borgia, Bianca Cappello, Faustina the Younger, the Sirens, Vittoria Accoramboni, Cleopatra, Salome (Medea's second appearance to Trepka is in the church of 'the decapitated, or as they call him here, decollated, John the Baptist' (66)). The description of her portrait, as Zorn points out, reworks Walter Pater's famous description of da Vinci's Mona Lisa.[34] These associations, however, are made by a man who admits of cases of 'insanity' in his own family (61) and repeatedly questions his own sanity – 'Am I mad?' (65). The first-person narrative voice is crucial here because at no point in these stories do we hear the female voice unmediated by the male narrator.

As 'Amour Dure' demonstrates, Lee understood very clearly the ways in which writing by men (whether 'history', Male Gothic, or Decadent tales) reflects and represents men's fears and desires, rather than an objective reality, and how this leads to a construction of 'Woman' as feared and desired other. In an essay on Charlotte

Perkins Gilman in *Gospels of Anarchy*, Lee stated this even more clearly. Developing Gilman's arguments about gender, she discusses the French concept of *La Femme*, essentialised as 'siren [and] man-destroying monster.'[35] As she argues,

> with all our literature about La Femme . . . we do not really know what women *are*. Women, so to speak, as a natural product, as distinguished from women as a creation of men; for women hitherto have been as much a creation of men as the grafted fruit tree, the milch cow, or the gelding.[36]

In this essay, the first version published in 1903 – the same year as *Penelope Brandling* – Lee credits Gilman's work with converting her (rather late in her career) to the 'real importance of what is known as the Woman Question'.[37] Lee's stories in *Hauntings*, however, suggest that she had already developed a sophisticated understanding of the ways in which 'The man makes the woman' but also, as she goes on to say, 'and the woman . . . in her turn makes the man; woman in the image of man, man in the image of woman'.[38] 'History', 'Amour Dure' suggests, is always 'hysterical', always a projection of desires and fears onto the other, whether male or female.

Murdering the phallic mother: 'Prince Alberic and the Snake Lady' (1896)

Part history, part legend, part fairy tale, 'Prince Alberic and the Snake Lady' is, I will argue here, disguised Female Gothic, an allegory of the Irigarayan 'murder of the mother' in the tradition of Sophia Lee, Ann Radcliffe and Elizabeth Gaskell, which demands we honour female genealogies. While the lack of a traditional Gothic heroine may seem to work against this reading, the rich suggestiveness of the text invites us to be canny readers in interpreting this uncanny and elusive tale. Given its publication in *The Yellow Book* in 1896, Margaret Stetz has argued that the story is an 'artistic and political gesture of homage' to Oscar Wilde, then serving two years' hard labour.[39] Other critics have offered more psychoanalytic readings. Using post-Freudian theory, Jane Hotchkiss reads it as a pre-Freudian exploration of the 'castration' of the feminine within patriarchy and Lee's alternative validation of the clitoral.[40] Mary Patricia Kane (2006) uses Lacanian theory to read it as a text which exposes the phallocentric logic behind myth and legend and the repression and control of the feminine in the figure of the 'uncanny mother'.[41]

The opening of 'Prince Alberic' stages an abrupt shift from fact to fiction, history to 'the Past', the real to the strange or fantastic:

> In the year 1701, the Duchy of Luna became united to the Italian dominions of the Holy Roman Empire, in consequence of the extinction of its famous ducal house in the persons of Duke Balthasar Maria and of his grandson Alberic, who should have been the third of the name. Under this dry historical fact lies hidden the strange story of Prince Alberic and the Snake Lady.[42]

The truth claims of 'dry historical fact', implied by the specific place and date,[43] are undermined by the 'strange' story of the 'Snake-Lady', with its promise of other kinds of truths. The concern here with inheritance and the extinction of the ducal 'house' is, of course, a classic theme of the Gothic, dating from Walpole's *Castle of Otranto*. 'History' here is the working out of patrilineal inheritance.

We are given no indication of what has happened to the parents of the orphaned Prince Alberic, who lives with his grandfather, Duke Balthasar Maria, in the 'Red Palace' at Luna. However, the first recorded action of the Duke is to remove from Alberic's apartments a tattered, Gothic tapestry to which the unloved child has become deeply attached. The tapestry depicts an Edenic natural world, which is the child's only image of the world outside the palace, and a knight on horseback with his arm clasped around a beautiful lady. Initially the lower part of the lady's body is concealed by a chest of drawers and a large ebony and ivory crucifix. When these are removed, Alberic sees that the lady 'ended off in a big snake's tail with scales of . . . green and gold'(187). He is told these figures are his ancestor, Alberic the Blond, and the Snake-Lady Oriana. The Duke orders it to be replaced by one depicting 'Susanna and the Elders' which the enraged Alberic cuts to pieces. This pattern of the pagan being 'covered up' by the Christian is common in Lee's fiction, and Duke Balthasar Maria's name doubly associates him with Christianity.[44] The removal of the tapestry representing a female figure to whom he is so passionately attached symbolically suggests a repetition of the orphaning of the prince, and foreshadows the later events of the tale.

Snakes and snake-humans frequently appear in Lee's writing and are usually associated with the feminine (in *Hauntings* Medea, Alice Oke, Dionea and Zaffirino are all described in snake-like terms). But it is the Prince's reaction to the Snake-Lady which is most striking. Instead of being repelled by the discovery that she is half-snake, he 'loved her . . . only the more' (188). Like 'Amour Dure', 'Prince Alberic' is richly intertextual, recalling multiple sources for snake-women including Keats's 'Lamia' (1819), Coleridge's 'Christabel' (1816) and Swinburne's serpent-like fatal women. In his 'reading' of the text of the tapestry, Alberic is reading against the grain of such male-authored texts, particularly those of the *fin de siècle*, which present the snake-woman as monstrous and devouring: the 'deadlier Venus incarnate' in Swinburne's words, 'a Lamia loveless and un-assailable by the sophist, readier to drain life out of her lover than to fade for his sake at his side'.[45] More positive sources for the snake-woman are E. T. A Hoffmann's 'The Golden Pot' (1814), where the hero is finally happily united with his Serpentina in an idyllic Atlantis, and the Melusina legend (which exits in several versions).[46] In one version, Count Raymond falls in love with a beautiful woman, has three sons by her but finally loses her when he disobeys her injunction not to look at her on a Saturday, and discovers, by spying on her in her bath, that she is a serpent from the waist down.

Banished to the 'Castle of the Sparkling Waters', the original ducal seat, Alberic discovers the natural world of the tapestry made real. He has two companions: a tame grass snake, and a woman who appears every day for an hour at sunset and who reassures him that she is 'not a ghost' but his 'Godmother' (202). She takes charge of his education, teaching him to read, to play, to ride, and 'above all, to love' (202) – 'mothering' him in what reads like a return to the plenitude of 'a primal womb, our first nourishing earth, first waters, first envelopes'.[47] It is his discovery of the full story of his ancestors, the two Alberics, which signals his final maturation, not as a Freudian

Oedipal rejection of/separation from the mother but through a union with her. According to legend, Alberic the Blond had released the Fairy Oriana from her imprisonment in the form of a serpent by kissing her, but had failed to fulfil the ten years' fidelity needed to complete the disenchantment, instead marrying a princess to fulfil 'his duty as a prince' (210). A second Alberic also failed the test, becoming a monk. The calls of the world (of paternal inheritance, and thus of 'history') and the Church supersede the needs of the imprisoned woman. The priest who retells the end of the story offers Alberic the traditional interpretation of the snake-woman, as 'this demon . . . a fairy – or witch, malefica or stryx . . . who had been turned into a snake for her sins' (210).

After hearing the legend, Alberic goes to the well by moon-light in which the trees seem 'twined and knotted like huge snakes around the world' and the trellises seem 'to twist and glide through the blue moonlit grass like black gliding snakes' (214). There, in a conscious repetition of his ancestor's action, he kisses the snake and slips into unconsciousness, from which he wakes to find himself with his head in his godmother's lap. Their idyll, however, is broken when Alberic is imprisoned in the Red Palace by his grandfather after he refuses to marry an heiress. The story ends with Alberic dead of voluntary starvation and the rumoured discovery in his cell, not of a dead grass snake killed by the Duke's followers, but 'the body of a woman, naked and miserably disfigured with blows and sabre cuts' (227).

The end of the story moves back out of myth/legend into 'dry historical fact', leaving the supernatural identification of snake with godmother implicit, and refusing to substantiate as fact the 'rumour' or 'tradition' of the dead woman's body: 'Be that as it may, history records as certain that the house of Luna became extinct in 1701, the duchy lapsing to the Empire' (227). Prince Alberic's grave is covered with a 'nameless slab' (227), and the damaged tapestry is transformed into chair covers and curtains in the porter's lodge. The story of Alberic and the Snake-Lady, it seems, is erased from accepted chronological history, existing only in almost unreadable traces, as 'rumour', 'tradition'. Yet, Lee's framing suggests, the 'dry historical facts' of traditional history are unable either to contain or to deny the emotional appeal of the vivid story within that frame.

Within the allegory of this text, Prince Alberic functions as a version of the Gothic heroine. His reaction to the portrait of his 'mother' in the tapestry, his response to natural landscapes, and his imprisonment by a father figure for refusal to marry, all replicate the characteristics of the Radcliffean Gothic heroine. Similarly, there are several recess-like spaces in the story. The Duke's regimented 'Red Palace' with its voyeuristic 'Twelve Caesars' and grotto is a nightmare version. The only real animal Alberic sees there is a dead, skinned rabbit in the kitchen. His vision of his grandfather's decapitated head stuck on a pole (actually a barber's block) is an image of castration which suggests the sterility of the Duke's regime. In contrast, the 'Castle of the Sparkling Waters' is an Edenic version, a womb-like space within which Alberic is nurtured and educated, surrounded by a lush fertile landscape and living animals. The grotto with its rationed 'spurt[ing]' waters (189) is contrasted with a deep well, next to which is 'a long narrow trough of marble [which] people used as coffins in pagan times' (194). It is carved with 'garlands and people with twisted snakes about them' (194), later referred to as 'serpent-bearing maenads' (214). It is from this trough that the snake first appears to Alberic, and it is from a similar carved 'sepulchre' (207) next to a fountain that Oriana first appeared to his ancestor, Alberic the Blond. The carved trough-coffin here is a trace of the pagan past within the present and the 'serpent-bearing maenads' (214) connect Oriana to Greek myth, specifically Dionysus.

It is Oriana's association with the serpentine, her uncanny snake-like lower half, which makes her symbolism both suggestive and difficult to read. Jane Hotchkiss argues that

> The Snake Lady . . . represents what psychoanalysis calls the 'phallic woman' but more accurately might be called the clitoral woman, the woman who has 'never already' lacked anything until patriarchal history reified its own parapraxis and claimed, as Freud often did, that there was 'nothing' where there was, in fact, the powerful and exclusively erotic . . . female organ of pleasure.[48]

Legend asserts that Oriana cannot die until her head is severed from her body. Her killing is a Freudian image of castration (although Lee never explicitly says that the body is decapitated, only 'miserably disfigured' (225)) which seems to enact patriarchy's murder of the mother. This identification of the Snake-Lady, the *femme fatale*, with the mother is the element missing from Lee's earlier stories. Furthermore, the maternal is identified with the divine – '*God*/mother'. In Lacanian terms, Mary Patricia Kane reads the metamorphosis of the snake following Alberic's kiss as 'a reunion with the God/Mother from whom Alberic and all of his ancestors have been separated as a necessary precondition to their assumption of identity in the phallocentric symbolic order'.[49] While the patriarchy represented by Duke Balthasar represses the feminine, Kane argues, this is an 'untenable position' (58) which leads to the fall of the Duchy of Luna.

While the snake-woman is an obvious figure for the phallic woman, she also has important mythic associations, notably with the Dionysiac indicated by those 'serpent-bearing maenads' carved on Oriana's sepulchre. Dionysus has a central importance in Lee's writing, as Catherine Maxwell has shown, partly stemming from her engagement with Walter Pater's Heine-influenced 'Denys l'Auxerrois' in which the exiled pagan god is torn to pieces by a mob in thirteenth-century France.[50] Lee herself referred to this theme of the exiled god as a 'kind of *haunting*; the gods who had it partaking of the nature of ghosts even more than all gods do, *revenants* as they are from other ages, and with the wistful eeriness of all ghosts . . . Now of all ghosts Dionysus is the one fittest for such sinister exile.'[51] She associated Dionysus with the feminine: 'Dionysus is a seducer of women, though little more than a woman himself.'[52] Thus, Maxwell reads the stories in *Hauntings* as 'revision[s] of the fatal woman motif, as an assertion of a specifically female form of Sublimity which is analogous to and rivals the Dionysian'.[53]

Lee's interest in Dionysus is even more suggestive in relation to 'Prince Alberic'. In an essay on Jane Harrison's work (which Lee is likely to have known), Marianna Torgovnick notes that in *Mythology* (1890) Harrison described the original myths surrounding Dionysus in which he was the son or consort of the Great Mother: 'Harrison saw Dionysus as a liminal figure presiding over the transition from Goddess worship to patriarchy and a male-dominated pantheon.'[54] Read in this context, Lee's story is an allegory of the *female* divine in exile after the imposition of patriarchy and a male-dominated pantheon, symbolised by Duke Balthasar and his twelve heads of Caesar. Prince Alberic is the son-consort of the Snake-lady, herself an embodiment of the 'Great Mother'. Dionysus, then, becomes important as a figure for the son who is mother-identified. In contrast to the denial and murder of the mother enacted by Orestes which I discussed in chapter 1, Lee celebrates the erotic mother—son connection as a source of plenitude.

One of Dionysus' most important feats as a divinity was to rescue his mother from Hades and make her divine.[55] Like Julia in *A Sicilian Romance*, Alberic chooses imprisonment with his 'mother' rather than to marry as his (grand)father wishes. Moreover, like Julia, he tries to 'deliver' his mother from her imprisonment by remaining loyal to her for ten years, an attempt to replicate Dionysus' feat. Like *The Recess*, 'Prince Alberic' enacts the repression of the feminine within patriarchy but it also symbolises the failure of the son to 'deliver' the mother from her oppression.

Recovering the mother? Penelope Brandling: A Tale of the Welsh Coast in the Eighteenth Century (1903)

A self-consciously revisionary piece of Female Gothic, or 'neo-Gothic' in Colby's phrase, *Penelope Brandling* looks back to Ann Radcliffe and is likely (as I will argue in chapter 5) to have been an important influence on Daphne du Maurier. It is important in Lee's *œuvre* because it is one of the few pieces where she uses a female first-person narrative voice (the other is 'The Doll' (1900)[56]), and it seems to be the only piece of her work set in Wales, the country where her mother was brought up. While Lee is usually described as 'English', she seems to have felt somewhat alien in England. As she put it, 'It's funny, though I feel so much more English than anything else (in fact only English) I cannot feel well in body or mind save on this sufficiently big and sufficiently aired and warmed continent.'[57] It was Italy she associated with the past which inspired much of her fiction.

Wales seems to have offered her something different, an imaginative space, like that of Italy, but connected to her maternal past. She visited Wales at least once. In 1882 she went to 'Llanfair' to stay with her cousin Adah Hughes, and while she was there she visited her mother's childhood home, Middleton Hall,[58] since burnt down and now the site of the National Botanic Gardens. The detailed descriptions in *Penelope Brandling* also suggest that she visited the Glamorganshire coast. Her attitude to Wales within the novel, however, is conflicted. On the one hand she uses it, as Radcliffe had used Italy and Sicily, as a 'Gothic' space which connoted primitiveness and barbarity. In *Penelope Brandling* the Welsh landscape is depicted as desolate and uninhabited, 'this vague country without landmarks, where everything appeared and disappeared in mist'.[59] In '[t]his heathenish country' (53), with its 'unintelligible' (42) Welsh language the reader is primed to expect Gothic horrors. On the other hand, using Wales as a setting appears to have released Lee to use a female first-person narrator and to explore issues of female identity and, particularly, maternity more directly than elsewhere.

Presented as a diary written by the eponymous heroine, *Penelope Brandling* has a framing narrative set in Switzerland in1822 but looks back to events in Wales between 1772 and 1774. It opens with the classic Gothic themes of genealogy and inheritance. The writer, Sophia Penelope Brandling, the widow of Sir Eustace Brandling of St Salvat's Castle in Glamorgan, sets out to explain to her 'children's children' (13) why the family has been 'so long cast in foreign parts and remote colonies, instead of its ancestral and legitimate home' (12) in Wales. The problematics of historiography are immediately highlighted as she remarks on the need for a written account, 'knowing how soon all verbal tradition becomes blurred and distorted' (11). The authenticity of her own account is presented as guaranteed by the fact that she can rely on a journal that she kept during these years for her mother.

Penelope's journal gives an account of her journey with her husband to his newly inherited ancestral seat, St Salvat's Castle on the Glamorganshire coast, following the death of his elder brother, Sir Thomas Brandling, and their stay there of eighteen months. The castle, in the best Gothic tradition, harbours a secret and Penelope becomes suspicious of the activities of Eustace's uncle Hubert, a clergyman, and the group of other male relatives who dominate the place. Under cover of pilchard fishing they are, in fact, a gang of wreckers who draw ships onto the treacherous coastline and plunder their cargoes. Increasingly isolated and able to confide only in her diary, Penelope becomes estranged from her husband, and starts to suspect him of being involved in or condoning the wrecking. Becoming pregnant, she suffers a miscarriage after witnessing a shipwreck. The initially sinister housekeeper, Mrs Davies, becomes an ally and tells her that Sir Thomas had actually been murdered by the wreckers. She is reconciled with her husband, and they plan to escape with the help of Mrs Davies, but are foiled by the return of Uncle Hubert who they had thought was away on a 'fishing' trip. Penelope shoots Uncle Hubert, Eustace blows up the castle, and, exiled from Britain as felons, they return to Switzerland to live with Penelope's mother until, after Eustace's death, their son returns to Britain to reclaim his inheritance.

An early reference to Walpole's *Castle of Otranto* (1764) signals that Lee was self-consciously revising the Gothic tradition, revising, indeed, its very origins:

> [St Salvat's] makes one think of castles, like that of Otranto, which one reads of in novels; nay, I was the more reminded of the latter work of fiction (which Eustace believes to be from the pen of the accomplished Mr Walpole, whom we knew in Paris), that there are let into the stonework on either side of the porch, huge heads of warriors, filleted and crowned with laurel, which though purporting to be those of the Emperors Augustus and Trajan, yet look as if they might fit into some gigantic helmet such as we read of in that admirable tale. (33–4)

Penelope's familiarity with Gothic fiction, like that of Austen's Catherine, alerts the reader to the ways in which this text plays with generic conventions. The 'huge heads', like the gigantic helmet of *Otranto*, suggest the possibility of a supernatural return of past secrets. Like the uncanny 'Twelve Caesars' in 'Prince Alberic', they also symbolise conquering patriarchal power. In Lee's work the Roman period is often presented as repressing the earlier Greek civilisation, with its extraordinary artistic achievements and its pagan gods. Augustus, the first Roman Emperor (and great-nephew of

Julius Caesar who subsequently adopted him), is perhaps best known for his victory over Antony and Cleopatra, and thus over the Egyptian culture Cleopatra represented. Trajan, emperor AD 98−117, conquered the Parthian empire. Neither left a direct heir.

The heads, however, are also one of the elements Lee takes from an actual place and documented history in the complex inter-weaving of fact, fiction and legend in this novel. The description of St Salvat's castle is closely modelled on St Donat's castle on the Glamorganshire coast, near Llantwit Major, which has the gate tower, escutcheon, lawned castle yard, battlements and turrets, and the mix of medieval and Tudor architecture all described by Lee. Similarly, the gardens of St Salvat 'which descend in great terraces and steps into the woods and to the sea' (34), the church and sea wall are those at St Donat's. The 'huge heads' which Penelope describes seem to have their genesis in the three terracotta roundels which are set into the walls of the inner court at St Donat's. Two of these represent the Roman Emperors Caligula and Marcus Aurelius, while the third represents an unidentified woman, possibly a Roman lady but sometimes said to be Cleopatra.

The history of St Donat's and of the Stradling family who owned it until 1738 stretches back to Romano-Celtic times. It is easy to see how this coastal castle, with its rich mix of recorded history and evocative, if contradictory, legend, must have appealed to Lee's interest in 'the Past' and the ways in which we engage with it. Her text draws on many elements, mixing fact and fiction. The present castle was built on what is thought to have been the site of an Iron Age fort connected with Caradog, or Caractacus, the leader of the British resistance against the Romans. From around 1298 when Sir Peter Stradling (possibly of Norman descent) married Joan de Hawey, the heiress of St Donat's, it was owned by the influential Stradlings. Parts of the original Norman concentric castle, dating from around 1200, can still be seen, although much of it has been replaced by Tudor building. In Lee's novel the Stradlings become the Brandlings − 'kings of this part of Wales in the time of King Arthur, crusaders later, and great barons fighting at Crecy and at Agincourt' and now 'dwindled into common smugglers' (66) − and St Donat's becomes St Salvat's. St Donat was the patron saint of shipwrecked sailors and their rescuers, while 'salvat' comes from

Latin, meaning 'saved'. Given to a castle which was the base for a gang of wreckers, Lee's invented name is clearly deeply ironic. The plot of Lee's novel fictionalises two stories about the Stradlings. In *Folk-Lore and Folk-Stories of Wales* (1909) Marie Trevelyan tells the story of how the heir, Sir Thomas Stradling, went on the Grand Tour in 1738 with a friend, Sir John Tyrwhitt, and was killed in a duel in Montpellier, almost certainly by Sir John. The two men had made an agreement before setting off that if one should die the other would inherit his estates.[60] According to some versions, Sir Thomas's body was brought home and set in the Great Hall where a mysterious fire destroyed the coffin as well as portraits of five generations of Stradlings.[61] Legend also has it that Sir Thomas had lost a finger from his left hand when a boy, and his old nurse, feeling the hands in the coffin, had discovered that the corpse had all ten fingers and therefore could not be Sir Thomas.[62] The Stradling family disputed Tyrwhitt's attempt to take possession, and the subsequent litigation lasted over fifty years. From 1862 the castle was owned by Dr Nicholl Carne, who had Stradling ancestry, and after his death in 1901, it was bought by Morgan Stuart Williams, who owned it when Lee's novel was published. In *Penelope Brandling*, the mysterious death of Sir Thomas Stradling becomes that of Sir Thomas Brandling, firstly attributed to 'a stab from a drunken sailor at Bristol' (18), then revealed as murder carried out by the wreckers when they thought he was about to betray them: he was 'taken out, a prisoner, to the deepest part of the channel, and drowned' (128). Again, a fire during his wake destroys Sir Thomas's supposed body together with the library at St Salvat's (although Hubert has first removed the family archives). Lee's Sir Thomas also has a devoted nurse, Mrs Davies, who realises that the body is false when she is not allowed to see it.

The second element Lee borrows is the long history of shipwrecks, smuggling, piracy, and wrecking on this rugged coastline. A key source here was probably Marie Trevelyan's *Glimpses of Welsh Life and Character* (1893) with its horrific account of the work of wreckers at St Donat's,[63] which I will discuss further below. Legends which connect the Stradlings themselves with piracy include the story that Sir Harry Stradling and his wife and child were captured by the Breton pirate Colyn Dolphin in 1449 and later ransomed.

Sir Harry later captured Dolphin and buried him up to his neck in a sea cave in St Tresilian's Bay (just along the coast) to drown in the rising tide. The sea cave was believed to have a tunnel leading to St Donat's Castle and used by smugglers. Sir Henry Stradling was himself believed to have been a smuggler. Later, in the sixteenth century Sir Edward Stradling was famous for having 'twelve brothers, most of them bastards, [who] have no living but by extortion and pilling (i.e. robbing) of the king's subjects',[64] who seem obvious precursors of Eustace Brandling's 'crew of Caliban uncles' (47).

Lee's novel draws on history, both written and oral, to create a Gothic fiction which foregrounds the female past missing in most of these accounts. As so often with recorded history, the Stradling women are shadowy figures who feature mostly in the legends and superstitions of the castle. Often even their names are in doubt. For instance, the perfume of lavender is supposed to accompany the ghost of a Lady Anne who allegedly haunts the castle, but historical records show no evidence of a lady of that name.[65] Another story is that during the Civil War, Parliamentary troops came to the castle. Lady Katherine Stradling, left there while her husband fought with the Royalists, stood with her baby in a window, and the soldiers, seeing them, left the castle alone.[66] Lee (like Sophia Lee) uses fiction to re-imagine the voice of such a historical woman.

Although it is Walpole who is named in the novel, Radcliffe is an equally important (albeit buried) influence. Lee deploys the classic Radcliffean scenario of the heroine imprisoned within a castle by a father/uncle villain, as well as foregrounding Penelope's response to the sublime landscape, and using the 'explained' supernatural. However, Lee makes radical – and possibly influential – changes to Radcliffean conventions. Firstly, her use of a first-person, rather than omniscient, narrative voice pushes Radcliffe's technique even further in terms of centralising the female point of view. Secondly, for Radcliffe's heroines marriage marks the *end* of their story, in a way which some critics see as an indication of her conservatism. In contrast, marriage is the *beginning* of Penelope's story as she moves from her mother's home to her husband's. Her marriage takes her into an almost exclusively male environment in her husband's ancestral home, and puts her into the power of a husband whom she begins to suspect of murderous activities. This plot becomes more typical in twentieth-century texts by women which write 'beyond the (marriage) ending'.[67] Both Daphne du Maurier's *Rebecca* (1938) and the modern Gothics of the 1960s (which I discuss in chapter 5), follow Lee's example in using a first-person narrator and a post-marriage plot. Thirdly, Lee's heroine not only becomes pregnant but suffers a miscarriage, both even now rarely the subject of literary writing. Finally, Penelope is more actively autonomous than Radcliffe's heroines. Her shooting of Hubert anticipates by seventy years Angela Carter's feminist reworking of Bluebeard in 'The Bloody Chamber' (1979), where the heroine's mother rides up to the castle to shoot the Bluebeard figure before he executes his wife.[68]

By presenting Penelope's narrative as an intimate journal addressed to her mother, Lee foregrounds the issue of the maternal and the connections between mother and daughter enabled by writing. Indeed, *Penelope Brandling* can be seen as Lee's 'letter' to her own mother who had died in 1896. Discussing her mother's influence, Lee noted that she cared for her own writing 'because in some indirect manner it is associated with her indescribable, incomparable person'.[69] Penelope's mother, née Sophia Hamilton and of Scottish origins, seems closely modelled on Lee's mother (whose first married name was Matilda Lee-Hamilton). 'Sophia' comes from the Greek, meaning 'wisdom', and is shared with Penelope, signifying a matrilineal genealogy. (Penelope's deceased father, Jacques de Morat, seems to have been French.) Penelope's other given name, also from the Greek, invokes, of course, Odysseus's resourceful, intelligent and faithful wife, whose tapestry-weaving makes her an appropriate model for a woman writer. The eighteenth-century setting of the novel is also closely associated with Lee's mother, as is Sophia's philosophical bent. Lee writes that her mother 'clung, even in the seventies, to certain eighteenth century words and pronunciations, and to heresies which I later identified as Voltairean, or derived from Rousseau and Tom Paine; and her politics were those of Charles James Fox.'[70] The opening pages of the novel depict a Rousseauesque pastoral upbringing that recalls that of Radcliffe's Emily with her father at La Vallée in *The Mysteries of Udolpho*. But this is a feminised version, centred on the mother, and it is marriage which breaks it up.

Indeed, given Eustace's initial lack of prospects, it is regarded as proof of Penelope's mother's 'high-flown and romantic temper, and of the unpractical influence of the writings of Rousseau and other philosophers' (14) that she allows the marriage. Eustace is 'merely a young Englishman of handsome person, gentlemanly bearing, an uncommon knowledge of the liberal arts and sciences, and a most blameless and amiable temper, but with no expectations of fortune in the future' (13–14). Despite his links to St Salvat's he is presented here, and throughout the novel, as 'English' not Welsh. As a younger son, with no status or responsibilities, he is easily absorbed into this maternal space. The couple's residence with Penelope's mother 'on her little domain of Grandfrey' (14), can be seen as an idyllic continuation of the daughter's pre-Oedipal merger with the mother – 'our existence of pastoral and philosophic happiness' (14).

But the needs of primogeniture override those of this maternal 'domain', and Eustace's succession to the position of (nominal) head of the Brandling family requires that Penelope separate from her mother: 'I suppose', she writes, 'it was that I was only then really ceasing to be a child though I had been married two years' (23). The journal remains a link between them, like an umbilical cord which stretches thinner and thinner but always holds. Arriving at St Salvat's, Penelope directly confides her 'childish fear of I know not what' in her journal, sure in the knowledge that her mother 'would know what it is, for the first time in my little life, to be without you' (32). Unwilling to write letters in case they are opened, she continues her journal because 'while I write I seem to be talking to my dearest mother, and to be a little less solitary' (62). It is this absolute confidence in her mother's nurturing maternal love, their connection symbolised by writing, which sustains Penelope throughout the violence she encounters at St Salvat's.

Like the castles and landscapes of Radcliffe's novels, St Salvat's offers Penelope two kinds of experience. Both are mediated through intertextual references which make Lee's novel a kind of metafiction as she explores the ways in which our experience of landscape and history is constructed through texts. On the one hand, like Radcliffe's heroines, Penelope responds to the sublime landscape and the romance of the castle sited 'on an utterly isolated little bay on this wild and dangerous coast' (36). This response is self-consciously mediated through her reading. Noting the moonlight pouring in through the 'vast cage-like window' of her room, Penelope writes: 'I tried to enjoy it like a play, or a romance which one reads: and indeed, the whole impression of this castle is marvellously romantic' (25). And she repeats 'a line of Ossian, at the beginning of the description of the pirates crossing the sea to the house of Erved' (26). More apposite than she realises, this irritates Eustace.

The choice of Ossian here, also a favourite with Ann Radcliffe, invokes a specifically Gaelic and female Gothicism. But given that early suspicions that these supposedly ancient Gaelic epics were forged by James MacPherson were confirmed in 1805, they also suggest Lee's meta-historical foregrounding of questions about the reliability of textual representations of the past. This places her firmly in the tradition established by Sophia Lee: as Anne Stevens notes, the subtitle of *The Recess; or, A Tale of Other Times*, is taken from the Ossian forgeries and thus signals the status of the historical novel itself as a kind of forgery.[71]

The setting of the castle resembles the female landscapes analysed by Ellen Moers in *Literary Women*.[72] The path down the terraces leads through a 'narrow ravine, lined with every manner of fern and full of venerable trees' (36) to the sea wall, on the other side of which, 'quite unexpected, is the white misty sea, dashing against a bit of sand, low pale rocks . . . and chafing, further off against the sunken reefs of this murderous coast'(37), Such secretive landscapes evoke, in Freudian terms, the 'complicated topography' of the female body.[73] Moers notes that they have nothing to do with the plot but 'surge . . . up, a kind of vision, when the heroine is alone. It is a time of feminine stocktaking, an atmosphere of apartness as much as a place.'[74] There are many such examples in Radcliffe's novels, and Lee's landscape similarly provides a space in which Penelope attempts to find solace in solitary reflection. The fact that this landscape is located in Wales, Lee's mother's country, makes it a doubly female and maternal space. Reading *Penelope Brandling* against Radcliffe allows us to see Lee's other travel and history writing with its interest in the 'genius loci',[75] not just in relation to Pater and Ruskin but also in a long literary tradition of *female* sensitivity to place and landscape.

The other side of Penelope's experience at St Salvat's, however, is the classic Gothic scenario of female imprisonment imposed by male violence. The castle which should be her new home – 'the house of [Eustace's] fathers' (26) – is dominated by the Revd Hubert Brandling, and the other uncles, Simon, Edward, Gwyn and David, and cousin, Evan. Even the 'mulatto' Spanish-speaking cook is male (49), the reason given for this all-male household being that they are all capable of manning a boat. The only women are a couple of serving maids who are described as the uncles' 'sultanas' (51), and the once-beautiful housekeeper, Mrs Davies, foster-mother and nurse of the late Sir Thomas. Increasingly, Penelope 'like a caged bird [who has] grown accustomed to my prison' (65), confines herself to the isolated apartments which had belonged to Eustace's mother.

The courtly and yet sinister Uncle Hubert, who seems 'somehow a creature from another planet' (41), is a Gothic villain in the tradition of Matthew Lewis's *The Monk* (1796). A clergyman and magistrate, he represents the evils enabled and covered up by the structures of religion and law. 'There are two natures in us, occasionally, and the one vanquishes and overwhelms the other,' he tells Penelope. 'In me . . . the fisherman for pilchards has got the better of the fisherman for souls' (57). In contrast to 'the crew of Caliban uncles' (47) who can barely speak English, Hubert is knowledgeable in mathematics, a skilled mechanic, 'passionately fond of music' (80), and loves to 'lard his speech with literary reminiscences' (42). He rarely holds services in the church, explaining that not only do few of the household understand English but the common folk are of 'Mr Wesley's sect' (54). When he does do so, Penelope is surprised to find that he is 'a preacher of uncommon genius' (55), although his extempore rhetorical style is 'Romish' (55) with 'no kind of real religious spirit' (55). Given that his non-English-speaking audience are mostly asleep, Penelope sees the 'utter and almost indecent inappropriateness' (55) of his performance. The incestuous desires underlying the behaviour of the archetypal Gothic uncle/father villain are foregrounded through Penelope's horror at his 'paternal sentiment' (80) towards her and the way he kisses her neck just before she shoots him.

The secret of St Salvat's is not merely the wreckers' occupation but the way that violence underpins and perpetuates patriarchy through a murderous repression of the feminine. Primogeniture promulgates the deathly hand of patriarchy. Hubert's driving emotion is a reverence for family history – 'I care about my ancestors,' he admits, 'perhaps more, to say the truth, than for my living kinsfolk' (68). While he allegedly risked his life to rescue the family archives from the fire which burned his murdered nephew's body, and left his own hands dreadfully burned, Hubert's admission that he removed the most valuable volumes before the wake indicates his guilt. The library is also the site of another Gothic incident – the discovery, while a wall is being altered, of nine or ten skeletons 'walled up erect in the thickness of the masonry' (70). While Hubert dismisses these as 'relics' of the 'games' of his ancestors from 'hundreds and thousands of years ago, when we were sovereign princes' (72), Penelope's response, 'I had thought it was scarce so far removed from us as all that' (72), reveals the continuity of this history of violence into the present.

In the face of this patrilineal violence, Eustace, 'a dreamer' (96) sent away as a child by his mother to protect him, seems paralysed, as if bound by a 'bad spell' (97). In relation to this, Penelope invokes the 'legend' of her mother's clan 'where the future chieftain, on coming of age, was put into possession of some secret so terrible that it turned him from a light-hearted boy into a serious and joyless man' (92). Lee was clearly struck by this legend (which is associated with Glamis Castle, where it allegedly originated when a malformed heir was hidden in a secret room) because she parodied it in 'The Hidden Door' (1886).[76] In *Penelope Brandling* the 'secret' is a metaphor for the system of patrilineal inheritance where the boy's passage into manhood involves the murderous repression of the feminine within himself. Repelled by this version of masculinity, Eustace seems unable to act or to forge another version for himself.

The violent repression of the feminine is figured in another central image, which reiterates the legend of 'Prince Alberic'. As a child, Eustace tells his wife, he used to watch at an overgrown pond with a broken statue of a nymph in the terraced garden, 'for the transformation into a fairy of a great water snake which was said to have lived in that pond for centuries' (35). One day his brother Thomas 'trapped the poor harmless creature and cruelly skinned it alive' (35). The blurring here of legend or myth – the 'great water snake' which is really a 'fairy' – with the reality of a snake which can be trapped and killed is typical of Lee's work. The motif of skinning (which recalls the skinned rabbit which terrified Alberic) is repeated when Evan horrifies Penelope by coming to dinner with 'hands unwashed and red from skinning, as he told us, an otter' (41). Like the snake, the otter is a liminal watery creature. Skinning becomes a symbol of masculine violence towards the feminine (the water snake is another version of Oriana) and the legendry.

The motif of skinning alive is repeated in Lee's story 'Marsyas in Flanders' (1927).[77] This is another version of the 'god in exile' myth. A statue of Marsyas, the satyr flayed alive by Apollo for challenging him in a musical competition, is mistaken for one of Christ but refuses to stay on the crucifix to which he is attached. The mythical Marsyas, Patricia Pulham points out, was a liminal figure associated with castration and linked to Dionysus. His flayed body, she suggests, is reminiscent of a foetus.[78] Thus, she suggests, Lee's version of Marsyas, with its refusal to stay on the cross, appears to 'embody that fluid sexuality that characterises a child's amorphous existence prior to the formation of a "fixed" subjectivity'.[79] The skinned water snake, then, represents both mother and unborn child.

The horrific climax of the novel brings together these motifs as the pregnant Penelope witnesses a shipwreck, then a possible murder, and subsequently miscarries her baby. Lee's depiction of a pregnant heroine is itself unusual and *Penelope Brandling* here engages explicitly with the concern with maternity which is at the heart of the Female Gothic. Like Mary Shelley's *Frankenstein* (1818), Lee's novel is a birth myth which metaphorically enacts the dilemma of the mother within patriarchy. These nightmarish passages utilise the supernatural imagery of the Gothic to figure parallels between Penelope's situation and the scenes she witnesses.

The climax begins when Penelope is awakened from 'dreams of shipwreck' (102) by moonlight which makes her room look 'more than ever like a great glass cage' (103), and then witnesses a real shipwreck. Nightmare and reality merge and the dreamlike scene is strangely surreal. The shipwreck is presented in strikingly gendered terms which enforce the parallel with Penelope's 'caged' position. Pitching and rolling, the ship has run onto one of the reefs: 'She seemed enchanted, or rather she looked like some captive creature struggling desperately to get free' (104). Lee's descriptions here may owe something to a similarly gendered and emotive account of wreckers at St Donat's in Trevelyan's *Glimpses of Welsh Life and Character.*

> Then, like a helpless and wounded bird, the vessel droops her pinions, and succumbs to the mercy of the storm. One more noble effort to save herself – one terrible attempt to mount the waves, and she rushes upon the rocky ledges, there to become the shattered spray of the merciless waves.
>   The wreckers of St Donat's gleefully rub their hands.[80]

Trevelyan describes a woman swimming strongly towards the shore who is killed by one of the wreckers. He strips off her jewellery, biting off her swollen fingers to remove the rings, then leaves her body under the rocks. Trevelyan notes oral traditions of this story 'whispered during [the man's] lifetime' and becoming 'a lasting reproach upon the infamous race of men known as "the wreckers"' (317). Whether as oral tradition or in Trevelyan's account, this story seems likely to have fed into Lee's text.

Following the account of the shipwreck there is a break of several months in Penelope's diary as a result of illness following a devastating miscarriage. After long hours of unconsciousness Penelope writes, 'my mind seems misty, and like what a ghost might be' (109). As with Gaskell's 'Grey Woman' (discussed in chapter 3), her experience has 'ghosted' her. The diary pieces together 'shreds of recollection' (109) of an event which seems so much of a nightmare that she doubts its reality. As in her earlier stories, Lee uses first-person narrative to retell a possibly supernatural effect or event which could be explained by the protagonist's mental state. We cannot be sure if what Penelope saw as her illness makes her an unreliable narrator. The last thing of which she is certain is that three days after the shipwreck she went down to sit on the sea wall. Meditating on her impending motherhood, she looks at a Celtic cross in the churchyard and wonders 'whether when it was made – a thousand years ago – women about to be mothers' had felt as she did (112). This seemingly irrelevant act of empathy with other

mothers-to-be through history, an invocation of a maternal genealogy, is important in relation to the following events.

The nightmarish horror Penelope witnesses seems to be the brutal
murder of a mother and child cast ashore by the shipwreck. At the
sea wall she sees three men wading among the rocks, and close under
the wall where she is sitting, what she first takes for a heap of sea-
weed 'but which, as my eyes fixed it, became – *or methought it became*
– something hideous and terrible; so that for very horror I could
not shriek (114, emphasis added). What 'it' is, or might be, as it
comes into focus is unspeakable, almost unseeable. The three men,
one at least of whom has no 'human face' because he is wearing 'a
loosely fitting black mask' (114), gather round the heap, touch it
with a boat-hook. One stooping down 'did I know not what' (115),
stuffing something into his pocket, then takes 'something narrow
which caught a glint of the sun' (115). Penelope thinks that the
water 'suddenly changed colour, but that must surely be my nightmare' (115). Then they lift it to carry it to the boat and Penelope
flees, to collapse, symbolically, by the pond where the water snake
had been killed:

> For as they took *it* up, the thing had divided in two, and somehow
> I had known the one was a mother and the other a child; one was I,
> and the other I still carried within me. And the voice which had said
> 'Better like that' was Hubert's. But as I write, I know it must have
> been a vision of my sickness. (116).

This is the climax of a series of images of the murder of the maternal
in the novel: the killing of the water snake and the otter, the broken
statue of the nymph, the wreck of the ship, some pearls which
Hubert earlier gave to Penelope and which probably came from a
shipwrecked woman.

Yet, as with so many of Lee's stories, particularly those using
first-person narrators, what we are reading is left obscure and that
obscurity is central to its effect. As Lee wrote in relation to 'Dionea',
'such a story requires to appear and reappear and disappear, to be
baffling, in order to acquire its supernatural quality. You see there
is not [*sic*] real story; once assert the identity of Dionea with Venus,
once show her clearly, and no charm remains.'[81] It seems unlikely

that a mother and child would survive three days on a beach after a shipwreck. Certainly Penelope, suffering from what we would now call post-traumatic stress disorder, doubts what she saw: 'that must surely be my nightmare,' she says repeatedly. But the night-marish element of the event, its haunting quality, suggests that we need to read it as a working out of the unconscious, of what has been repressed.

The separation of mother and child in Penelope's nightmare vision can be read as a revision of Lacan's account (following Freud) of the need for separation of mother and child in order that the child should enter the Symbolic Order ruled by the Law of the Father. The separation of Penelope and her mother at the beginning of the novel is triggered by an earlier murder, of Sir Thomas, and this is replayed in the scene on the beach. 'For as they took *it* up,' Penelope writes, 'the *thing had divided in two*, and somehow I had known the one was a mother and the other a child' (116, my emphasis). This division into two is a violent one, enforced by the phallic knife of the paternal figure, and the repression of the con-nection to the mother is figured as an Irigarayan 'murder' which is deathly to the child as well. Like Sophia Lee and Gaskell, Lee suggests the need for women to retain their connection to the mother, and the need for them to 'mother' each other, to 'deliver' each other from imprisonment.

The complex relationship between 'self' and 'other' (whether male/female, or mother/child) is at the heart of the Gothic. The Female Gothic has been variously read as being about the fear of sameness (engulfment by the mother) or the fear of difference either of the male (violence) or of the mother (separation). As I have noted, it was Lee who introduced the concept of 'empathy', a sympathetic identification with the other, into English. The use of a female first-person narrative voice allows Lee to depict an act of empathy with the victimised woman, who is 'self' rather than 'other' (as in the male-narrated stories in *Hauntings*). As Penelope puts it: 'one was I, and the other I still carried within me' (116). Carrying an unborn 'other' in her womb, Penelope is both self and other. But she is also able to map this connection between self and other onto another woman, through their experience of a violated maternity.

To kill a child is also to kill a mother, destroying her identity *as mother*. Thus Penelope's miscarriage destroys her newly emerging sense of herself as a 'mother'. This connects her to another bereaved mother, the housekeeper Mrs Davies, who regarded her foster-son, the murdered Sir Thomas, as her 'son of the heart' (127). In a key scene, Mrs Davies, who has 'been as a mother' (119) to Penelope through her illness, brushes her hair 'with wonderful tenderness' (118) and they see each other's faces 'reflected in a mirror' (118), suggesting a surrogate mother–daughter relationship. It is Mrs Davies who shields Penelope from the wreckers, and she engineers the couple's escape from the castle. Her Welshness also connects her to Lee's own mother, although, as I have suggested, Lee's attitude to Wales and the Welsh is ambivalent and the other (male) Welsh characters in the novel are all villains. (Eustace, as I have noted, is presented throughout as 'English'.) Mrs Davies, however, is killed by Hubert, yet another murdered mother, and her body burned in the fire.

Lee's novel advocates female autonomy and action, including the refusal to be complicit in systems of oppression. While on one level it is caused by trauma, Penelope's miscarriage can be read as a refusal to perpetuate a patrilineal inheritance, to 'mother' within a violent system: 'no child of mine shall ever be born into slavery and disgrace such as, I feel, is ours,' she writes (97). Her discovery that Eustace is not involved in the wrecking enables a rapprochement, but given his incapacity for decisive action and his scruples about protecting the family name (156), she cannot rely on him to free her. In contrast, Penelope is, as Uncle Hubert recognises, 'a *virago*, a warlike lady' (174). It is Penelope Hubert bargains with, knowing that she is 'capable of making her husband respect [an oath]' (175). Eustace has given her a pistol which he implies she should use on herself if captured: 'I have no right to let you fall alive into the hands of those villains,' he tells her (169). Instead, Penelope shoots Hubert, telling him: 'in the name of God Almighty, whose ministry you have defiled, and whose law you have placed yourself outside, I take it upon myself to judge and put you to death as a wrecker and a murderer' (178).

Penelope's speech indicates the 'wrecking' of the institutions of religion and law, both made hollow shams by Hubert's abuse of patriarchal power. With the burning of St Salvat's (which parallels the fall of *Otranto*) she fulfils her desire to 'clean out this Augean stable, and burn out these wasp's nests' (53). While St Salvat's, which symbolises the male line, is destroyed, it is Penelope who is the 'saviour' of the text, rescuing both herself and her husband. Moreover, the destruction of the castle which makes them 'outlaws and felons' (188) whose lands are 'held over for our possible heirs' actually enables a reunion with Penelope's mother as they return to Switzerland. It is at 'Grandfrey, my dear dead mother's little property' (189) that Penelope spends her widowhood and it is there that she writes her final account of events, and waits for death.

As another rewriting of Walpole's *Castle of Otranto*, *Penelope Brandling* blocks and reverses the negative cycles of history depicted in Sophia Lee's *The Recess*. The letter-journal Penelope writes for her descendants, unlike that of Lee's Matilda, is a positive narrative of the successful overcoming of oppression and violence and the upholding of maternal values and connections. Vernon Lee's *œuvre* offers an extraordinarily complex and detailed engagement with the puzzles of 'the Past', and a particularly sophisticated understanding of the ways in which our understanding of history is almost always gendered. Yet the neglect of *Penelope Brandling*, as well as much of the rest of her work (the bulk of which remains out of print), suggests the erasure of Lee's own importance in the tradition of (Gothic) historical fiction. The critical focus on her as a writer influenced almost solely by male figures has made it difficult to place her in relation to other women writers. As I have argued, Ann Radcliffe is a literary 'mother' whose hitherto buried influence can be seen in Lee's work. It is also possible that *Penelope Brandling*, with its own emphasis on maternal genealogy, may have had an important influence on later writers, through (as I will argue in the next chapter) the work of Daphne du Maurier.

5

Displacing the Past: Daphne du Maurier and the Modern Gothic

ॐ

We can never go back again, that much is certain. The past is still too
close to us. The things we have tried to forget and put behind us
would stir again, and that sense of fear, of furtive unrest, struggling at
length to blind unreasoning panic – now mercifully stilled, thank God
– might in some manner unforeseen become a living companion, as
it had been before.

Daphne du Maurier, Rebecca (1938)[1]

The Female Gothic is always 'going back': texts are haunted by their
predecessors and, in turn, haunt their descendants. This uncanny
echoing is particularly intense in the relationship between the work
of Daphne du Maurier, particularly *Rebecca* (1938), and the so-
called 'modern Gothic' or 'drugstore Gothic' developed by Victoria
Holt and others in the 1960s. Just as critics have repeatedly drawn
attention to the ways in which *Rebecca* is 'a Cornish Gothic resetting
of *Jane Eyre*', the modern Gothic has been characterised as a 'cross-
breed of *Jane Eyre* and Daphne du Maurier's *Rebecca*'.[2] A huge and
calculated publishing success story, particularly in North America,
the formulaic nature of the modern Gothics was signalled by their
lurid covers featuring infinite variations on the same theme of a
young frightened woman overshadowed by a looming house, castle,
or château. Their unashamed intertextual debts to the Brontës

and du Maurier were used as a marketing tool: Victoria Holt's *The Legend of the Seventh Virgin* (1965), for instance, was advertised as 'A tale of gothic intrigue that captures the haunting evil of "Wuthering Heights" and the suspense of "Rebecca".'[3]

Yet this repeated emphasis on similarity – the promise to readers that in buying a modern Gothic they would be getting 'more' of *Jane Eyre* or *Rebecca* – obscures important differences, notably the ways in which Victoria Holt repeatedly displaces her plots into the past. The mesh of intertextual relationships I want to discuss is wider than the straight descent from *Jane Eyre* (1847) through *Rebecca* to Holt's *The Mistress of Mellyn* (1960) implied by much discussion of the modern Gothic. A web rather than a line, it also connects to Sophia Lee's *The Recess* (1783–5), Austen's *Northanger Abbey* (1818), *Wuthering Heights* (1847), Vernon Lee's *Penelope Brandling* (1903) and du Maurier's other Gothic historical novels – *Jamaica Inn* (1936), *The King's General* (1946), and *My Cousin Rachel* (1951).

As Patsy Stoneman has shown, famous texts become a kind of 'common property' within a culture and are 'transformed' in ways which go beyond the sense in which all literature is intertextual:

> Famous texts, like *Jane Eyre* and *Wuthering Heights*, which are repeat-edly plundered . . . acquire a different status, rather like that of a fairy-tale, which we might describe as mythological, This status depends partly on some inherent significance in the original text, and partly on the process of reiteration itself.[4]

Reduced to its basic elements, the plot of *Jane Eyre* (which itself reiterates Cinderella and Bluebeard) has become 'a staple of popular romance'.[5] Stoneman's study identifies two questions to ask about these modern myths. The first is, 'What is it in the original story which gives it such enduring interest?'[6] Such a question inevitably, as she notes, turns us towards Freudian readings, but these offer not a single answer but more questions: 'why does the Oedipus complex itself endure?' The other question is to do with the relationship of each transformation to the history of the society which produces it.[7] These two questions are at the heart of my own discussion of the relationship between history and the Gothic.

In repeatedly plundering *Jane Eyre* (1847) and *Rebecca*, the most important change Victoria Holt makes is to displace the basics of their plots back into the past. While neither *Jane Eyre* nor *Rebecca* is a historical novel (in the sense of being set sixty years or more in the past), almost all the thirty-two novels of Victoria Holt, the most successful of the modern Gothic writers, are historical in that sense. The classic 'governess/companion who falls in love with her employer and is haunted by his first wife plot' of *Jane Eyre* and *Rebecca* is explicitly rewritten as 'history' by Holt. Why? The fact that Holt locates this plot back into the nineteenth century of Charlotte Brontë's novel – what we usually call the 'Victorian' period – reinforces the connection with *Jane Eyre*. But it naturalises and obscures what is a more unexpected move than it at first seems.

The Female Gothic is, of course, always concerned with 'history', even when it is set in the present, because it is obsessed with a past which keeps returning, just as Rebecca's boat – *Je Reviens* – resurfaces. As Mary Ann Doane has argued, 'In psychoanalysis, the past is aggressive – it returns, it haunts, it sometimes dominates the present. In historiography, the past is static, inert – qualities which make it, in effect, more knowable.'[8] It is this difference between the past of the psyche and that of traditional historiography which I want to tease out in my readings of these novels. This is also partly a difference between public history and private experience and the ways in which these are recorded and valued.

We read *Jane Eyre* as 'historical' now because it is a nineteenth-century novel. The contemporaneousness of the 1930s setting of *Rebecca* should perhaps be more obvious since it is closer to us. Both novels, however, make powerful use of retrospective first-person narratives as well as Gothic motifs of haunting, both techniques which conjure up a sense of pastness. The case is slightly different with *Wuthering Heights*, another key intertext for du Maurier and the modern Gothic. *Wuthering Heights* is a historical novel in the Scott tradition although it is rarely discussed as such. Readers often fail to notice that it opens with a date, '1801', which is seventeen years before the birth of its author, and that the story of Cathy and Heathcliff is set a generation earlier in the 1770s. While he notes this and the influence of Walter Scott, Ian Jack nevertheless concludes that 'of course [*Wuthering Heights*] is not a historical novel except in the sense that it is set in a period earlier than that of its publication.'[9] Writing in 1981, Jack seems to be working with a

Lukácsian definition of the 'historical novel' here but these uncertainties about exactly what constitute a 'historical novel' are
telling in relation to assumptions about gender.
In fact, both *Wuthering Heights* and *Jane Eyre* were probably
influenced by *The Recess*. April Alliston notes the 'correspondences'
between *Wuthering Heights* and *The Recess*:

> Brontë also wrote her novel around the problem of female and
> maternal inheritance, with a plot that is unusual in that it, like Lee's,
> includes both the mother's and the daughter's histories . . . The
> structural peculiarities of *Wuthering Heights* also strikingly resemble
> those of *The Recess*, for both are doubled: Brontë devoting one of the
> split halves to each Cathy, while Lee devotes one half of her strangely
> split narrative to each of her twin heroines.[10]

Wuthering Heights, like *The Recess*, is historical in the sense that it is
concerned with matrilineal genealogies. It is this focus on female
inheritance (rather than the kinds of public and political history Jack
seems to be searching for), which so often draws women writers to
the Gothic historical novel. And, as I have already argued in relation
to Gaskell, women often look to literary texts for a female history
which is left out of history books. Moreover, *The Recess*, Janina
Nordius has argued, is also a likely influence on *Jane Eyre*: both novels
feature a wedding scene interrupted by news from Jamaica which
renders the marriage unlawful (incest in *The Recess* and bigamy in
Jane Eyre).[11] Both texts depict the imprisonment of women: the attic
in which mad Bertha Rochester is immured is another version of
Lee's recess. Tracing the antecedents of the modern Gothic back
through *Wuthering Heights* as well as *Jane Eyre* makes more explicit
its descent from the female Gothic *historical* novel as developed by
Sophia Lee. Taking a long view along this matrilineal genealogy
illuminates the consistency with which women writers have returned
to Gothic tropes as the most eloquent expression of women's inheritance within and exclusion from androcentric history. But it also
exposes the ways in which these tropes mean differently in each
period.
The 'reiteration' of earlier texts connects to the uncanny repetition at the heart of the Female Gothic. It is frequently further
doubled within each text through the use of pairs of women –

mothers and daughters, twin sisters, first and second wives. Moreover, this reiteration is situated within the 'coherence' of Gothic conventions analysed by Eve Kosofsky Segwick,[12] whereby even a glancing allusion keys the reader into a Gothic frame of mind. The marketing of the modern Gothics exploited this coherence. The central reiteration is of what Holland and Sherman summed up as 'woman-plus-habitation and the plot of mysterious sexual and supernatural threats in an atmosphere of dynastic mysteries',[13] endlessly pictured in those formulaic covers. But it is not just the plot but the names of characters (Catherine, Bevil, Favel, Rockwell) and houses (Menfreya, Mellyn, Pendorric, Kirkland Revels), as well as the landscape (the Cornish coast, the Yorkshire moors) which reiterate past texts, reinforcing the reader's sense that she has read this somewhere before.

Daphne du Maurier's Gothic historical novels

Daphne du Maurier's fiction returns repeatedly to those two key Female Gothic motifs I have been discussing – the 'murder of the mother', and imprisonment in a womblike-tomblike 'recess' – and it is these which become central to Holt's modern Gothic. However, as Avril Horner and Sue Zlosnik have shown, du Maurier's novels do not fit the usual formula of the Female Gothic:[14] du Maurier eschews the affirmative closure of the happy ending, and she often uses a male narrative voice associated with the Male Gothic. Horner and Zlosnik identify a 'critical confusion' over the differences between 'Gothic romances of the best-selling pulp variety' and 'a gendered genre entitled "Female Gothic"', which might include texts like *Jane Eyre*.[15] It's that 'critical confusion' I want to adddress in focusing on the ways Holt rewrites du Maurier.

It is tempting to read these Gothic motifs simply in relation to du Maurier's own biography. Both du Maurier's potentially lesbian desires and her desire to write are imaged in Gothic terms in a much-quoted passage from one of her letters:

> And then the boy realised he had to grow up and not be a boy any longer, so he turned into a girl, and not an unattractive one at that,

and the boy was locked in a box forever. D. du M. wrote her books and had young men, and later a husband and children, and a lover . . . but when she found Menabilly and lived in it alone she opened up the box sometimes and let the phantom, who was neither girl nor boy but disembodied spirit, dance in the evening when there was no one to see.[16]

The phantom boy – the masculine that has to be repressed – is an interesting reversal of the ghosted women in Gaskell's stories. It evokes the figure of Rebecca, the 'first Mrs de Winter', who 'ought have been a boy' (253), and whose murdered body is locked in the cabin of her drowned boat. The coffin-like 'box' is also reiterated as the central image of *The King's General* (1946), where the effeminate Dick dies trapped in the secret buttress room.

Whatever its biographical origins, I want to stress the self-conscious literariness of du Maurier's writing. One of the most striking things about du Maurier's *Myself When Young: The Shaping of a Writer* (1977) is the intensity and the breadth of her reading. Her juvenile diary is peppered with the refrain 'I read also'.[17] Without the university education of her male peers, this is a woman who made herself into a writer through avid reading of other writers' work. Equally striking is the way she made use of that reading to understand her own identity and place in the world. As a child she explored her ambivalence towards her rather distant mother though identifying her as the Snow Queen or Snow White's wicked stepmother: 'If I could turn into Kay, and M [her mother] could become the Snow Queen, then who was I really, where did I belong? The Snow Queen was an enemy, like that other queen, who looked into a mirror.'[18]

This is an example of the ways in which children, as Bruno Bettelheim shows in *The Uses of Enchantment* (1976), use fairy tales to understand complex psychological relationships in their world.[19] The difference lies in du Maurier's self-conscious recognition of the place of this process in her 'shaping as a writer'. Her conclusion that 'Evil women were more terrible than evil men,'[20] which positions the mother as an 'enemy' who must be vanquished, is a theme to which her mature writing returns. Her transformation into the male Kay (not Gerda) foreshadows her invention of a male alter ego, Eric Avon, who 'remained in my unconscious, to emerge in later years

– though in quite a different guise – as the narrator of the five novels I was to write, at long intervals, in the first person singular, masculine gender'.[21]

Later, enmeshed in an over-close relationship with her father, the celebrated actor-manager Sir Gerald du Maurier, and a semi-affair with her older, married cousin Geoffrey, du Maurier used history in a similar way. Kissing Geoffrey, she mused, was 'so like kissing D [Gerald]. Perhaps this family is the same as the Borgias. D. is Pope Alexander, Geoffrey is Cesare, and I am Lucretia. A sort of incest.'[22] Groaning 'Daddy, Daddy!' as she emerged from anaesthetic at the dentist, she concluded: 'So it was not the Borgia brother but the Borgia father that the unconscious self demanded.'[23] Fairy tales and history provide narratives which she uses to make sense of unconscious desires, but she is unusually conscious of both those desires and the processes through which they manifest through texts.

As in Vernon Lee's work, the unconscious often seems so close to the surface of du Maurier's novels that they cry out for Freudian readings. Thus Tania Modleski's reading of Hitchcock's film of *Rebecca* as 'an oedipal drama from a feminine point of view'[24] makes perfect sense. If Maxim is an obvious father figure, Rebecca (a boyish Snow Queen) takes the place of the Oedipal mother-rival who must be destroyed if the daughter-narrator is to take her place as 'Mrs de Winter'. Rebecca's serpentine qualities – '"She gave you the feeling of a snake"', says Ben (162) – connect her with Lee's Snake-Lady, the phallic mother. In her comparison of the film with the novel, Karen Hollinger argues that 'du Maurier's vision of an essentially unresolved, female oedipal dilemma is transformed into the film's vexed but ultimately successful resolution of its heroine's oedipal crisis'; ultimately, the film celebrates 'the final triumph of patriarchy over female power'.[25] Yet, as Stoneman reminds us, such readings raise other questions: why the Oedipus complex? How does this relate to history? For du Maurier is equally obsessed with history and uses the Gothic to explore women's disinherited place in patrilineal narratives.

Du Maurier's first historical novel, *Jamaica Inn* (1936), begins as classic Radcliffean Female Gothic, but may also have been indebted to Vernon Lee's *Penelope Brandling*. While I have found no definite evidence that du Maurier read Lee's novel, there are striking similarities which suggest that du Maurier was self-consciously reworking the conventions of this Female Gothic tradition. Like *Penelope Brandling, Jamaica Inn* takes its inspiration from a real building with a troubled history, set in an 'alien' country (6). The orphaned protagonist, Mary Yellan, arrives at Jamaica Inn, an isolated building with 'secrets . . . embedded in its walls' run by her uncle Joss Merlyn, a 'great husk of a man, nearly seven feet high'.[26] Her coach journey towards the Inn through the hard, barren landscape of Bodmin moor, obscured by mist and 'lashing, pitiless rain' (7) and with trees 'bent and twisted from centuries of storm'(7), recalls the desolate Wales through which Penelope travels to St Salvat's. Like Penelope, Mary finds herself imprisoned, with one other woman for company. Aunt Patience is a 'living ghost' 105), her youth and beauty erased (like that of Gaskell's 'grey woman' or Lee's Mrs Davies), by marriage and her knowledge of the inn's secret. That secret – the 'phantom figures' and 'shrouded wagons' (71) – is not just, as Mary first suspects, smuggling, but the more sinister practice of wrecking. As in *Penelope Brandling*, ships are lured onto the rocks, survivors murdered and the spoils 'salvaged'.

While Lee's suave uncle Hubert is also the clergyman villain, du Maurier splits this figure into two. This split develops a duality in Lee's novel, where Hubert tells Penelope, 'There are two natures in us.'[27] Joss Merlyn initially appears to be the wreckers' leader, but is actually controlled by Francis Davey, the albino vicar of Altarnun. If Hubert is 'somehow a creature from another planet' (41), Francis with his halo of white hair, 'strange eyes, transparent like glass', and soft voice, is 'a freak of nature' (87). While his ghostly appearance marks him out as otherworldly, abject even, his status as a gentleman and a clergyman leads Mary to mis-recognise him, regarding him as her rescuer. In this he is the prototype of what Joanna Russ calls the 'Shadow-Male' of the modern Gothic of the 1960s, the man 'invariably represented as genteel, protective, responsible, quiet, humorous, tender and calm' who is ultimately 'revealed as a murderer'.[28] Du Maurier further complicates this pattern through the doubling of Joss Merlyn with his brother Jem, the 'worst of the family' (64).

Like Austen's Henry Tilney, Davey brings the forces of male rationalism to bear on Mary's story of violence at Jamaica Inn, telling her '"this is the nineteenth century you know, and men don't murder one another without reason"'(91). Under the cold influence of his 'unbelief', her 'ridiculous and highly-coloured' story becomes 'an elaborate piece of nonsense' (92) told by a hysteric. It is '"too much of a fairy tale"' (92) which would never stand up in a court of law. As in *Northanger Abbey*, the Gothic narrative (like fairy tales) expresses the truth, as the villainous vicar knows only too well. Indeed, the Gothic landscape of *Jamaica Inn*, like that of Gaskell's 'Grey Woman', is saturated with violence towards women: Mary is locked up, tied up, beaten up and threatened with rape and murder, while Aunt Patience is stabbed to death, not by Joss, but by Francis Davey.

As in *Penelope Brandling*, the wrecking of a ship is associated with the symbolic murder of a mother and her child. As Irigaray comments: 'once the man-god-father kills the mother so as to take power, he is assailed by ghosts and anxieties.'[29] Thus Joss Merlyn is haunted by the alcohol-sodden nightmares:

> 'There was a woman once, Mary; she was clinging to a raft, and she had a child in her arms; her hair was streaming down her back . . . She cried out to me to help her, Mary, and I smashed her face in with a stone; she fell back, her hands beating the raft. She let go of the child and I hit her again; I watched them drown in four feet of water.' (116)

This confession disinters Mary's own memory of a shipwreck witnessed when she was a child, the gendered imagery of which reiterates that of Vernon Lee and Marie Trevelyan (discussed in chapter 4): '[Mary] saw a great white ship like a bird rolling help-lessly in the trough of the sea, her masts broken short and her sails trailing in the water beside her' (118). The secret of *Jamaica Inn* is, like that of Bluebeard and *Penelope Brandling*: 'patriarchy's secret founding truth . . . women as mortal, expendable matter/*mater*.'[30] But the man-god-father who is responsible for the murder is not the brutal Joss, but, as in *Penelope Brandling*, the cultured clergyman.

Both Francis Davey and Hubert Brandling are cynical non-believers whose abuse of their position exposes a hollowness at the heart of established Christianity. Davey's caricature of himself with a wolf's face preaching to a congregation who have sheep's heads, each bearing the 'expression . . . of an idiot who neither knew nor cared' (232), takes a step further Hubert's indecently inappropriate preaching to an non-English-speaking audience, most of whom are asleep. Davey sees himself as a '"freak in nature [and] a freak in time"' (243). Having sought peace and silence in the 'dogma of Christianity' he finds that '"the whole foundation is built on a fairy tale. Christ Himself is a figure-head, a puppet thing created by man himself"' (243). Like Vernon Lee, du Maurier presents the past as a palimpsest: beneath the foundation stone of the aptly named Altar/nun church '"lie the bones of [the congregation's] pagan ancestors, and the old granite altars where sacrifice was held long before Christ died on his cross"' (248). While Lee associates the pagan past with the repressed feminine through the symbolic water fairy, however, du Maurier associates it with ghost-like Francis Davey. Abducted by him to a cave on Roughtor, Mary sees his gods, 'monsters of antiquity': 'Their faces were inhuman, older than time, carved and rugged like the granite; and they spoke in a tongue she could not understand, and their hands and feet were curved like the claws of a bird' (254).

Cornered, Davey stands 'poised like a statue' on a 'wide slab like an altar' and then '[flings] out his arms as a bird throws out his wings for flight' and falls (258). The pagan past here is not the feminine fluidity of Lee's water snake but the stony cruelty of a bird of prey, deeply inimical to women. Christianity is merely a 'fairy tale . . . created by man [sic] himself'. Both have at their heart, du Maurier intimates, the denial of the creative and maternal function of women: as Mary reminds Francis Davey, he has '"killed my mother's sister"' (250).

Recorded history is more important in *Jamaica Inn* than a casual reading may suggest: the novel is set in the reign of George IV at the moment when the establishment of coast guards to patrol the coast will, Davey tells Mary, create '"a chain across England . . . that will be very hard to break"' (152). It is, she thinks, 'the dawn of a new age, when men and women would travel without fear' (153). In one sense, the novel suggests, the wreckers are a thing of the barbaric past, like the pagan gods. But the contemporary idiom of the writing and the focalisation through Mary bring the novel into the present in ways which suggest its continued relevance.

Moreover, the ending of the novel is ambivalent, and this ambivalence is located in the figure of Jem Merlyn (whose name, like that
of his brother, ominously associates him with a bird of prey).

While Lee provides Penelope with an indecisive and ineffectual
husband, reminiscent of Radcliffe's bland heroes and initially of
Davey himself, du Maurier offers a much more ambivalent figure
in Jem. She also offers a more incisive exploration of the physical
(and incestuous) attraction which underlies the battle between
Gothic heroine and villain. Jem is an uncanny copy of his brother,
'what Joss Merlyn might have been, eighteen, twenty years ago'
(63). If Joss is the 'Borgia father' of du Maurier's family romance,
then Jem is the 'Borgia brother'. Jem stands for 'everything [Mary]
feared and hated and despised; but she knew she could love him'
(122). This as an irresistible biological urge, 'no choice made with
the mind' (122). His close physical resemblance to Joss shows Mary
'that aversion and attraction ran side by side; that the boundary line
between them was thin' (126). Francis Davey's sexless recognition
of Mary's '"dash of fire"' (245), which reiterates Hubert's admir-
ation of Penelope, is mirrored by Joss's assertion that if he'd been
younger '"I'd have courted you, Mary . . . aye and won you too, and
ridden away with you to glory"' (187). The merging of the two
brothers is symbolised by Joss's mouth, 'so like his brother's' (175),
when he kisses Mary. Furthermore, for some time, Mary suspects
that it is Jem who masterminds the wrecking, and the 'idea of a dual
personality' (192) deeply troubles her. Here the doubled Joss–Jem
is a prototype for the dangerous lover of the modern Gothic, the
Super–Male (as Russ calls him)[31] the heroine suspects of wanting to
murder her. The ending of the novel reveals Jem's innocence in a
move that is played out obsessively in Victoria Holt's later novels.
Having informed against Joss, it is Jem, not Mary, who shoots Davey.
While the end of *Jamaica Inn* looks on the surface like the affirmative
closure of the Female Gothic, as Mary rides off with Jem towards
the Tamar '"because I must"' (266), it is actually deeply ambivalent.

Both *The King's General* and *My Cousin Rachel* revisit these
Female Gothic themes, offering more detailed explorations of the
recess and the murder of the mother. Both, like *Rebecca*, take their
inspiration from Menabilly, the 'house of secrets'[32] Du Maurier
famously fell in love with and lived in for a central part of her

writing life. Since the house belonged to the Rashleigh family, the 'fairy tale' of her tenure was haunted by the sense of an ending: 'Perhaps it is the very insecurity of the love that makes the passion strong,' she wrote in 1946, 'Because she is not mine by right. The house is still entailed, and one day will belong to another.'[33] As always in the Gothic, ownership of the (female) house passes down the legitimate male line, and du Maurier, neither Rashleigh nor male, was always a 'trespasser in time'.[34] She could inhabit the house, learn her stories, and re-create her in fiction, but never own her. The delegitimising of female inheritance has its most lethal expression in *Rebecca*, of course, where Maxim de Winter kills Rebecca to prevent an illegitimate child inheriting Manderley.

Living at Menabilly inspired two of du Maurier's best historical novels. *The King's General*, based on the life of Sir Richard Grenville, has been praised as 'excellent' by Grenville's biographer Ian Roy.[35] Du Maurier did considerable work in the Rashleigh archives and the novel is based on the lives of real people (including Honor Harris, the narrator-protagonist) and set against a detailed account of the Civil War which drew on letters to the Rashleighs from key figures, including King Charles I and the Grenville brothers, Sir Bevil and Sir Richard.[36] Given this basis in archival research it is (as with *The Recess*), the interventions du Maurier makes in recorded history through what she called her 'blend of fact and fiction' which are important.[37]

The framing of the story through the retrospective first-person narrative of Honor Harris, her love for Richard Grenvile, and the use of a contemporary idiom (as in *Jamaica Inn*), can all mislead the reader into thinking that this is merely a historical romance. In fact, *The King's General* is a bleak exploration of women's exclusion from recorded history, particularly during wartime. Very much a novel of the mid-1940s, it uses the Civil War to explore the divisions between non-combatant women who can do little except wait passively for the 'relentless tramp of enemy feet' (133) and men who 'are really bred to war and thrive upon it' (185). Crippled in a fall from a horse just fifty pages into the novel, Honor warns the reader who thinks that she makes 'an indifferent heroine to a tale' (54) to close the book. Her 'crippled' status acts as a metaphor for her gender – that which ostensibly makes women 'indifferent' subjects for history. But it also, ironically, frees her from traditional female roles (including that of romantic heroine, since she will never marry Richard), allowing her to 'take a leading part in the drama' (55) and to take on the 'role of judge and witness' (55) – the role of female historian, in fact.

The genesis of the novel came from the story (retold in the novel's 'Postscript') that in 1824 builders at Menabilly had discovered a secret room in a buttress which contained 'the skeleton of a young man, seated on a stool, a trencher at his feet, and . . . dressed in the clothes of a Cavalier, as worn in the Civil War'(349). This haunting image of live burial is at the heart of du Maurier's novel, and it is this which is reiterated in the modern Gothic, although there it is (as I will argue below) regendered so that it is a woman who is repeatedly buried alive. The imaginative leap du Maurier takes is to make this entombed Cavalier the son of Richard Grenvile. There is no evidence for this (Ian Roy notes a report that Grenville's only legitimate son, Richard, was hanged as a highwayman, while the Rashleigh family believed the skeleton to be that of a Grenville cousin[38]) but it enables du Maurier to symbolise the brutal repressions involved in certain kinds of masculinity, at their most extreme in wartime, and the complicities in which this involves women. Nicknamed 'Skellum' (German for 'a vicious beast' (78)[39]) for his ruthless brutality as a solder, Richard despises his effeminate and artistic son Dick. Tellingly, Dick's pathological fear of bloodshed stems from a violent quarrel between his parents when Richard struck his mother and her blood fell on Dick, then a baby in her arms. Taking on the role of surrogate mother, Honor tries – and fails – to protect Dick from his father.

Like Bluebeard's prohibited room, the secret room in the buttress conceals the horrors at the heart of patriarchy. Originally built to subdue the lunatic brother of Jonathan Rashleigh, it is then used by Jonathan to hide plate for the Royalist cause. Discovering the room, Honor hides Dick Grenvile in it for hours on end when Menabilly is occupied by Roundheads. She herself sees the space only once, when she is carried down there by Richard, and realises with horror what Dick has endured there: 'Six foot high, four foot square, it was no larger than a closet, and the stone walls, clammy cold with years, icy to my touch' (335). At the end of the novel, when Richard and Dick escape through the secret tunnel, Dick stays in the room (it is unclear whether he chooses this or is abandoned by Richard because Dick betrayed the Royalist uprising), and dies there. It is this which haunts Honor who wakes in the night to 'the sound of a boy's voice calling my name in terror, to a boy's hand beating against the walls' (15). As Horner and Zlosnik have noted, Dick is 'quite literally, a boy in a box', and the sexual ambiguity he represents in the novel is 'punished by containment of the most horrific kind'.[40] In biographical terms, they suggest, Dick represents du Maurier's fears about the walling-up of her own ambiguous desires.

As a kind of female historian, Honor is only too well aware of the fate of women's stories. Her account of events is written to record the name of 'a boy whose name will never now be written in the great book at Stowe [the Grenville family home]' (346). But 'while my Richard's 'Defence'[41] is discussed by the world and placed on record for all time amongst the archives of this seventeenth century, my apologia will go with me to the grave, and by rotting there with me, unread, will serve its purpose' (16). Honor's unread 'apologia' rotting in the grave reiterates the fate of Dick in the buttress, both casualties of the masculinity represented by 'my Richard' and upheld by mainstream history.

If *The King's General* is a bleak account of the historical legacy of striated gender roles, *My Cousin Rachel* is an even bleaker analysis of the murderous effects of the patrilineal descent of property, power and narrative structures. Horner and Zlosnik have brilliantly read this novel as 're-enact[ing] the matricide which Luce Irigaray believes to be the foundations of our culture: "the whole of our western culture is based upon the murder of the mother."'[42] Set in a vaguely delineated nineteenth century, the novel is bracketed by the repetition of the opening lines which initially seem to invoke a past barbaric violence now safely civilised: 'They used to hang men at Four Turnings in the old days. Not any more though.'[43] It opens with the image of a gibbet and the rotting body of a man executed for murdering his wife for being a 'scold' (6). But 'that was no excuse to kill her,' comments Ambrose, cousin-guardian of the narrator Philip, 'If we killed women for their tongues all men would be murderers' (5). His 'we' signals the hegemony of the male viewpoint (enacted in the novel through the first-person narrative viewpoint of Philip), the 'othering' of women, and the symbolic potential in 'all men [to be] murderers' who silence and disinherit women.

When Ambrose unexpectedly marries the widowed Rachel in Italy and then himself suddenly dies, Philip becomes obsessed with the idea that she has poisoned Ambrose. Here, as in *Rebecca*, du Maurier uses an unreliable narrative voice to trap the reader in Philip's point of view and to show how Philip constructs Rachel 'as a wicked woman in the Gothic mode'.[44] Falling in love with her, he hands over his patrimony to her and then, devastated when he realises that she has no intention of marrying him, contrives her death through a fall. Rachel's guilt is left undetermined – she may or may not be a poisoner. As Horner and Zlosnik argue, *My Cousin Rachel* can be read as Male Gothic, reflecting in Williams's words, 'patriarchy's night*mère*', a 'primitive anxiety about "the female", specifically the mother'.[45] 'The 'ultimate horror' for the feminist reader, they suggest, 'lies in Philip's own subjectivity'.[46]

To put this slightly differently, Philip believes that he is in an Oedipal plot where the death of his 'father' means he can marry his 'mother'. In fact, he is following an Orestian plot, killing the 'mother' he believes has murdered his 'father'. Du Maurier's repeated doubling of Philip and Ambrose – the dying Rachel calls Philip 'Ambrose' (302) – suggests the interchangeability of father and son in this plot. One answer to the question 'Why Oedipus?', then, is 'Not Oedipus but Clytemnestra'. It is not the Oedipal murder of the father by the son, but the 'murder of the mother' by the man-father-god and the complicity of the child, whether daughter or son, that haunts du Maurier's texts.

Rebecca's daughter: 'Victoria Holt' and the costume Gothic

The success of the popular modern Gothic novel for women, a 'bonanza for publishers',[47] began in North America in 1960 with the publication of Victoria Holt's *Mistress of Mellyn* and republication of Phyllis Whitney's *Thunder Heights*. It peaked between 1969 and 1974. Jerry Gross, then at Ace Books, republished *Thunder*

Heights because his late mother, Helen Gross, told him 'that she'd been reading the same copy of "Rebecca" over and over because they didn't make books like it any more'.[48] Notwithstanding the Brontëan title, Whitney cited du Maurier as inspiration: 'I loved "Rebecca" and that sort of reading,' she said, 'so I decided to try that sort of writing.'[49] In Britain Eleanor Hibbert, then best known under her pseudonym 'Jean Plaidy', was persuaded by the American agent Patricia Myrer to revive the Gothic novel. Hibbert described *Mistress of Mellyn* as 'the sort of book I loved to write, because I had read so much of the Brontës, over and over again, and Wilkie Collins, and all that sort of thing'.[50] Hibbert used several different pseudonyms: 'Jean Plaidy' for her biographical–historical novels based on royal women, 'Victoria Holt' for the modern Gothics, and 'Philippa Carr' for her series of historical Gothics. While 'Plaidy' was taken from a Cornish beach, 'Holt' was (rather appositely) taken from her bank, and 'Victoria' subliminally suggests a 'Victorian' setting. The true identity of 'Victoria Holt' was kept a secret for the first six books, and many readers were apparently convinced that it must be a pseudonym for du Maurier because the atmosphere of *Mistress of Mellyn* was similar to that of *Rebecca*.[51] Victoria Holt came to dominate modern Gothic sales, closely followed by Whitney.[52]

The formulaic nature of the modern Gothic was a calculated marketing ploy, an attempt to replicate the elements of long-standing best-sellers. 'Victoria Holt' was characterised by her British publisher Fontana as 'The supreme writer of "gothic" romance, a compulsive storyteller whose gripping novels of the darker face of love have thrilled millions all over the world'.[53] The compulsion to repeat is at the heart of the modern Gothic phenomenon, and the metaphor of addiction was frequently used to describe it. Emma Mai Ewing uses the term 'Gothic mania' and notes that readers described themselves as 'gothic addicts'.[54] 'Once you begin to read,' said one of Hibbert's readers, 'it is like a drug for which, without in the least meaning to, you form an addiction.'[55] Indeed, it was not only Hibbert who could not remember details of her 200 or more novels; neither could her readers, who made secret marks in the backs of library copies so that they could tell which they'd read.[56]

As Juliann Fleenor reminds us, 'There is not just one Gothic but Gothics.'[57] The notorious slipperiness of the term 'Gothic' enabled

it to be applied to a range of novels by a disparate group of writers
– among them Holt, Whitney, Norah Lofts and Mary Stewart –
who actually write different kinds of novel. Indeed, Norah Lofts
rejected the label: 'Strictly speaking I don't think I belong in the
romance or gothic class.'[58] While Holt's novels are usually set in the
nineteenth century,[59] Whitney's are mainly, with the exception of
Thunder Heights,[60] set in the present day, as are those of Mary Stewart.
The distinction between past and present settings is blurred, however, by the formulaic covers where the flowing garments featured
on the covers of the modern novels such as Holt's *Bride of Pendorric*
(1963) or Whitney's *The Winter People* (1969) are indistinguishable
from the 'period' gowns on the historical novels.

Holt's novels return to the historical roots of the Gothic, the sense
in which the Gothic is a 'mode' of history, a gendered narrative of
the past. They are, however, more accurately 'costume Gothics', the
vagueness of their 'Victorian' settings connoting a 'past' which is
defined mainly by the fact that it is not the present. The blurb for
Mistress of Mellyn is typical of the way in which the word 'Victorian'
is deployed to evoke *Jane Eyre*: 'To become a governess was the
only course open to a lonely Victorian girl.'[61] History is evoked
through place and space. The signifiers of 'pastness' are mainly
costume, country houses, architectural details like priest holes,
horse-drawn carriages and servants, all connoting what Catherine
Bennett calls 'a pre-National Trust sort of past'.[62] Only in rare
instances – as in *Menfreya* (1966) where the heroine marries an MP
– is there any inclusion of actual historical fact.[63] The use of identical
covers on modern and costume Gothics suggests that the basic
Gothic plot of girl-plus-habitation is extremely portable, equally at
home in the nineteenth or mid-twentieth century. This is not to say
that the historical setting is unimportant, as Hibbert's explanation
for their success indicates: 'it is about the past, and people really
want to escape from the present, which may seem rather drab to
them.'[64] Given Hibbert's parallel career as 'Jean Plaidy', it is not the
case that she was historically ignorant or uncaring, but rather that
she chose to exclude specific historical detail. This was another
marketing decision – Hibbert saw the Holt books as written for
'the housewife in the mid-West of America, who has never heard of
Louis XV and doesn't want to'.[65] 'Englishness' here connotes 'history'.

The vaguely historical setting produces a dreamlike atmosphere in which the psychological past – repressed emotions of fear and desire – becomes all important. This reiterates the atmosphere of *Rebecca*, with its famous dream opening: 'Last night I dreamt I went to Manderley again' (5). The triangle plot of *Rebecca* is typical of inter-war novels of female rivalry which responded to a very specific historical phenomenon: the inter-war population imbalance which provoked a media frenzy over the lack of men for the so-called 'surplus' of women to marry.[66] (Hibbert was herself a second wife, which may be part of her obsession with such plots.) Yet *Rebecca* has very few specific historical markers indicating its contemporanity, although it is saturated in a sense of the lost past: 'We can never go back again, that much is certain' (8). In *Mistress of Mellyn*, Holt rewrites *Jane Eyre* back through *Rebecca*, displacing her plot into a 'Victorian Cornwall' which functions as a fantasy space. As Martha muses,

> In this moorland country it was possible to believe in fantastic dreams: as some told themselves that these tracts of land were inhabited by the Little People, so I told myself that it was not impossible that Connan TreMellyn would fall in love with me. (163)

The past here serves a symbolic function, which is not straightforwardly nostalgic or conservative. Rather it directs us towards the ways in which the modern Gothics endlessly play out a psychological drama which Russ suggests replicates the Freudian family romance: 'Heroine plays daughter, the Super-Male is father, and the Other Woman/First Wife plays mother.'[67] Russ found that the key elements she identified in this pattern – brooding House, passive Heroine, brusque Super-Male, sexual Other Woman, murderous Shadow-Male, Young Girl – were remarkably constant in the novels she examined. The Other Woman, 'the heroine's double and opposite', Russ notes, is usually involved in the '*Buried Ominous Secret*' connected to the Super-Male which the heroine has to unravel.[68] Russ does not discuss the role of setting in the modern Gothic but the doubling of the heroine and Other Women/First Wife suggests that Mary Anne Doane's characterisation of the past of psychoanalysis as 'aggressive – it returns, it haunts, it sometimes dominates the present' is apposite here. It is this doubling which most closely signals the modern Gothic's obsessive reiteration of *Rebecca* and *Jane Eyre*.

Despite Hibbert's citing of nineteenth-century novels as the inspiration for *Mistress of Mellyn*, du Maurier's work was more influential than she acknowledged. But the seemingly straight line which connects *Jane Eyre*, *Rebecca* and Victoria Holt is actually a jagged one. The first book Hibbert published under the pseudonym 'Jean Plaidy' was *Together They Ride* (1945). Set in eighteenth-century Cornwall, this blends a *Jamaica Inn*-style tale of wreckers with the dual-house cross-class romance of *Wuthering Heights*, spiced with a hero-disguised-as-a-highwayman straight out of Georgette Heyer's early novels. The climactic scene where the hero realises he is involved with wreckers replays Mary's experiences in *Jamaica Inn*. Treloary sees a ship which had 'broke[n] her back on Satan's Teeth' struggling in 'a heavy sea with white-flecked waves', and then attempts to save a drowning woman who is murdered by one of the wreckers.[69] The novel ends, like *Jamaica Inn*, with the two lovers riding off: 'Neither of them looked backwards as they crossed the Tamar.'[70]

Holt's early novels, then, rework a wider range of texts than previously assumed: *Mistress of Mellyn* reiterates *Rebecca* and *Jane Eyre*; *Kirkland Revels* (1962), with a heroine called Catherine who is nearly incarcerated in a lunatic asylum, draws on *Wuthering Heights*, Mary Elizabeth Braddon's *Lady Audley's Secret* (1862) and Wilkie Collins's *The Woman in White* (1860);[71] *Menfreya* (1966), with its lame heroine, husband named Bevil, and buttress room, transposes elements of *The King's General* into the late nineteenth century. Three of the key elements Holt borrows from du Maurier's work are obsessively repeated, however: the first-person narrative voice; incarceration in a recess-like space (originating in *The King's General*); and the murder of – and by – the 'mother'.

One of the defining features of the Holt novels is her use of a first-person narrative voice for the heroine (Whitney's *Thunder Heights*, for instance, uses third-person narration). This powerful device for creating reader identification with the heroine is used in both *Jane Eyre* and *Rebecca*. However, du Maurier's innovation in *Rebecca* is to make the nameless narrator unreliable in her misreading of the situation at Manderley. In this du Maurier draws on her reading of Austen's *Northanger Abbey*, for which she wrote a sympathetic and astute Introduction in 1948. Arguing that Austen was 'poking fun' at her readers rather than sneering at Radcliffe, du Maurier notes that 'we as readers, are misled in precisely the same fashion that Catherine was misled.'[72] Like Catherine, the gauche narrator of *Rebecca* takes her expectations from books where 'men knelt to women' in the moonlight to propose marriage (57). To her Maxim de Winter is a Gothic figure, like a portrait of 'a certain Gentleman unknown' from 'a past of whispers in the dark, of shining rapier blades, of silent exquisite courtesy' (18). Like Catherine, she is misled by her romantic imaginings and Du Maurier uses the first-person narrative to ensure that we too are misled. In *Rebecca* the unreliable first-person narrative becomes a textual 'recess', into which the narrator and the reader are locked, unable to see beyond its imprisoning boundaries. The revelation that Maxim did not love Rebecca, indeed, that he killed her, releases the narrator (and us) from one misreading – the 'real Rebecca took shape and form before me' (284) – only to imprison us in another.

Holt uses this first-person narrative voice in a way that facilitates reader-identification, but her heroines are closer to the feisty independence of Jane Eyre than the gaucherie of du Maurier's narrator. They all have names for a start, tend to be outspoken, even tart, and are often described as unconventionally unfeminine. Martha in *Mistress of Mellyn* has eyes which are 'too bold' (5). The caustic Harriet in *Menfreya* feels 'a real outsider' (116) because of her lame leg, but is determined to 'retain my own personality' in marriage and not 'become a slave of her menfolk' like her mother-in-law (166). Passionate and ambitious, Karensa in *The Legend of the Seventh Virgin* is a working-class 'cottage girl' with a grandmother everyone believes to be a witch.

This unconventionality is what attracts the hero to the heroine. It fits the pattern Louise Weston and Josephine Ruggerio found in the modern Gothics they examined, where the hero displayed more positive attitudes towards the non-traditional heroine than towards the minor female (often the villainess), who was more traditional.[73] Weston and Ruggerio see the rewarding of the non-traditional heroines as offering 'an intermediate step on the way to female liberation',[74] but they do not analyse the differences between historical and modern-day settings (although their sample included Holt, Stewart and Whitney). However, Fawcett Vice-President Leona Nevler attributed the success of the modern Gothics to their theme of 'the woman who is victimised by the fact that she's a woman': the heroines of the historical Gothics were usually 'very bright', she noted, but because they were female had to become 'governesses or whatever'.[75] Women readers who 'seethe inside', she thought, 'respond to these heroines'.[76] It is, then, the 'modern' (even 'feminist') women in the costume Gothics who are rewarded, even if their behaviour is anachronistic in nineteenth-century terms. Holt's first-person narrative voice with its modern idiom facilitates an identification with the victimised heroine, which allows a carthartic release of that 'seeth[ing] inside'. At the same time, the historical setting reassures readers that such victimisation is safely in the past and can be 'put behind' them. Through this combination of historical setting and first-person narrative, the novels both express *and* defuse women's frustration.

Although the house/castle/château is a key element in the costume Gothic, Holt repeatedly deploys an image of women's imprisonment within an even smaller space, often within the house, which recalls Sophia Lee's womb-tomb-like recess as well as Gaskell's women buried alive. This space is associated with a woman from the past, often fatally incarcerated in it, with whom the heroine identifies to the extent that she fears the same fate may overtake her. The climax of the novel is usually the heroine's entrapment in this space, from which she is rescued by the hero. In *Mistress of Mellyn* this is the priest's hole in which Martha finds herself imprisoned with the decaying corpse of Connan TreMellyn's first wife, Alice. The doubling between heroine and Other Woman borrowed from *Rebecca* is pronounced here. Martha's 'You are haunting me, Alice' (209), is a direct reiteration of her literary predecessor's comment: 'Perhaps I haunted [Rebecca] as she haunted me' (244). In the priest's hole, Martha feels herself merging with Alice, as du Maurier's narrator merges with Rebecca in her final dream:

> During that time I spent in that dark and gruesome place I was not sure who I was. Was I Martha? Was I Alice?
> Our stories were so much alike. I believed the pattern was similar. (247)

The process of matrilineal history is played out through the fear of repeating the fate of an incarcerated and murdered (m)other woman. As Tania Modleski has astutely noted, the heroine's 'uncanny sensation' that the past is repeating itself through her expresses two anxieties: 'it is not only that women fear being *like* their mothers, sharing the same fate, but that in an important sense, they fear *being* their mother,' in the sense of failing to separate from her.[77] (That the name of Eleanor *Alice* Hibbert's mother was also Alice suggests Hibbert was playing out her own personal psychological dramas.)

It is this 'pattern', or 'story', which is obsessively repeated in Holt's early books. In *Kirkland Revels*, Catherine is about to be incarcerated in the lunatic asylum where the woman she believes to be her mother has been locked up for the last seventeen years, when she is rescued by Simon Redvers. *The Legend of the Seventh Virgin* opens with the discovery of 'the bones of a walled-up nun', in the walls of St Larnston Abbas (5). The legend is that six novices and a nun 'had ceased to be virgins' (5) and were punished, the nun being immured in a tiny chamber in the wall. When the twelve-year-old Kerensa climbs into the chamber, 'I really believed that I was the seventh virgin, that I had extravagantly cast away my chastity and was doomed to a frightful death' (10). This foreshadows her adult life, when she is about to be bricked into the same wall by the villain and thinks, 'All that I have done has brought me to this, just as all [the nun] did brought her to this same spot' (27). What Kerensa has done is to marry a man she did not love, and although she is rescued by the man she loves, he does not marry her. This is one of the few Holts not to have the traditional marriage ending but Kerensa realises that she has metaphorically shut herself away from the possibility of love by her own actions: 'I had been walled up for years, shut away from all that made life good' (283). In the contemporary-set *Bride of Pendorric*, Favel is told the legend of the Brides of Pendorric, who are cursed to haunt the house until the next bride dies and takes their place.[78] She then finds herself locked into the Pendorric family vault, a motif repeated in *The Curse of the Kings* (1973), where Judith is trapped in the Egyptian Pharaoh's tomb her archaeologist husband is excavating, and in *The House of a Thousand Lanterns* (1974), where Jane is shut into the tomb presided over by the goddess Kuan Yin, under the eponymous house.

The origin of this motif of live burial in Dick's incarceration in the buttress room in du Maurier's *The King's General* is clearest in *Menfreya* where Harriet becomes obsessed with the legend of a governess who was the mistress of an earlier Bevil Menfrey. Hidden in a buttress room the governess died in childbirth and subsequently is said to haunt the house. The current governess, the woman with whom Harriet suspects her own Bevil may be in love, speculates that 'the wife murdered her' (205). Although a shaken Harriet insists, 'That's not in the story' (206), Jessica argues that, 'It makes a better story' (207). Harriet's own identification with the earlier wife is signalled by her wearing (in a reiteration of *Rebecca*) of a distinctive topaz dress which Lady Menfrey is shown wearing in a portrait. (The confused historicity of these novels is typified by the fact that although the dress is described as medieval, the governess is described as eighteenth-century.) But while Holt borrows the motif of burial alive in the equivalent of the buttress room from *The King's General*, she re-genders it so that it is repeatedly, indeed, obsessively, women who are entombed alive.

We are back here to what Freud suggests is 'the most uncanny thing of all':[79] being buried alive, which is a transformation of the phantasy 'of intra-uterine existence'.[80] While she doesn't mention this in her analysis, Modleski notes two of the other possible sources of the uncanny given by Freud – 'the fear of repetition and the fear of castration' – but she then makes an extraordinary theoretical leap which connects to my own argument: 'suppose we view the threat of castration as part of a deeper fear – fear of never developing a sense of autonomy and separateness from the mother';[81] both fears thus represent the 'more primal fear of being lost in the mother'.[82] Given that women, according to Nancy Chodorow, have more problems separating from the mother, Modleski argues, their 'sense of the uncanny may actually be stronger than men's'. Modern Gothics then, she suggests, 'serve in part to convince women that they are not their mothers'.[83] While Holt's obsessive return to the womb-tomb recess appears to confirm Modleski's powerfully suggestive analysis, this seems to me to tell only half the story of these deeply ambivalent books.

If the house/castle represents patrilineal power and status, the tomb-like recess (crypt, wall chamber, tomb, buttress room) which

lies beneath it represents the heroine's fears of what might happen
to her because she is a woman. Her matrilineal inheritance is the
maternal 'womb' which is the foundation underlying patriarchal
culture, and which Irigaray suggests has been erased through the
murder of the mother. This connection is made explicitly in *Legend*,
where Kerensa in childbirth thinks that 'the agony of the walled-up
nun could not have been greater than mine'(161). Historically,
these texts repeatedly insist, women *have* been locked up, entombed
alive, incarcerated in lunatic asylums, and thus the protagonist is
justified in her fears. Initially, this looks like a repetition of the
symbolic 'murder of the mother' I have traced in earlier plots, the
erasure of the maternal. Certainly, the focus of fear in these texts is
usually the enigmatic husband/fiancé who is linked with the secret
the heroine has to uncover. This fear is represented as paranoid and
unspeakable: 'How could I say', asks Martha in *Mistress of Mellyn*,
'I suspect the man I am engaged to marry of being involved in a
plot to murder me' (238). And the heroines repeatedly attempt to
convince themselves that their fears of history repeating itself are
imaginary: 'The past could not intrude like that on the present,'
Harriet asserts in *Menfreya* (213).

That the metaphor of incarceration was also common in non-
fiction writing in the period suggests that the costume and modern
Gothic were feeding on and into common preoccupations in the
1960s. Nora Johnson's *Atlantic Monthly* article 'The Captivity of
Marriage' (1961) analyses 'the housewife syndrome', the 'gap
between what she thought marriage was going to be like and
what it really is like'.[84] Suggesting that 'Wives are lonelier now
than they ever used to be,' she notes that the disillusioned housewife's sense of futility also brings guilt 'because of her belief in
the magic medicine of love'.[85] While Johnson focuses on the conflicting feelings surrounding children, and the way they threaten
the mother's autonomous identity – 'She wants to give everything
to the baby; she wants equally to hold on to herself' – she also notes
the sense of being 'trapped' in a relationship from which all 'mystery'
has gone.[86] Holt's novels repeatedly enact this attempt to hold
on to an autonomous identity, but they also suggest that it is only
by solving the mysteries of the past that the heroine can move
forward.

That the motif of 'captivity' symbolises modern women's fears about marriage is often made surprisingly clear in the novels. 'I want to marry you', Connan tells Martha in Mellyn, 'because I want to keep you a prisoner in my house' (212), while Harriet in *Menfreya*, remarks that 'some husbands I have heard can be jailors' (93). There are echoes here of *Rebecca*, where Jack Favell asks the narrator, 'Like being buried down here?' (169), and Maxim makes the Bluebeard-like comment: 'There is a certain type of knowledge I prefer you not to have. It's better kept under lock and key' (211). That some very conflicting emotions are being expressed here is indicated in *Menfreya* when, after an incident of marital rape, Harriet recognises that this is Bevil's 'symbolic' way of telling her that he is 'the master', but concludes that 'the only thing I should not be able to endure would be his indifference' (169).

Holt's costume Gothics offer her readers the 'magic medicine of [heterosexual] love' as a panacea to the ills of marriage. It is almost always the hero who releases the heroine from live burial: it is Connan, the fiancé she suspected of trying to murder her, who releases Martha from the priest's hole (*Mellyn*); Simon who prevents Catherine being locked up in the asylum (*Kirkland*); Bevil who rescues Harriet from drowning in a flooded cellar (*Menfreya*); Tybalt who releases Judith from the pharaoh's tomb (*Curse*); Joliffe who opens the door to free Jane from the temple tomb (*Lanterns*); and Kim who lifts Kerensa from the wall chamber (*Legend*). Each release signals the end of fears about the man in an almost orgasmic over-flow of joy: 'Tybalt was holding me in his arms and I thought: I did not die of fear, but I shall die of bliss' (*Curse*, 246). There are none of the traces of lesbian desire identified in *Rebecca* by Mary Wings in Holt's novels.[87]

If the hero is the rescuer, it is most often an/other woman who is responsible for the heroine's incarceration (not the Shadow Male as Russ suggests). In *Mellyn* it is Celestine who covets the house; in *Pendorric* it is the heroine's mother-in-law, Barbarina; in *Lanterns* it is the sinister Chan Ho Lan who wants to restore the house to its rightful owners. Perhaps the most interesting example, however, is *Menfreya*, where the person who confines the heroine in a flooding cellar to drown is not the pregnant governess, but Harriet's nurse, and surrogate mother, Fanny. Convinced that Bevil and Jessica are having an affair, and Jessica intends to poison Harriet, Fanny plans an easy death for Harriet and herself. As Harriet reflects: 'Poor Fanny, the gentle murderess who had killed for love' (246). Holt, then, doubles the 'murdered mother' (the dead women in the past) with a murdering '(m)other' in the present.

Reading Holt's novels back against du Maurier's rewriting of *Jane Eyre* is instructive, because *Rebecca* uses the insights of *Northanger Abbey* to deviate from Brontë's novel. Speculating about Austen's novel, du Maurier records her fancy that 'General Tilney may have beaten his wife',[88] but in *Rebecca* she makes real Catherine's speculations about wife murder. While Rochester only locks up his 'intemperate and unchaste wife',[89] Maxim shoots his through the heart, characterising her as '"vicious, damnable, rotten, through and through . . . not even normal"'.[90] Furthermore, while Jane leaves Rochester when she discovers his conduct towards his wife, du Maurier's narrator not only connives at Maxim's act but rejoices in it as proof that 'He did not love Rebecca' (297). This makes her, as she recognises, complicit in the murder: 'I too had killed Rebecca' (297). Du Maurier has one further speculation about General Tilney: the 'rather shaming impression' she has always had, 'that at one time he fancied Catherine as a bride for himself instead of for his son'.[91] The Oedipal family romance is reversed: Maxim is the 'father' ('Borgia father', indeed) who kills the 'mother' so that he can move on to the 'daughter'.

In her costume Gothics, Holt repeatedly invokes and then swerves from the central revelation of *Rebecca* – the fact that Maxim *is* a wife-murderer and that the narrator is complicit in this. While Austen leaves her reader in no doubt about the symbolic meaning of Catherine's suspicions, du Maurier's text literalises the murder of the '(m)other'. In contrast, Holt's novels repeatedly reassure the reader that their paranoia is unfounded, that in Harriet's words in *Menfreya*, the 'web of suspicion in which I become entangled was of my own weaving' (250). Holt de-historicises and de-radicalises the text she rewrites, stripping *Rebecca* of its ambivalence. She does this by displacing its plot into a faux-Victorian past which allows her to invoke the happy ending of *Jane Eyre*. In Holt's costume Gothics while the murdered 'mother' is safely in the past, the murdering 'mother' in the present is vanquished by the husband who rescues the heroine, releasing her from the womb-tomb in which she has been incarcerated. Nevertheless, the obsessive repetition of this plot in thirty-two books suggests a fear that cannot finally be put 'behind' either Holt or her readers, but has to be repeatedly exorcised through the act of rereading.

The uses of history: Philippa Carr's historical Gothics

In 1972, the year that the publication of Kathleen Woodiwiss's *The Flame and the Flower* launched the erotic historical blockbuster which would supersede the modern Gothic in the best-seller lists, Eleanor Hibbert began another series of books under the pseudonym, Philippa Carr. These were what she called 'historical Gothics', combining the conventions of her costume Gothics with the 'real' history of her Plaidy novels. While Hibbert retained the brand of 'Victoria Holt', the post-1972 Holt books use a different plot, often featuring an adventuress in an exotic setting, and adapting elements of the historical blockbuster.

The eighteen Philippa Carr novels form an elongated family saga, known as the 'Daughters of England' series, and trace a female line from the Reformation to the Second World War. The novels use the female first-person narrative voice of the costume Gothics but place this against a more detailed historical background. They are presented as journals kept, as part of a family tradition, by the women of the family. Since women's names change on marriage, the family tree given at the start of each novel is unusual in that it does not follow the patronymic. As Arabella Tolsworthy's mother tells her when she gives her the journals going back to her great-great-great-great-grandmother, Damask Farland, "'These journals cover not only the lives of your ancestors but tell you something of the events which were of importance to our country . . . They will make you understand why our ancestors acted in the way they did.'"[92]

Within this format Hibbert set herself a quite extraordinary task: to retell the history of post-Reformation Britain through the female line. Although these novels have been almost entirely ignored by critics, they are interesting (if not altogether successful) in that their combination of the Holt and Plaidy techniques brings together the aggressively haunting past of the psyche with the static past of historiography. They take the psychoanalytic plot of the modern Gothic out of the 'Victorian' past and back to the sixteenth century. In doing so, they offer a fascinating insight into the uses of history for women readers.

The first novel, *The Miracle of St Bruno's* (1972), sets Damask Farland's story against the background of Henry VIII's marital history and its political fallout.[93] History for women, Carr seems to suggest, begins with the ur-story of the Bluebeard king. The fates of his wives – 'divorced, beheaded, died, divorced, beheaded, survived' as the mnemonic goes – suggest that history is a nightmare within which women are trapped. The Gothic myth of origins Carr suggests here is confirmed by Anne Williams, who has drawn attention to the way in which the story of Henry VIII's femicidal desire for an heir is echoed in the plot of *The Castle of Otranto*. These Gothic affinities, she suggests, indicate the ways in which the patriarchal family is fundamental to the shape of English political history.[94] For women, Carr's novels suggest, the Gothic provides a way of emplotting history which makes sense of their experience of it.

The eponymous 'miracle' is the appearance of a real baby boy in the nativity crib in the Abbey of St Bruno's on Christmas morning. Named Bruno, the boy is brought up to believe in his own divinity by the monks. After the abbey is dissolved by Thomas Cromwell's men, Bruno disappears, reappearing years later as the new owner of the abbey. The story, however, is told by Damask, who first meets the 'Holy Child' when they are children and later marries him. She bears him a daughter but miscarries the son he wants. The secret she uncovers is that Bruno is not divine, but the illegitimate child of her promiscuous nurse, Keziah, and a monk named (in a reiteration of Lewis's *The Monk*) Ambrose. Furthermore, she discovers that Bruno has fathered two children by her cousin Kate. Like her namesake in *Wuthering Heights*, Kate refused Bruno when he was poor and married the much older but wealthy Lord Remus. To avert an unknowingly incestuous marriage between her daughter Catherine and her half-brother Carey, Damask threatens to make known the contents of Ambrose's written confession. After attempting to poison her, Bruno is killed when a jewelled statue of the Madonna hidden in a chamber beneath the abbey falls on him.

The Miracle at St Bruno's deploys the key conventions of Holt's costume Gothic: first-person narration, a potentially murderous husband, a haunted house (Damask sees what she thinks is the ghost of a monk in the abbey grounds) and a recess-like chamber. But the uncanny sense of matrilineal repetition in the Holt novels is replaced here by an overt series of parallels between the fictional characters and real historical figures. Each of Henry's Queens is invoked as a possible model for Kate and Damask, figures whose fates offer a warning to other women.

Initially ambitious Kate identifies with Anne Boleyn, imagining herself into *becoming* the future Queen. '"[Anne Boleyn] says, 'No, your mistress I will not be; your wife I cannot be'. Which shows how clever she is." Kate threw up her hands as if warding off a persistent lover. She was Anne Boleyn.' (26).

After Anne's fall, '[Kate] was now Jane Seymour, but the role of meek Jane . . . did not suit her as well as that of proud Anne Boleyn' (54). Later Kate compares Katherine Howard with Keziah, commenting, 'Oh how differently I should have managed my affairs if I had been in her place!' (219). By this stage, Damask is obsessed by the parallels between Anne Boleyn's fate and her own similar failure to provide a male heir to Bruno. When she miscarries a boy Damask reflects: 'surely the King himself had not looked more thunderous [than Bruno] when he stood over his sad Queen's bed' (245). The parallels between these six tragic Queens and 'ordinary' women are repeatedly pointed up in the novel: '"How near Queens are to death," I said. "How near we all are to death," replied Kate' (250).

Carr's novel suggests the ways in which women readers might use history to play out their own psychic dramas. Du Maurier used history in exactly this way, mapping the incestuous tensions in her family through allusions to the Borgias. In her essay 'True romances' Carolyn Steedman draws on both Freud's 'Family romances' and Bettelheim's *The Uses of Enchantment* to suggest that considering what 'children do with history', the ways in which they may use the manipulable figures of history like those of fairy tales to map out their personal dramas, can help to 'reveal the uses we make of a common past'.[95] For Freud, the child's phantasy of being an adopted child whose real parents are of 'much higher social standing'[96] is part of the drama of separation. The replacing of the real parents by grander people is a way of exalting them. Steedman's concern is with the class issues raised by the fact that children have access only to 'a highly conservative historical romance'.[97] The schoolchild's preference for glamorous Mary Queen of Scots over a poor hand-loom weaver reflects the way the Queen (like the figures from fairy tale and myth) can be used to play out elements of her own family romance. But for Steedman, the crucial difference lies in the fact that history (unlike fairy tale and myth) is 'real':

> History does not allow children to leave aside the categories of 'true' and 'not-true', as fiction does . . . it really did happen. And history is terrifying. There is nothing within the historical romance to mediate the abandonment of most children who use it: the message that they must finally read is that they, no more than their parents, are not kings and queens and brave knights. They are the poor peasant, the nameless Saxon . . . the serving maid, the rabble.[98]

For Steedman, the conservative historical romance marks out the very terms of the working-class child's exclusion.

Where then does this leave us with historical *fiction*, particularly women's Gothic historical fiction? Carr's novels suggest that for women they might provide the kind of mediation Steedman argues is missing from history itself. Kate and Damask's phantasies of being queens act as stand-ins for the reader's, mediating and dramatising these kinds of family romance and offer a series of possibilities. Contemplation of the fates of Henry's six queens allows a proto-feminist assertion that 'Life is cruel for a woman' (224). However, this stress on similarity between women collapses together such disparate figures as, for instance, the sixteen-year-old Queen Katherine Howard, the Protestant martyr Anne Askew and the fictional serving maid Keziah, in ways which are hugely problematic.

The parallels drawn between the fictional Bruno and Henry VIII are equally important. Refusing to accept he is the child of Keziah and Ambrose, Bruno insists on his divine status as a Messiah in what reads like an extreme case of the Freudian family romance. He rejects not only Keziah, but also his grandmother, the witch Granny Salter who put him into the crib, his half-sister Honey and his daughter Catherine. When Damask refuses to accept his divinity, he attempts to murder her. 'I am guilty of heresy, then' (322). Damask says when he disputes her story of his birth. The parallels between Bruno, who takes 'Kingsman' as his surname, and Henry VIII suggest the deathly nature of male power to women and the fraudulent nature of men's claim to divine status. *The Miracle at St Bruno's* dramatises not only the matricide Irigaray claims underlies Western culture but also the male claim to divinity (what Irigaray calls 'man-god-father') which that entails. By moving into 'real' history Hibbert also reverses the implications of her costume Gothics. The 'murderer' here is not the (m)other woman but Damask's husband. 'Whom could one trust?' she asks. 'It seemed only my mother' (346). In the final scene in the inevitable recess-like space, Bruno is killed by a representative of the female divine mother, the Jewelled Madonna, buried there to save her from Cromwell's men. A former monk suggests that this is the 'Madonna's answer': 'A new reign is almost upon us' (350). As Mary Tudor dies, Elizabeth is released from Hatfield to take the throne. Here Carr races through Tudor history to bring us to the succession of the woman the reader knows will be known as the 'Virgin Queen', a Protestant sovereign who takes to herself the symbolism of the Catholic Virgin which remains in the underground chamber. The finale of the novel, then, enacts what could be seen as the revenge of the murdered mother and the beginning of a new female sovereignty.

While du Maurier is a writer whose stature has been consistently underestimated, Hibbert's varied *œuvre* is equally fascinating in some ways, not least in her status as a phenomenal best-seller. Indeed, the success of both writers illustrates the capacity of the Gothic as a mode of history which can be used to play out the psychic dramas of women who feel that they are trapped and victimised because of their gender. We should not underestimate the importance of such popular historical novels, and Hibbert uses a Gothic history to articulate a dissatisfaction with women's lot and the beginnings of a proto-feminism in the early 1960s. In comparison with du Maurier, however, Hibbert's ultimate conservatism can be seen in what she erases from *Rebecca* — the spectre of lesbianism, which was to be reborn to spectacular effect in the novels of Sarah Waters.

6

Queer as History? Sarah Waters's Gothic Historical Novels

ye

Pa used to say that any piece of history might be made into a tale: it was only a question of deciding where the tale began, and where it ended. That, he said, was all his skill. And perhaps, after all, the histories he dealt with were rather easy to sift like that, to divide up and classify – the great lives, the great works, each of them neat and gleaming and complete, like metal letters in a box of type.

Sarah Waters, *Affinity* (1999)[1]

As a writer, Sarah Waters is interested in the 'queerness' of history: history, that is, not as 'neat and gleaming and complete' as a box of type, but as 'strange', 'odd', 'eccentric', 'of questionable character', 'shady', 'suspect', and, of course, 'homosexual'.[2] Her historical novels use the Gothic to play knowing games with the shifting meanings of the word 'queer', nudging the modern reader into an acknowledgement of the complexities of historical process. The word functions as a touchstone, signalling her re-creation of a re-pressed lesbian past and the way in which this project alters, or indeed, 'queers' ('puts out of order'), our perceptions of history. If historical fiction, as Waters herself has said, 'tells us less about the past than about the circumstances of its own production – reveals, if nothing else, the historiographical priorities of its author, or its author's culture',[3] then what do Waters's novels tell us about our own attitudes to history, gender and sexuality? As the most recent manifestation of the tradition of female Gothic historical fiction, their extraordinary popularity with both general readers and critics, suggests its continuing importance.

The Gothic historical novel, as I have argued, has from its beginnings in the eighteenth century been a kind of metafiction which foregrounds the textuality and subjectivity of history. Lesbian writers, as Waters has herself put it, have long enjoyed a 'special affinity'[4] with the historical novel and Waters further exploits this. Her use of the Gothic historical mode enables her introduction of explicitly lesbian material into the literary forms of the past. As Paulina Palmer has argued, 'One of the chief attractions that Gothic holds for the writer of lesbian fiction is its tendency to question mainstream versions of "reality" and to interrogate the values associated with them.'[5] 'Gothic and "queer"', she suggests, 'share a common emphasis on transgressive acts and subjectivities.'[6] Waters's play with the word 'queer' to evoke the 'shadow presence' of the lesbian, Lucie Armitt argues, carries with it the 'sense of uncanniness which lesbians have historically provoked within patriarchy'.[7] What Terry Castle called 'the apparitional lesbian', a figure 'always in the margins, hidden from history' because 'she has been "ghosted" – or made to seem invisible – by culture itself'[8] is re-materialised in Waters's fiction. As a mode of history which uses fantasy to undo the 'real', Gothic historical fiction allows lesbian writers to question and counter the values of mainstream histories and thus contemplate alternative futures.

Waters's novels engage in strikingly self-reflexive ways with the two Gothic motifs I have centralised: imprisonment in a recess-like space, and the haunting nature of matrilineal relationships. The motif of imprisonment is central to all her novels: Millbank prison, which is doubled by both the spiritualist's cabinet and the claustrophobic middle-class home, in *Affinity*; the lunatic asylum, doubled by Briar and the thieves' house in Lant Street in *Fingersmith* (2002); Wormwood Scrubs prison in *The Night Watch* (2006), paralleled by bombed-out houses and more mundane spaces, like the train lavatory in which Reggie and Viv meet; the big house, Hundreds Hall, with its attic nursery in *The Little Stranger* (2009); even in *Tipping the Velvet* (1998), Nan is 'kept' in Felicity Place by Diana

Lethaby as 'her *boy*'.[9] Linked to this motif of incarceration are the ambivalences around matrilineal inheritances central to the three novels I want to discuss: *Affinity*, *Fingersmith* and *The Little Stranger*. The dense intertextuality of Waters's work explores the ways in which history is textually constructed, a 'tale' shaped, as she puts in it *Affinity*, by historians' decisions about where the 'beginning' and 'end' should be (7). Moreover, we understand history in part through literary fictions: we 'read' the nineteenth century through the Brontës or Wilkie Collins, particularly if we are women. *Affinity* and *Fingersmith* are faux-Victorian novels,[10] while *The Night Watch* and *The Little Stranger* reiterate the forms of the 1940s. Waters's sophisticated play with generic conventions, particularly those of the Gothic, exposes, subverts and exploits the ways in which some histories fit more neatly than others into the 'boxes' (or plots) familiar to readers. Her understanding of these issues is informed by a familiarity with 1990s literary and cultural theory which comes out of the doctoral thesis she completed in 1995: 'Wolfskins and togas: lesbian and gay historical fictions, 1870 to the present'. It is partly this theoretical underpinning which has made her work so popular with literary critics, although it is, as Cora Kaplan notes, very lightly worn, worked into the novels without 'any pedantic aftertaste'.[11]

'Thinking about how we write history – the pleasures of writing about history,' Waters has said, 'was my way into writing fiction.'[12] For Waters, this is intimately linked to the question of sexuality. While Waters's work, particularly *Affinity*, has featured centrally in what has become a rich body of work on neo-Victorian fiction,[13] less attention has been paid to the fact that she is working within a tradition of lesbian historical novels which she traced in her thesis, including writers like Sylvia Townsend Warner, Mary Renault, Bryher and Maude Meagher. And, as she has noted, 'the plundering and selective rewriting of historical narrative is something at which lesbians and gays have always been particularly adept.'[14] Thus, 'Utilised for a specifically gay agenda, historiographic metafictional techniques expose the provisionality of (historical) representation.'[15] That sense of the provisionality of structures of gender, sex, sexuality and class is central to her work: 'It's a fundamental thing of mine', she has said, 'that history is a process, and in a sense a good historical novel is a celebration of that.'[16] Angela Carter's work has also been an important influence on Waters's work, particularly the fin-de-siècle *Nights at the Circus* (1984) and the Gothic fairy tales of *The Bloody Chamber* (1979).[17] Waters's novels revisit Carter's assertion that 'our flesh arrives to us out of history, like everything else does,'[18] but they do so from a lesbian sensibility missing from Carter's work.

Moreover, Waters's novels exploit the fact that it has been easier to slip controversial material – abortion, lesbian or gay sexuality, politics – past censorship under cover of a good historical costume. The title of her thesis alludes to Naomi Mitchison's response to the censorship of the first novel she wrote with a contemporary setting: 'In some of the stories in *The Delicate Fire* there is, I would have thought, far more overt sex than in *We Have Been Warned*, but apparently it's all right when people wear wolfskins and togas.'[19]

'To look beyond the wolfskins and togas of the women's historical novel is, sometimes', Waters writes in her essay on Maude Meagher's *The Green Scamander*, 'to find the controversial lesbian body.'[20] While much lesbian fiction has been marginalised and ignored, Waters has used historical settings to bring lesbian sexuality to mainstream audiences, not least through the television adaptations of her novels. In one sense Waters has benefited from a wider trend. As Christian Gutleben commented of retro-Victorian novels in general in *Nostalgic Postmodernism* (2001), 'The emphasis on the ill-treatment of women, homosexuals, or the lower classes is not at all shocking or seditious *today*; on the contrary it is precisely what the general public wants to read.'[21] But Gutleben's rider that this represents 'an aesthetics of the politically correct'[22] hints at a residue of unease in a culture which is, perhaps, happier to read of the ill-treatment of 'women, homosexuals, or the lower classes' in the past than to confront it in the present.

The 'neo-' or 'faux-Victorian' novel benefits from a kind of coherence (like that of the Gothic) which comes from its apparently harmonious blend of form and content: the conventions of the nineteenth-century realist novel are being used to depict the nineteenth century. Hence, certain words – like 'Victorian', or the presentation of Waters as 'a modern-day Charles Dickens or Wilkie Collins'[23], invoke familiar preconceptions about the past. It is partly this coherence which allows Waters to use the insights of the twentieth century to make explicit the buried subtexts of the original novels. But it can also obscure the fact that Waters's faux-Victorian novels are historicised in ways that the originals were not. Part of the 'sensationalism' of the novels of Wilkie Collins or Mary Elizabeth Braddon was precisely that they situated their Gothic secrets, not in the distant past, but in the domestic interiors of the contemporaneous present.

This historicising can blind us to the ways in which Waters's texts refract our own preoccupations. As she has suggested, 'In our efforts to trace and recover our own cultural histories we should, perhaps, be more sensitive to the particular shape of the historical fantasies of earlier generations of female writers.'[24] As a particularly self-reflexive form of fantasy, her novels not only use history to play out *our* fears and desires (not those of the Victorians or the 1940s), but also draw our attention to that play, through the use of Gothic conventions and the word 'queer'. It is in teasing out the ways in which our histories reflect our present fantasies that psychoanalysis is so valuable and this is particularly true in relation to Waters's work.

Affinity: the darkened rooms of history

In *Affinity,* the story of middle-class Margaret Prior and Selina Dawes, the spiritualist medium whom Margaret visits in Millbank prison and falls in love with, Waters explores the possibilities of the Gothic as a metaphorical language which can express the repressed. Margaret's narrative opens with a meditation on history as she reflects upon her historian father's comment that 'any piece of history might be made into a tale' (7). Wondering how to begin the history of Millbank prison, with its curious shape and twisting passages, when she cannot even remember the date it was built, she concludes that her father 'would not start the story . . . with a lady and her servant, and petticoats and loose hair'(7). The petticoats symbolise both the restrictions and the insights Margaret's gender brings to her role as a female historian: when she has to stop to free her skirts as she enters the prison she looks up to see 'the pentagons of Millbank' (8). Seen in the diagram on her desk the pentagons look like 'petals on a geometric flower' (8), but up close Millbank is terrifying, as if it has been designed 'expressly to *drive* its inmates mad' (8). The opening of the novel thus prepares readers for a different kind of history: female rather than male, fiction rather than fact, Gothic rather than rational. Millbank is another version of Sophia Lee's recess, symbolising the ways in which women have been hidden from, locked-up in, and driven mad by, history.

Although Waters does not append a bibliography to *Affinity*, a key influence appears to have been Alex Owen's *The Darkened Room: Women, Power and Spiritualism in Late Victorian England* (1989).[25] Waters cited *The Darkened Room* in her thesis to explain the 'appeal of the spiritualist movement for lesbians in particular'.[26] Owen's study is remarkable not only for its wealth of documentary evidence but also for the way in which it uses psychoanalysis and post-structuralist theory to analyse complex relations between power, gender and class. It is informed by the understanding that: 'Histories are made and remade, and bear the marks of current concerns and preoccupations.'[27] Nineteenth-century spiritualist mediumship was facilitated by the conventions of female passivity and, Owen argues, 'can be read as a language of ambivalence and resistance' which spoke of 'the fractured and contradictory nature of feminine subjectivity'.[28]

The seeds of Waters's novel can be seen in the world Owen depicts, where a lower-class girl like Florence Cook who became a medium could transgress both class and gender norms. If Waters's Selina resembles Florence, another key source, Tatiana Kontou has established, was the American medium Susan Willis Fletcher's account of her imprisonment for fraud in *Twelve Months in an English Prison* (1884).[29] During séances, women could become 'men' through the materialisation of male spirit controls. Owen records that Mary Rosina Showers, for instance, had a male spirit control called 'Peter' 'who spoke with a deep sonorous voice from within the cabinet'.[30] Selina's control, 'Peter Quick', also evokes Peter Quint, from Henry James's *The Turn of the Screw* (1898) and his punning surname hints at ambiguity. Male spirits often showed aggression to male sitters at a séance and sweet-talked the women,[31] as Waters's Peter Quick does in the novel (152). If, as Owen, suggests, 'the spirits can be seen as representations of psychical reality in much the same way as a fantasy might'[32] then the live crab Peter Quick drops into a mocking male sitter's lap is an all-too-physical revenge fantasy. Owen also provides evidence which hints at same-sex relationships between women. The relationship between Nellie Theobold and her family's cook, Mary, based on their spiritualism, and Florence Marryat's account of feeling the naked body of Cook's spirit control, 'Katie King',[33] both suggest erotic possibilities which Waters makes explicit in the relationship between Selina and the maid, Ruth Vigers.

Waters's imaginative use of this kind of material in *Affinity* has interesting parallels with Gaskell's fictionalisation of the Salem witch trials in 'Lois the Witch' (see chapter 3). Spiritualism, Owen records, began in 1848 in rural upstate New York with two young girls, Katherine and Margaret Fox, then twelve and thirteen years old.[34] Hearing knockings and rapping in their reputedly haunted house, the sisters devised a code to communicate with the spirit. Their activities precipitated the fashion for spiritualism. Two hundred years earlier such activities might have been interpreted rather differently. As Boyer and Nissenbaum point out, girls in Northampton who behaved in a similar way to the Salem girls in 1735, just forty years later, precipitated a religious revival rather than a witch hunt.[35] The differences in interpretation here illustrate shifts in the narratives available to give meaning to seemingly irrational behaviour. Where Waters differs from Gaskell's rationalist approach, is that Waters leaves open the possibility that Selina has, or thinks she has, actual supernatural powers.

Made up of two diaries, one written by Margaret, who is recovering from a suicide attempt brought on by the marriage of the woman she loves, and the other by Selina during her earlier period as a medium, *Affinity* exploits the restrictions of first-person narration to misdirect the reader. As with *Rebecca*, Margaret and the reader are imprisoned within a textual recess, beyond which they cannot see until the twist of the final pages. Only in retrospect can we correctly, and perhaps only partially, interpret the pages of Selina's diary. While Selina records instructions on how to keep a flower from fading or make an object luminous (74) which suggest she is a fake, her diary never admits that 'Peter Quick' is a fraud. Only by interpreting the evidence, such as Mrs Brink's reaction to the appearance of 'his white legs' (2) when she interrupts the séance, can we guess that 'Peter' was Ruth Vigers. Earlier entries – like her vision of a 'necklace' of dead babies' faces around their mother's throat, with space for two more (55) – suggest that Selina sees, or thinks she sees, spirits. It is left to the reader to decide whether Selina's diary is a deliberate fabrication. If it is, then, as Jeannette King points out, the novel subverts the convention that diaries provide privileged insight into a character's most secret thoughts and thus undermines 'the basic assumption of Victorian realist fiction that language is a medium which can convey fact, the truth, one of the assumptions also of Victorian science'.[36]

This is, of course, also one of the basic assumptions of Victorian history, undermined by the post-structuralist insight that 'history is inaccessible to us except in textual form.'[37] As a female historian, Margaret is alert to the ways in which we construct our own histories: the women's histories in Millbank have been told so many times that 'the telling of it has made a kind of story of it' (40), while her mother's story of Helen coming to the house to see Stephen, rather than Margaret, has been 'told that way so many times [that] I am half-way to believing it myself' (103). But Margaret's discovery that her maid Vigers has been Selina's accomplice all along forces us to recognise the unreliability of Margaret's narrative. Her diary, begun in an attempt to write a book that was factual, 'only a catalogue, a kind of list' (241) to disprove Arthur's contention that women only ever write '*journals of the heart*' (241), has been shaped, after all, by the 'crooked passage' of her heart across its pages (241). Moreover, the recording of her passion in its pages, written privately in her darkened room but secretly read by Vigers, has facilitated Selina's escape. Like the memoirs of Lee's heroines, Margaret's diary reveals the ways in which desire drives and deforms narratives: 'There never was a cord of darkness, never a space in which our spirits touched,' Margaret realises. 'There was only my longing' (348). Like Margaret, we have been seduced into wanting the happy ending. As with *The Recess*, the difficulty of interpreting a history which is only accessible through (often fragmentary or contradictory) texts is vividly dramatised, but so too are our own cultural blind-spots.

As a title the word 'affinity' ('relationship', 'structural resemblance', 'likeness' (*OED*)), directs our attention to the importance of the Gothic as a metaphorical mode in the novel. Owen notes the concept of 'spiritual affinity', associated with free love, in spiritualist circles.[38] Selina uses the word as a euphemistic metaphor for same-sex desire when she tells Margaret that, 'You were seeking me, your own *affinity*' (275). This title metaphor has a range of meanings in the novel which include the relationships and resemblances between characters (Margaret and Selina, Ruth and Selina, Mrs Prior and the prison matron) and places (the prison and the house), and the affinities between texts (including the two diaries), between history and fiction, and between the nineteenth and twentieth centuries.

The metaphor of 'affinities' thus offers a way of thinking about the relationship between past and present in historical fiction. In discussing her attraction to the nineteenth century as a Gothic 'psychological landscape', Waters suggests:

> I've sometimes thought that it's a way of addressing issues that are still very current in British culture, like class and gender, and sub-merged sexuality or sexual underworlds. Things that we think we're pretty cool with, and actually we're not at all, and we keep wanting to play these out on a bigger scale, precisely because they're still very current for us.[39]

This resonates with Cora Kaplan's description of the Victorian and Edwardian periods as 'our fairy-tales' or 'our middle ages' in her 1978 Introduction to *Aurora Leigh*:[40] 'There', Kaplan writes, 'in fancy dress, the still-present hierarchies of class and gender are displayed without shame, unsuppressed by the rhetoric of equality which glosses our own situation.'[41] While in Victorian literature, Kaplan argues, class conflict and gender inequality were the 'spoken subjects' and sexuality the 'erotic subtext', the opposite is true of twentieth century texts: 'In modern fiction sexuality is the spoken subject, power relations the subtext which must wear a fig leaf.'[42] In *Victoriana* (2007), Kaplan revisits these insights and argues that nineteenth-century novels such as *Jane Eyre*, *David Copperfield* or *The Scarlet Letter* 'have displaced Greek and Roman classics or the biblical narrative in providing the mythic structure of the early staging of our own modernity'.[43] In *Affinity* Margaret uses Barrett Browning's poem to imagine a future narrative for herself and

Selina, using Aurora as a secret name for herself (114) and obtaining a passport for Selina in the name of Marian Erle so that they can travel to Italy. Her claim to an affinity with the poet, however, is brutally dismissed by her mother who tells her: 'You are not Mrs Browning, Margaret . . . You are not, in fact, Mrs Anybody. You are only *Miss* Prior' (253). Even more brutally, Margaret's supposed affinity with Selina is exposed as a fiction when Selina uses the passport to elope with Ruth. Like du Maurier and Holt, then, Waters is exploring the use of history as a psychological landscape to play out psychic dramas.

Waters's novel exposes the dangers of assumptions about our own 'affinities' with the Victorians. Alert to the erotic subtext of the nineteenth century, we, like Margaret, fail to read the clues which reveal that Margaret's servant Vigers and Selina's Ruth are one person. Here Waters takes the Gothic theme of one woman 'haunting' another, whether as mother, double, rival or lover, which is so 'particularly suited to lesbian recasting',[44] and gives it a further twist. While Terry Castle theorises the lesbian as 'ghosted' by culture, Waters shows how we may now see the lesbian, but still fail to see the servant in front of us. Invoking the metaphor of the ghost as a figure for the women prisoners (20), spinsters (58) and Margaret herself (289, 307), Waters de-spectralises the lesbian body. In a scene that reiterates *Rebecca*, Selina explores the room which used to belong to Mrs Brink's dead mother. Half expecting to see the dead woman, she turns and does see a woman: 'But it was only Mrs Brink's maid Ruth. She had come quietly . . . *like a real lady's maid, like a ghost*' (119, emphasis added). The clues are there but it is only on a second reading that we can see them. The submerged elements given Gothic expression in Waters's novels are, then, as much to do with the unspoken power relations of class as with gender and sexuality. The final twist reveals that a novel we think is about the submerged sexuality of the Victorians is about submerged and un-articulated issues of class in our own time.

Margaret's apparently limpid, realist narrative is, in fact, embedded within and broken into by Selina's unstable and enigmatic diary. The novel opens with three and a half pages, dated 3 August 1873, which record Selina locked into her room after the alleged assault on Madelaine by Peter Quick. And it ends with another page, dated 1 August 1873, which foregrounds the question of the reader. Lying on Selina's bed smoking 'one of Peter's cigarettes', Ruth asks: "'Why are you writing?" & I tell her I am writing for my Guardian's eyes, as I do everything. *"Him"*, she says, & now she is laughing.' (351). Ruth's final command, "'Remember . . . whose girl you are'" (351) hints at her position as the 'reader' of both Margaret and Selina's narratives, the puppet-master/mistress who exploits her ghostly invisibility as a servant to control others. As the parodically Freudian cigarette suggests, however, to exercise control she has to adopt the (ghostly) trappings of masculinity. A kind of ghost narrative, resistant to rational historical interpretation, Selina's pages haunt Margaret's journal.

The central image of women's imprisonment, Millbank, is re-iterated in a series of other spaces: the room in which Selina is confined, the spiritualist's cabinet, Margaret's own home where she is drugged with chloral or laudanum, and, at the heart of the prison itself, below the level of the Thames, the 'darks' (178) used for solitary confinement. Near the dark cell lies the chain room which contains handcuffs, hobbles, gags, straitjackets, as well as 'other nameless, complicated instruments whose purposes [Margaret] could only, shuddering, guess at' (179) which date from Millbank's earliest days. These instruments of torture and restraint in the Gothic womb-tomb space beneath Millbank are testaments to the historical con-finement and abuse of women. When Selina is confined to the 'darks', Margaret climbs into her own closet. There she seems to merge with Selina in a scene which collapses the dark cell into the spirit-medium's cabinet:

> I was with *her*, and close to her, so close — what did she say once? *closer than wax*. I felt the cell about me, the jacket upon me –
> And yet, I seemed to feel my eyes bound, too, with bands of silk. And at my throat there was a velvet collar. (257)

This merger with another woman in a recess-like space, the motif repeatedly used by Victoria Holt, which seems to Margaret to confirm her 'affinity' with Selina, is exposed by the later events in the novel as a fiction. Moreover, all these confining spaces are controlled by women: Ruth orchestrates Selina's confinement in the cabinet; the prison is overseen by the principal, Miss Haxby; and Margaret's virtual imprisonment in her own home is overseen by her mother. Indeed, at one point Margaret almost calls Mrs Haxby '*Mother*!' (267). The final line – 'Remember . . . whose girl you are' (352) – emphasizes Ruth's control of Selina, and of the plot.

Yet, while *Affinity* problematises the notion that women have natural 'affinities' with each other, it also hints at women's desire for the lost or repressed maternal. The first spirit Selina sees (or says she sees), as a thirteen-year-old girl, is that of her dead mother (109). And Mrs Brink gives Selina a home in return for her material-ising the dead mother who died when Mrs Brink was a child. Mill-bank itself, that bastion of male confinement of women, is gendered female by the Porter:

> 'She's a grim old creature, ain't she miss? . . . And she's leaky . . . It's this ground, this wretched ground. Nothing will grow in it, and nothing will sit in it straight – not even a great old, grim beast like Millbank.
> . . . Would you think . . . that such a thing as that could wriggle about so devilishly on its foundations? . . . some nights, Miss Prior, when there ain't a breath of wind, I have stood where you are standing now and heard her *groan* – plain as a lady.' (312)

If the repressed feminine or maternal is, as Irigaray suggests, the 'foundations' or 'substration' on which the 'edifice' of patriarchy is built,[45] then Waters's novel suggests that it is on far more shaky ground than we often assume. The outwardly neat and rational pentagons of Millbank's design turn out to have a 'queer geometry' (235) after all. The pentagons have cracked open, locks shift and windows shatter, and even 'gallons of cement' (312) poured into the foundations have not prevented 'her' from moving. 'She'll come down one day, I am certain of it,' says the Porter, 'and take the lot of us with her!' (313). It is the desire for the lost maternal and a concern with matrilineal histories I want to trace further in *Fingersmith*.

Fingersmith: matrilineal histories and the redemptive mother

In *Affinity* Margaret, telling her former lover Helen about her visit to Millbank, asks her if she remembers 'Mr Le Fanu's novel about the heiress who is made to seem mad?' and remarks, '"I did think for a while: Suppose Mother is in league with Mr Shilitoe, and he means to keep me on the wards, bewildered?"' (29). Sheridan Le Fanu's *The Rose and the Key* (1871) is about an heiress, Maud Vernon, who is incarcerated in a lunatic asylum so that her mother can claim her daughter's inheritance for her illegitimate son. A prime mover in the plot against Maud is the servant, Mercy Cresswell, who facilitates her incarceration. *Fingersmith* takes its inspiration from this scenario, as well as the complex substitution plot of Wilkie Collins's *The Woman in White* (1860), and several other Victorian novels, including Le Fanu's *Uncle Silas* (1864), also featuring a heroine called Maud, and Mary Elizabeth Braddon's *Lady Audley's Secret* (1862). Contemporary in their settings at the time, these texts are rewritten as 'history' by Waters through the lenses offered by twentieth-century theory and fiction, particularly Angela Carter's *The Sadeian Woman* (1979) and her faux-Victorian reworking of Bluebeard, 'The Bloody Chamber'. In addition, *Fingersmith* rewrites the mistress–servant dynamic of *Affinity* as a love story with a (potentially) happy ending.

Reading Waters's novel against *The Rose and the Key* and *Lady Audley's Secret* brings into focus *Fingersmith*'s concern with the allegedly determining nature of matrilineal inheritance. The failure of maternal love is at the heart of Le Fanu's novel: 'Why am I cursed with this cruel yearning for her love?' Maud thinks of her unloving mother.[46] During Maud's childhood, Lady Vernon was 'an embodiment of power', a 'phantom' who only appeared in the nursery when Maud became unmanageable,[47] and in adulthood she confines Maud in an asylum. In *Lady Audley's Secret*, the bigamous anti-heroine attempts to escape conviction for the murder of her husband by asserting that she has inherited insanity from her mother. Like her mother, she ends her days incarcerated in a lunatic asylum. Madness and matrilineal inheritances appear to be inextricably linked in a female Gothic tradition which goes back, as I have argued, to *The Recess*. But in *Fingersmith* Waters rewrites this plot.

The two heroines, Sue Trinder and Maud Lilly, are both haunted by the belief that they have inherited their mother's characters and are thus bound to repeat their fates. Petty thief Sue, brought up by the baby farmer Mrs Sucksby, has been told that her mother was a murderess who died on the gallows. Upper-class Maud, brought up by her uncle to assist him in cataloguing his collection of pornography, has been told that her insane mother died in a lunatic asylum. Enlisted in a plot to defraud Maud of her inheritance through marrying her to 'Gentleman' (Richard Rivers), Sue acts as her maid but finds herself incarcerated in the lunatic asylum in Maud's place. The supposedly determining nature of their biological maternal identities is figured in images of blood: 'Bad blood comes out' (80), asserts Sue, while Maud, believing that her birth killed her mother, imagines the scene of her birth in the madhouse as 'slick with blood . . . that falling blood – *drip drop! drip drop!* – the beat telling off the first few minutes of my life, the last of hers' (179–80). It is the revelation that they have been swapped at birth, that Sue is the daughter of Marianne Lilly and Maud of Mrs Sucksby herself, which frees both girls from the trammels of the 'fiction' (337) fabricated by their mothers. By incarcerating Sue Lilly in the asylum, Mrs Sucksby had planned to take both halves of the fortune Marianne Lilly had intended to be shared between the two girls. But in the final confrontation after Sue escapes, someone – either Mrs Sucksby or Maud – stabs Richard. Mrs Sucksby takes the blame and is hanged for murder, and the novel ends with Maud earning her living through writing lesbian pornography, and teaching Sue how to read.

In her perceptive article on *Fingersmith*'s matrilineal 'fictions', Nadine Muller links these both to neo-Victorianism's relationship with the nineteenth century and to the familial metaphors of third-wave feminism, wherein second-wave feminists are seen as the 'mothers' of their third-wave 'daughters'.[48] What these have in common and what *Fingersmith* highlights, she argues, is 'their shared interest in how fragments of the past shape their presents, and how an acknowledgment thereof can lead to fruitful re-definitions of established customs and politics'.[49] However, *Fingersmith* is the latest intervention in a Gothic matrilineal history which goes back even further, beyond even the 'first wave' of feminism, to the end of the eighteenth century. What this long view suggests is that grand/ daughters who do not find appropriate ways of remembering their grand/mothers' past may be condemned to repeat it.

Waters's introduction of explicitly lesbian sexuality into literary forms where it was previously repressed signals that she is (to borrow Jameson's phrase) '(re)textualising' the 'prior texts' of history.[50] In *Fingersmith* she rereads the nineteenth century partly through the work of a second-wave feminist, Angela Carter's 'The Bloody Chamber', a Gothic retelling of Bluebeard in the first person set in fin-de-siècle France.[51] Carter aimed in her revisioned fairy tales to 'extract the latent content from the traditional stories and to use it as the beginnings of new stories'.[52] To reveal the buried nexus of gender, sexuality and power in the original 'Bluebeard', Carter uses the language of pornography, depicting the bride discovering her new husband's collection of rare books with their pictures of women used and abused. Waters takes this technique to an extreme in *Fingersmith*. Indeed, at one point Waters reworks a key image from Carter's story: Maud thinks of herself in her uncle's library as being 'like a curious wife at the keyhole of a cabinet of secrets. But I am inside the cabinet, and long to get out' (204). While the 'controversial lesbian body' is de-spectralised in *Affinity*, Waters uses both the language of pornography and the paraphernalia of historical costume, the encaging corsets and crinolines of the 1860s, to make it flesh in *Fingersmith*.

The ambiguity of the ending, with Maud becoming a writer of pornography herself, has troubled critics like Cora Kaplan: do we read it as a libertarian celebration of female sexuality as she suggests in *Victoriana*?[53] Or does Waters intend us to see, as Kaplan suggests in a later article, that 'the structure of [Maud's] desire and the conditions of production under which she writes are made and managed by the social and economic world she inhabits'? [54] In the context of 1980s and 1990s feminism, *Fingersmith* can be read as a serious intervention in debates around pornography.[55] Waters herself has suggested it was an attempt to write what Angela Carter in *The Sadeian Woman* termed 'moral pornography', to 'at least gesture towards the possibility that women could write their own porn themselves'.[56] As Carter asserts in her provocative engagement with de Sade, 'Pornographers are the enemies of women only because our contemporary ideology of pornography does not encompass the possibility of change, as if we were the slaves of history, not its makers.'[57]

History as process is central to this analysis. '[R]elationships between the sexes', Carter asserts, 'are determined by history and by the historical fact of the economic dependence of women upon men.'[58] If, as she puts it, 'Flesh comes to us out of history,' then our sexuality is 'never expressed in a vacuum' but always dictated by class, religion and race, thus exposing the historical construction of what we regard as our most intimate desires. In this context Maud's decision can be read as a determination to be a 'maker' (or a writer) not a 'slave' of history.

Developing Carter's thinking, *Fingersmith* shows that desire between women is also determined by the socio-historical structures. The matrilineal 'fictions' of origin which encase Sue and Maud are spun not only by their mothers, but also by Mr Lilly and Richard Rivers. If we move back from the pornography Maud writes (which we never read), to the central sexual encounter between Sue and Maud, which is told twice (first from Sue's point of view, and then from Maud's), then we can approach this rather differently. In her analysis of *The Green Scamander*, Waters astutely notes how Meagher's novel, under cover of its historical trappings, 'coerces its readers into a position from which textual fulfilment will only be secured by the erotic union of two women'.[59] Waters achieves a similar feat, although she seduces rather than coerces her readers, and this may be the secret of her success. She achieves this through her strategic deployment of first-person narrative under the cover of a historical setting. Here she has learned not just from novels like Meagher's but also from the gay and lesbian historical romances of the 1980s, which appropriated and revised historical narratives to draw attention to their own status as fantasy.[60] In *Affinity* the reader's desire for that erotic union between women is created through Margaret's diary, but then frustrated by the final denouement. In *Fingersmith* Waters uses the intimacy between mistress and maid — Sue's dressing and undressing of Maud, her care of Maud's body — to build erotic tension. The slow growth of Sue's feelings for the girl she has been told is 'Not queer [but] an innocent' (30) facilitates the growth of the reader's desire for (textual) union.

The erotic encounter between Sue and Maud, told from Sue's point of view, is a narrative of seduction as Sue explains to the 'innocent' Maud what she will be expected to do with Rivers on their wedding night: "'He will want,' I said after a moment, "to embrace you'" (139). From a verbal explanation this moves to a physical demonstration of kisses and intimate touchings until, approaching the moment of climax, Sue 'forgot to think of Gentleman': "'You pearl," I said. So white she was! "'You pearl, you pearl, you pearl'" (142). In this triangulated scene of desire the invocation of Rivers acts a kind of alibi, facilitating the desire between women which is thus constructed as only a rehearsal for the 'real' heterosexual encounter to come: "'It wants Mr Rivers,'" says Sue in reply to Maud's acknowledgement that "'You have made me feel it. It's such a curious, wanting thing'"(141). In the morning Sue denies her part in Maud's 'dream', substituting Rivers in her place: "'In your dream? I don't think so miss. Not me . . . I should say Mr Rivers.'" (144). The spectral presence of Rivers here acts as a go-between, much as 'Peter Quick' does in *Affinity* when he orchestrates kisses between Selina and Miss Isherwood (261–2).

In the retelling of this scene from Maud's point of view, it is coloured by her reading of pornography, including lesbian encounters: 'May a lady taste the fingers of her maid?', Maud thinks, 'She may, in my uncle's books' (256). No longer constructed as innocent, Maud actively provokes the encounter, which plays this time as a cliché from her uncle's collection: 'it is easy. After all, this is how it is done, in my uncle's books: two girls, one wise and one unknowing' (281). Yet, despite Sue's instructions to 'Think more of Mr Rivers' (282), Maud finds that Sue's fingers seem 'to quicken and draw me, to gather me, out of the darkness, out of my natural shape' (282). The word 'quicken', like the word 'queer', is a loaded one in Waters's novels where she frequently uses it to express the coming into knowledge of lesbian desire. In *Affinity* Margaret's desire for Selina makes 'a little *quickening* within me' (163). The word recalls Terry Castle's reading of the famous ending of *The Well of Loneliness* (1928) where, in Castle's words, Stephen 'undergoes a quickening – her "barren womb" becomes "fruitful." And . . . the ghosts begin to speak through her, as in one ecstatic and thunderous voice: "Give us also the right to our existence".'[61] In this context, of course, 'Peter *Quick*'s name takes on even more resonance, as a metaphor for the materialisation of lesbian desire.

This 'quickening', or materialisation, of desire, is the transformative moment for both Maud and Sue: '*Everything . . . is changed,*' Maud thinks, 'I think I was dead before. Now she has touched the life of me, the quick of me; she has put back my flesh and opened me up' (283). This image of 'opening', along with Sue's words, '*You pearl*', recall the oyster in *Tipping the Velvet*. There, Norman Jones argues, Waters uses the figure of the oyster which must be prised from its shell, not only as an erotic image which parallels the action of 'tipping the velvet', but also as an image of the exploration of lesbian history and its 'mysterious secrets'.[62] *Tipping*, he argues, 'symbolically refigures the vagina not as an empty vessel to be filled with significance but rather as a kind of full yet mysterious treasure trove – not unlike the oyster'.[63] In *Fingersmith* Waters deepens this lesbian erotic, replacing the dildo of *Tipping the Velvet* (which acts, like Peter Quick or the invocation of Rivers, as an signifier of the missing man in the triangle) with the 'fingers' which 'quicken' Maud.

The erotic triangle Waters delineates in *Fingersmith* maps onto and revises the Sedgwickian triangle of homosocial bonding which Terry Castle identifies in Sylvia Townsend Warner's historical novel *Summer Will Show* (1936). In Warner's novel, also set in the nineteenth century, Sophia Willoughby goes to Paris to reclaim her husband from his mistress, Minna Lemuel, and there falls in love with Minna herself. Castle engages with Eve Kosofsky Sedgwick's contention that male canonical texts, such as Flaubert's *L'Éducation sentimentale* (1869), typically foreground a plot of male homosocial desire, an erotic triangle in which, due to taboos on homosexuality, male bonding is facilitated or mediated through the body of a woman. *Summer Will Show*, Castle argues, reverses this as Sophia and Minna's bonding elides the man who has brought them together from the triangle altogether. Castle sees this undoing of the canonical plot of male homosociality through 'subverted triangulation, or erotic "counterplotting"' as 'characteristic of lesbian novels in general.'[64] In her own critique of Castle's reading Waters rightly argues that in taking Warner's novel as an 'exemplary "lesbian fiction"', Castle fails to acknowledge 'a distinctly lesbian tradition of historical fiction and speculation' in which Warner's novel has a place but 'not, perhaps, a privileged one'.[65]

Waters's novel has, however, more in common with Warner's equally revisionary novel than this critique might suggest. *Summer Will Show* also uses the oyster, although rather more elliptically, as an image of lesbian desire:

> 'I will stay if you wish it.'
> It seemed to [Sophia] that the words fell cold and glum as ice pellets. Only beneath the crust of thought did her being assent as by right to that flush of pleasure, that triumphant cry.
> 'But of course,' said Minna a few hours later, thoughtfully licking the last oyster shell, 'we must be practical.'[66]

Both Waters and Warner, then, suggest that the hard, deadened shell of history can be prised open to reveal the living (or 'quick') story of female desire hidden within.

In *Fingersmith* Waters depicts a triangle of female bonding which is facilitated by the spectral presence of Rivers. In a further ironic twist it is Rivers himself who names Maud's desire to her, to overcome her distaste for him: '"You've a heart, instead, for little fingersmiths?"' (276), he asks her. And he uses this knowledge to force Maud to perform heterosexuality in the interests of the plot to snare Sue: '"Excuse my whiskers. Imagine my mouth hers"' (276). Neither Maud nor Sue can act on their desire because at this point they are still both ensnared in what has become Rivers's plot: 'I have surrendered myself to Richard's plan,' Maud thinks, 'as I once gave myself to my uncle' (288). They are also entrammelled in the plots of pornography where lesbian desire is merely a prelude to, or a substitution for, heterosexuality, a point reinforced when Mr Lilly has Maud read to Rivers from a book which 'tells of all the means a woman may employ to pleasure another when in want of a man' (279).

If lesbianism is unspeakable, Waters shows, it has nevertheless left its traces in history not only in the texts of pornography, but also in those of the lunatic asylum. What Maud's narrative reveals is that the rationale for incarcerating Sue-as-Maud, what labels her mad, is Rivers's account of the 'gross attentions' she has paid to her 'maid': "'Must we oblige Miss Smith," he asks, "to rehearse the words, the artful poses – the caresses – to which my distracted wife has made her subject?"' (301). In the asylum, the nurses are certainly aware of the reason for 'Mrs Rivers's' incarceration. When the nurses play an obscene game of lying on Sue to compare their weights, Nurse Bacon leers, "'Like it do you? . . . No? We heard you did"' (442). Sue's resulting paroxysm is explained to the doctor as a lewd dream: 'she was saying a lady's name, and moving as she slept' (443). The treatment – or punishment – for this is to tie Sue to a frame and drop her, fifteen times, into a bath of cold water.

This torture recalls what Maud Vernon witnesses in the asylum in Le Fanu's *The Rose and the Key*, where another inmate is tied to an iron chair and nearly killed by a heavy downpour of water. 'This peculiar use of the shower-bath in the treatment of the insane', Le Fanu's narrator comments, 'is no fiction'.[67] He cites the example of a medical superintendent who caused the death of a male patient through such treatment. But he also links it to historical abuses suffered by women when he remarks (ironically) that, if one could ignore the suffering and danger, then this scene 'might be witnessed as merrily as, in old times, men stood by and laughed at the duck-ing of a witch'.[68] By the time Le Fanu was writing in 1871, the asylums were undergoing reform, but the use of 'baths of surprise' was documented as an abuse of the recent past by John Connolly, head of Hanwell Asylum in 1856.[69] Like Gaskell's 'Lois the Witch', Waters's novel reminds us of the stark reality of historical abuses of women. If history has its uses as a fantasy space, we must bear in mind that the Gothic expresses the nightmarish aspects of the past for many women.

Both Sue and Maud are physically incarcerated in the final section of the novel – Sue in the asylum, Maud at Lant Street – as well as entrapped within the plots fabricated by Mr Lilly, Rivers and Mrs Sucksby. It is in the unravelling of these that Waters gives another twist to the triangulation of desire. What frees them is the killing of Rivers, the man who has manipulated both of them. The male element in the erotic triangle is not just elided but bloodily mur-dered. In Sue's account it is impossible to tell who actually stabs him: 'I do not know if Mrs Sucksby, when she darted, darted at him or only – seeing Maud fly – at her. I know there was the gleam of something bright' (502). Later she thinks that 'it was [Maud's] hand I remembered seeing dart and flash'(510). It is, however, Mrs Sucksby, 'looking the picture of a murderess from one of the penny papers' (508) who confesses to the murder and is hanged for it. Like the mother in Carter's 'The Bloody Chamber' who shoots Bluebeard as he is about to behead his bride, Mrs Sucksby kills (metaphorically or literally) the man who threatens her daughter(s), and, further, sacrifices herself to save them. In doing so she frees them from both the male-authored plot of heterosexuality (ironically, there are hints that Rivers is homosexual) and from the female-authored plot of matrilineal inheritance.

While she seems initially a grotesque out of Dickens, Mrs Sucksby can be read as a figure of redemptive maternity. Her name encompasses a range of meanings, both nurturing and exploitative: 'to give suck to', 'suckle', 'suckling', 'sucker' (*OED*). It also hints at the fact that she becomes a source of 'succour' for her daughters, as does her unused first name, 'Grace', revealed only after the stabbing (502). By using two daughters, one biological and one adopted, and by reversing their positions so that they grow up unaware of their true identities, Waters frees them from the determining matrilineal plots of the Female Gothic. But she is also able to split and explore the daughter's ambivalence towards the mother's body through Sue's passionate attachment and Maud's revulsion towards Mrs Sucksby. Sue's outburst on seeing Mrs Sucksby undressing Maud – 'She has taken everything from me . . . She has made Mrs Sucksby love her, as she made – Oh I'll kill her' (476) – collapses together the desire for the mother with the desire for the other woman. The incestuous implications are made clearer as she asserts that 'The person who cheated me worst is lying at the moment in my own bed, with my own mother's arms about her' (477). This is contrasted with Maud's horror, not knowing that Mrs Sucksby is her biological mother, at the sight of Mrs Sucksby undressing to share her bed, and kissing a lock of Maud's hair (347). 'Why must you smother and torment me, with your grasping after my heart?' (391) Maud asks, just before she recognises her own face in the contours of Mrs Sucksby's.

In her essay 'The bodily encounter with the mother', Irigaray argues that the 'relationship with the mother is a mad desire, because it is the "dark continent" *par excellence'*.[70] It is the ultimate taboo in Western culture: 'Desire for her, her desire, that is what is forbidden by the law of the father, of all the fathers.'[71] And this 'first body, this first home, this first love' is replaced by a male language which 'privileges the masculine genre [le genre masculin] to such an extent as to confuse it with the human race [le genre humain].'[72] This lack of symbolic representation constructs the mother as a 'devouring monster'[73] who (to borrow Waters's term) 'smothers' her daughters in failing to separate from them. In contrast, Irigaray argues that women must retain their love for their mother in order to retain their identities. More, she argues that we must 'discover the singularity of our love for other women . . . if we are not to remain the servants of the phallic cult, objects to be used by and exchanged between men, rival objects on the market'.[74] The plot constructed by Mrs Sucksby and Marianne Lilly positioned Sue and Maud as objects to be used by men – by Rivers and Mr Lilly – as Mrs Sucksby acknowledges when she tells Maud that they had been 'wrong' (543). Like Clytemnestra, Irigaray's exemplary mother, who kills the man who 'sacrificed [her] daughter to conflicts between men',[75] Mrs Sucksby kills Rivers because he threatens her daughter(s), and in doing so redeems both herself and them. Erasing the man from the erotic triangle of desire, she leaves the two heroines to construct their own plots. Behind the lesbian body in *Fingersmith* is the desire for the lost/absent mother who is finally reclaimed by and redeems her daughter.

The Little Stranger: the unborn desires of male Gothic

Waters's most recent novels, *The Night Watch* (2006) and *The Little Stranger* (2009), are set in the 1940s. This move allows us to see Waters not just as a neo-Victorianist but as a writer engaged with history on a broader scale. These novels can be situated in a current turn towards the period of the Second World War, including books like Ian McEwan's *Atonement* (2001), Dan Rhodes's *Resistance* (2007) and Simon Mawer's *The Glass Room* (2009). The passing of Scott's 'Sixty Years Since' means that the 1940s are now clearly 'history', receding into textual evidence, particularly for writers of

Waters's generation who 'remember' the war through their parents' memories. Moreover, 9/11 in 2001 refocused attention on a history that had been prematurely declared over by theorists like Francis Fukuyama.[76] Waters herself noted the coincidence of beginning her serious research on the blitz for *The Night Watch* on 11 September 2001 and how 'after that, bombs or the threat of bombs, seemed to be everywhere.'[77] As the current media invocations of 'austerity Britain' suggest, our affinities with the dour exhausted post-war period now seem ripe for exploitation.

Described by Waters as a 'sort of supernatural country house whodunnit – a "Whose poltergeist is it?"',[78] *The Little Stranger* blends together and 'queers', the genres of historical novel, ghost story, detective story and country house novel. Set in 1947 and told in the first person by Dr Faraday, it is the story of his dealings with the Ayres family – Mrs Ayres and her grown-up children, shell-shocked Roderick and spinster Caroline, who live in the dilapidated Georgian Hundreds Hall in Warwickshire. First called out to treat the maid, Betty, who seems terrified by the house, Faraday is drawn into a series of events – a spooked dog, scorch marks on the ceiling, writing on the walls, mysterious fires, bells ringing, crockery falling, a ghostly voice heard through a speaking tube – which suggest supernatural causes and which escalate into tragedy. Rational and logical, Faraday refuses to accept Caroline's insistence that the family is haunted by a poltergeist. By the end of the novel, Roderick is incarcerated in a nursing home, Mrs Ayres has committed suicide, and Caroline, who has broken off her brief engagement to Faraday, has mysteriously fallen to her death from the second-floor landing. The ending is left open: Waters has said that her interest is not in whether ghosts exist or not but in 'why the supernatural draws us: what it offers us, in the way of catharsis or consolation, or in the articulation of the unspeakable'.[79]

Perhaps most impressive is that fact that, at 499 pages, *The Little Stranger* is a novel-length ghost story. Most ghost stories are, as I noted in chapter 3, just that – *short* stories. And Waters exploits to the full the ways in which intertextuality is a kind of haunting. As she says,

> The ghost story tradition is full of echoes. Haunted houses resemble each other, curses work themselves out along similar lines, and each

new Gothic narrative somehow recalls the ones before it. Writing *The Little Stranger* I found myself unconsciously invoking the touchstones of the genre, giving little nods to Dickens, to Poe, to Shirley Jackson and Henry James.[80]

Hundreds Hall, like all haunted houses, is 'a psychological structure as well as an actual one'.[81] Like Udolpho, St Salvat's, Manderley or Jamaica Inn, it is imbued with the secrets of its inhabitants, both dead and living. In *The Little Stranger*, this tradition is meshed with that of the country house detective novel, where the house becomes a microcosm of the social spectrum and everyone, servants and family, is a suspect.

The 'rational' solution is, of course, the marker of the detective story which, as a genre, must eschew the supernatural. Waters has recorded that her original inspiration came from Josephine Tey's detective novel, *The Franchise Affair* (1948), itself based on an eighteenth-century case.[82] In Tey's novel a certain post-war middle-class hysteria is evident in reactions to the case of the alleged kidnapping of a working-class girl, Betty Kane, by the shabby genteel Mrs Sharpe and her grown-up daughter Marion, who supposedly lock her in an attic in their house, the Franchise, to force her to be their servant. The problem is solved by the '*douce* country lawyer and gentleman',[83] Robert Blair, who is motivated by his class sympathy for the Sharpes, and who falls in love with Marion. The affinities with Waters's novel are both obvious, and slightly misleading. The anxieties provoked by post-war shifts in the English class structure are visible, for instance in Faraday's worries about the new National Health Service and the Ayres' distaste for the new housing being built on Hundreds' land, but Waters's sympathies lie in a different place. While Blair's problem is mainly to prove that the working-class Betty Kane is promiscuous and a liar, Waters leaves us guessing even after the final line: not only 'Whose poltergeist is it?' but, even, 'Is it a poltergeist?'

Following Faraday through his ratiocinative deductions, we as readers also use the intertextual 'clues' to interpret the novel, directed (or misdirected) by familiar generic conventions. Among the many other texts invoked in the novel, and acknowledged as influences by Waters in various places, are Charlotte Perkins

Gilman's 'The Yellow Wallpaper' (1892), M. R. James's ghost stories with their scholarly bachelor narrators, *Jane Eyre* (1847) and *Wide Sargasso Sea* (1966), *Wuthering Heights* (1847), Toni Morrison's *Beloved* (1987), du Maurier's *Rebecca* (1938), the country house tradition, and detective fiction, including that of Agatha Christie. The echoes of these, as with Waters's other books, embed *The Little Stranger* within a history which is textually constructed through literary representations.

The ghost story has a tangential relationship with the Gothic novel. As I noted in the Introduction, one of the defining characteristics of the Female Gothic is that, following Radcliffe, the supernatural is usually given a rational explanation. *Fingersmith* and *Affinity* follow in this tradition, with *Affinity* exploiting it to misdirect the reader. In both novels Waters also centralises a female point of view, another defining characteristic of the Female Gothic. It is the language of the Gothic, which Waters uses in these earlier novels to particularly superb effect, the motifs of spectrality, haunted houses and hunted heroines, which provide a coherent metaphorical matrix which can be both exploited and queered to figure the structures of gender, class and sexuality which both construct and constrain us.

The Little Stranger is rather different. At first glance it seems a departure from Waters's usual terrain, not least because it contains no obviously lesbian character. Yet in the story of Caroline Ayres and Hundreds Hall we can see the typical 'woman-plus-habitation and the plot of mysterious sexual and supernatural threats in an atmosphere of dynastic mysteries'[84] of the Female Gothic. Furthermore, Lucie Armitt has drawn our attention to the clues which suggest that Caroline, who is 'referred to locally as "rather hearty" [and] a "natural spinster"' (9), is the 'apparitional lesbian' in this text: Waters, Armitt remarks, hides the lesbian, '"in full view"'.[85] It is Waters's use of a (potentially unreliable) *male* narrator which obscures these elements. The centralising of the male point of view, the unexplained supernatural (the poltergeist), the tragic plot and uncertain closure, a focus on female suffering (Mrs Ayres's suicide and Caroline's death), and on horror rather than terror, are all elements which mark *The Little Stranger* out as 'Male Gothic' rather than 'Female Gothic'. In fact, the novel *The Little Stranger* most resembles in its (un)canny mixing of the two modes is du Maurier's *My Cousin Rachel* (1951) as discussed in chapter 5.

Waters's poltergeist is (probably) not a ghost in the usual sense of the word. Instead, she draws on the 'post-Freudian' interpretation of the poltergeist as 'an acting out of psychological distress . . . "a bundle of projected repressions"', in the words of Hereward Carrington and Nandor Fodor in *Haunted People* (1951).[86] Hundreds is haunted not by the dead but by 'the unconscious aggressions and frustrations of the living'.[87] In the novel, Caroline shows Faraday copies of Gurney and Myers's *Phantasms of the Living* (1886) and Catherine Crowe's *The Night Side of Nature* (1848) to convince him that Hundreds is haunted by a poltergeist. 'Poltergeist', she tells Faraday, is

'just a word . . . for something we don't understand, some sort of energy, or collection of energies. [Gurney and Myers] talk about "phantasms". They're not ghosts. They're parts of a person . . . Unconscious parts, so strong or so troubled they can take on a life of their own.' (364)

Faraday's response to Caroline's theory is to assert his own rational and scientific credentials – '"I'm a doctor!"' (366) – and to treat her as hysterical.

Faraday's colleague Dr Seeley, however, suggests that Myers's theory is a 'natural extension of psychology'; that if one subscribes to the principle of a personality divided unto conscious and subliminal selves then it is possible to conceive that the '"dream-self could, in certain circumstances, *break loose*: detach itself, cross space, become visible to others?"' (379). He goes on to articulate the image that provides the title of the novel:

'The subliminal mind has many dark, unhappy corners, after all. Imagine something loosening itself from one of those corners. Let's call it a – a germ. And let's say conditions prove right for that germ to develop – to grow, like a child in the womb. What would this little stranger grow into? A sort of *shadow-self*, perhaps: a Caliban, a Mr Hyde.' (380)

To interpret what lurks in the 'dark corners' of history, Waters seems to be suggesting, we need to turn away from the rational and scientific to the psychoanalytical.

The problem is that the source of the 'little stranger' who haunts Hundreds could be any one of the characters, Caroline suspects that the shell-shocked Roderick, by this time shut up in a nursing home, is at the root of it: "'suppose it's my brother, doing it all . . . You know how unhappy he could get, how frustrated'" (364). Roderick himself had believed that he was the source of an 'infection' (165) which he must keep from his mother and sister. Dr Faraday counters Caroline's theory with the possibility of Betty, arguing, "'You've only had trouble, haven't you, since she's been in the house?'", a suggestion Caroline dismisses with the comment: "'You might as well say we've only had trouble since you've been in it!'" (365). Readers of Tey's *The Franchise Affair* and, of course, *Affinity*, will be drawn to Faraday's suspicion of Betty. Seeley himself argues that "'it's generally women, you know, at the root of this sort of thing'" (380). He points the finger first at Mrs Ayes, "'the menopausal mother: that's a queer time, psychically'" (38). And, indeed, Mrs Ayres thinks the trouble is caused by the spirit of her daughter Susan, dead from diphtheria at the age of seven, drawn back by her mother's desperate longing for her. But finally Seeley concludes that Caroline herself is the obvious suspect, a deduction which tallies with Armitt's reading of Caroline as an 'apparitional lesbian'.

However, another clue to the mystery is not a ghost story, but the far more prosaic detective novel by Agatha Christie, *The Murder of Roger Ackroyd* (1926). Set in the ubiquitous country house, it is narrated in the first person by a doctor, James Shepperd, who is, in the final pages, unmasked by Poirot as the murderer. The novel features a shell-shocked young man, Ralph Paton, who is hidden in a mental asylum by Dr Shepperd; a 'queer' servant girl who turns out to be married to Ralph; and Shepperd's spinster sister Caroline, who reads, in his opinion, 'too many trashy novels' yet who is the most perceptive person in the novel.[88] A reading of Christie's novel, like a reading of *My Cousin Rachel* or Vernon Lee's 'Amour Dure', might lead us to look more carefully at the supposedly rational scientific man who narrates the text and to wonder what unrealised desires lie buried in the dark corners of his psyche. Does Waters hide the murderer, like the lesbian, 'in full view'?

As with so much of the historical Gothic, property ownership is at the heart of *The Little Stranger*. Faraday's overwhelming passion is not for Caroline but for Hundreds Hall. He falls in love with Hundreds when he first visits it as a boy during an Empire Day fête in 1919 with his mother, formerly a nursery maid at the house. Exploring the house, he is overtaken by a desire to 'possess a piece of it' (3), and uses a penknife to prise a plaster acorn from a decorative border on one of the walls. Finding this 'queer little thing' (3) in his pocket his tearful mother puts it on the fire. That Empire Day fête marks the beginning of Hundreds' decline: Susan Ayres dies soon after, followed by Colonel Ayres, and Faraday's mother dies when he is fifteen, killed by a succession of miscarriages. Thirty years later, Faraday's return to the decaying house up an over-grown drive evokes the dream opening of *Rebecca*. While this may seem at first to identify him with du Maurier's naïve narrator, we should also remember the murderous impulses the love of Manderley unleashes in Maxim. The image is repeated in disturbingly sexualised terms during his courtship of Caroline:

> My mind would go softly across the darkened miles between us, to slip like a poacher through the Hundreds gate and along the over-grown drive; to nudge open the swollen front door, to inch across the chequered marble; and then to go creeping, creeping towards her, up the still and silent stairs. (325)

While Caroline agrees to marry Faraday to get away from Hundreds, he takes it for granted they will live in the house, and is distraught when she breaks off their engagement and puts the house up for sale.

Faraday's narrative gives us all the clues we need to identify the 'ravenous shadow-creature, [or] "little stranger"' (498) which has consumed Hundreds and its inhabitants, but, to recognise them, we need to 'queer', to 'put out of order', the accepted conventions of history, psychology and genre. On the night Caroline dies, calling out 'You!' (482) before she tumbles to her death at 2 a.m., Faraday tells us he is slumbering in his car near the overgrown pond where he first tried to kiss her, just a couple of miles from Hundreds. Exhausted after dealing with an appendicitis emergency, he begins to 'feel out of time and out of place, an absolute stranger' (472):

> And in the slumber I seemed to leave the car, and to press on to Hundreds . . . I saw myself cross the silvered landscape and pass like smoke through the Hundreds gate. I saw myself start along the Hundreds drive.
>
> But there I grew panicked and confused – or the drive was changed, was queer and wrong, was impossibly lengthy and tangled with, at the end of it, nothing but darkness. (473)

At the end of the novel Faraday visits the derelict Hundreds whenever he has time, letting himself in with the keys he has retained. As he remarks, if the house is haunted the ghost does not show itself to him: 'For I'll turn, and am disappointed – realising that what I am looking at is only a cracked window pane, and that *the face gazing distortedly from it, baffled and longing, is my own*' (499; emphasis added). Conditioned by generic and societal conventions to assume that '"it's generally women . . . at the root of this sort of thing"' (380), we may well be looking through instead of at the clues in the narrative. Like du Maurier's Philip Ashley, Faraday can be read as a male hysteric whose desires have deathly consequences (real or supernatural) for any woman who comes between himself and the property he desires. The enigmatic title metaphor, taken from a jocular nineteenth-century euphemism for an unborn or new-born child (*OED*), offers the most important clue to the interpretation I want to offer here. Anne Williams argues that, 'Male Gothic conventions imply that the focus of horror is not merely "the female" in general, but more specifically, her most mysterious and powerful manifestation as mother or potential mother.'[89]

In *The Little Stranger* the language and imagery of pregnancy are repeatedly equated with the uncanny, female instability and horror. Seeley's argument that the poltergeist is like 'a germ' which develops 'like a child in the womb' is echoed in Rod's belief that the thing is '"breeding"' (423), and Faraday's speculation: 'Suppose, unconsciously, [Caroline] had given birth to some violent shadowy creature, that was effectively haunting the house?' (400). The masculine equation of female reproduction with madness is bitterly articulated when Caroline says to Faraday: 'I'm not going crazy . . . Though I'm not sure you wouldn't quite like that, too. You could keep me upstairs in the nursery. The bars are already on the windows, after all' (448). As a doctor it is Faraday who has the power to diagnose others as 'mad', 'unbalanced' or 'hysterical': he arranges Rod's admission to the nursing home, is in the process of arranging for Mrs Ayres to be admitted when she dies, and it is his testimony at the inquest which convinces the judge that Caroline was unbalanced and had committed suicide.

Yet there are clear traces of male hysteria in the book, not only in Rod's shell-shock but also in Faraday himself, as well as traces of homoerotic attraction between Faraday and Rod. In an early scene Faraday uses his electrical apparatus to treat Rod's disabled leg: 'The knee was as pale and bulbous as some queer root' (55), he notes as he manipulates it but the treatment makes it 'hot and moist' (59). Caroline's offhand comment that the machine is 'Like something of Dr Frankenstein's' (60) reminds us of Shelley's classic Gothic birth myth, about the male desire to usurp the function of reproduction. And Rod's later vehement reaction when Faraday touches his wrist – '"Get your hands off me! . . . when you're not doling out your doctor's advice to me you're making a grab at me with your filthy doctor's hands' (197) – suggests something more than class tensions. In the light of this, Faraday's engagement to Caroline can be read as another version of the Sedgwickian triangle: the woman as a symbolic substitute for the real (male) object of desire. Perhaps Waters is hiding not only the lesbian but the homosexual in full view?

There are traces of an even more deeply buried desire in the text: the tabooed desire for the mother's body which Irigaray locates at the heart of Western culture. The final image of Faraday gazing at his own reflection in a cracked window pane recalls Anne Williams's argument that 'Male Gothic is a dark mirror reflecting patriarchy's nightmare, recalling a perilous, violent and early separation from the mother/mater denigrated as "female".'[90] Faraday's initial introduction to Hundreds is through his mother's position as nursery maid there – a role in which her mothering was co-opted and commodified by the class system. Hundreds is haunted in this sense by Faraday's mother, a working-class woman who has left almost no trace in history. The Ayres show him a family photograph in which his mother may feature with the other staff but he cannot determine which of two possible women in identical uniform is her. Yet, he is 'more moved by the unexpected appearance of my mother's face – if it *was* her face – than I would have expected' (30). This ghostly trace of his mother is later reiterated in his reaction to the speaking tube which connects the nursery with the kitchen: 'I had the sudden irrational idea that, in putting my ear to the cup, I would hear my mother's voice' (334).

Here the haunted house can be read as an image of the mother's body, the body which the subject both fears and desires to return to. Hundreds' shady uterine passages and central hall, with its pink and liver-coloured marble and serpentine banister, are topped with a breast-like dome of 'milky glass' (31). Given that it is unrealised maternity which kills Faraday's mother, through that succession of miscarriages, the construction of the unborn child as a monster or poltergeist takes on another layer of meanings. Seeley argues that Hundreds has been 'defeated by history' (498), as the Ayres fail to adapt to the changing times. Faraday's final 'possession' of Hundreds, however hollow, is both a class revenge against the gentry who laugh at the 'very people' who have 'made and maintained' (27) Hundreds by their labour, and a symbolic return to the mother's body which has been denied to him by class and gender structures.

The Little Stranger exposes the fear and desire for the maternal at the heart of our culture and the ways in which these intersect with issues of class, gender and sexuality. To 'see' this, Waters's work suggests, we need to turn not to rational and scientific analyses but to other discourses, among them psychoanalysis and the Gothic, which have the potential to articulate what is otherwise unspeakable. The anxieties expressed in *The Little Stranger*, like those in Waters's earlier novels, are closer to us than we may think and the class and gender structures that we assume belong to the world of *Upstairs Downstairs* or *Downton Abbey* still define our identities in ways which are both complex and mundane. The tussle for ownership of Hundreds Hall is a microcosm of a wider struggle over England itself, or rather – given Waters's birth in Neyland in south Wales – Britain itself, which is still ongoing.

Waters's sensitivity to these issues perhaps has its roots in the upward mobility of her own family: 'My nan was a nursery maid,' she has recalled. 'Most people weren't in big houses. They were maids of all work . . . that's just what most young people did. They went into service. The war swept all that away.'[91] (In this context the Ayres's dismissal of one former servant as a 'moron' (27) takes on rather a different light.) In the same interview, Waters compared the 'chaos, violence and disorder of war to a giant poltergeist' and commented: 'For me there's always a lot of free-floating anxiety, which seems resonant of our times. We just don't quite know what to be anxious about.'[92] In her use of the Gothic, Waters has found the ideal lens through which to focus and analyse our 'free-floating anxieties', about class, gender and sexuality, and their persistence through and in history. Her Gothic historical novels offer us not 'queer history', but, to borrow a term from Scott Bravmann which she quoted approvingly in her thesis, '"*queered* history"', a meta-history that is, which '"takes issue with historiography itself"'.[93]

Afterword

> Every image of the past that is not recognised by the present as one
> of its own concerns threatens to disappear irretrievably.
>
> Walter Benjamin, 'Theses on the Philosophy of History'[1]

The Gothic historical mode, as I have argued, has allowed women
writers to offer a symbolic critique of the ways in which women
have been left out of recorded history and the psychological effects
of this exclusion. Legally constructed as 'civilly dead' for much of
the period I have been discussing, women writers have developed
the language and imagery of the Gothic – spectrality, live burial, the
haunted house, the womb-tomb 'recess', the murdered mother – to
symbolise the fact that that they, and their mothers and daughters,
have been denied a matrilineal genealogy and full subjectivity.

History (both recorded history and the unrecorded past) is important because it reminds us that the cultural and social structures we
take for granted are in fact provisional and contingent. Even patriarchy itself may be, as Luce Irigaray suggests, a temporary stage,
though a long one. As Sarah Waters points out,

> if you take a longer view and just remind people that these things are
> always in process, they're not fixed, and gender's never fixed, and
> how we feel about women changes all the time, and how we feel

about sex and sexuality and class, these things change all the time . . .
historical fiction can dramatically enact that.[2]

Historical fiction has been particularly important for women because,
as Virginia Woolf put it, 'the history of England [for which we can
read Britain, Europe, the world] is the history of the male line, not
of the female.'[3] Within mainstream history women have tended to
feature only in certain roles – as queens, witches, nuns, spiritualists
– or as *femmes fatales* like Vernon Lee's Medea da Carpi. Historical
fiction has allowed women writers to reassess these figures, and to
show how they are often 'hysterical' constructions, reflecting the
anxieties and desires of male historians and otherwise disempowered
women.

Yet the seemingly endless reiteration of the plot of entrapment
in the costume Gothics of Victoria Holt also offers a warning. As
Alex Owen writes in her study of nineteenth-century spiritualism,
'We must not permit ourselves to become trapped in darkened
rooms of our own making.'[4] Owen is discussing what she sees as
the essentialism of radical feminist spirituality, but there is a wider
warning here about the dangers of reiterating the patterns of the
past. Through re-imagining the past we can – and should – also be
imagining alternative futures.

Notes

1: Introduction

1   Virginia Woolf, 'Women and fiction' (1929), in *On Women and Writing*, ed. Michèle Barrett, (London: The Women's Press, 1979), p. 44.
2   Luce Irigaray, *Thinking the Difference: For a Peaceful Revolution*, trans. Karin Montin (1989; London: Athlone, 1994), p. 110.
3   Hayden White cites Northrop Frye's use of 'metahistory' as a synonym for 'speculative philosophy of history', in *Tropics of Discourse* (1978; Baltimore and London: Johns Hopkins University Press, 1985), p. 76.
4   Irigaray, *Thinking the Difference*, p. 110.
5   Blackstone, *Commentaries on the Laws of England* (7th edn, 1775), quoted in Mary R. Beard, *Woman as Force in History* (New York: Macmillan, 1946), pp. 78–9.
6   Ibid., pp. 80, 77.
7   Mary Spongberg, *Writing Women's History since the Renaissance* (Basingstoke: Palgrave Macmillan, 2002), pp. 1–2, emphasis added.
8   Bonnie G. Smith, *The Gender of History: Men, Women and Historical Practice* (Cambridge, MA and London: Harvard University Press, 1998), p. 3.
9   Christina Crosby, *The Ends of History: Victorians and 'the Woman Question'* (New York and London: Routledge, 1991), p. 1, emphasis added.
10   Ibid.
11   Virginia Woolf, *A Room of One's Own* (1929; London: Granada, 1977), p. 45.
12   Joan Wallach Scott, 'After History', *Common Knowledge*, 5/3 (1996), 25.

13 Mary Ann Doane, *Femmes Fatales: Feminism, Film Theory, Psychoanalysis* (New York and Routledge, 1991), p. 91.

14 Montague Summers, *The Gothic Quest: A History of the Gothic Novel* (1938; London: Fortune Press, 1968) includes a chapter on 'Historical Gothic', pp. 153–201; Devendra P. Varma, *The Gothic Flame* (1957; New York: Russell and Russell, 1966), includes a chapter entitled 'Historical-Gothic School: The Heirs of "Otranto"', pp. 74–84.

15 David Punter, *The Literature of Terror*, vol. I: *The Gothic Tradition*, 2nd edn (London and New York: Longman, 1996), p. 52.

16 Patricia Waugh defines metafiction as 'fictional writing which self-consciously and systematically draws attention to its status as an artefact in order to pose questions about the relationship between fiction and reality.' *Metafiction* (London and New York: Routledge, 1984), p. 2.

17 Rosemary Jackson, *Fantasy: The Literature of Subversion* (1981; London and New York: Routledge, 1998), p. 4.

18 Sheila Rowbotham, *Hidden from History: Rediscovering Women in History from the Seventeenth Century to the Present* (1973; New York: Random, 1976); Elise Boulding, *The Underside of History: A View of Women through Time* (Boulder, CO: Westview, 1976).

19 Sir Walter Scott, *Waverley* (1814; Oxford: Oxford World's Classics, 1998), p. 3.

20 Ibid., p. 4.

21 Ibid., p. 5.

22 Ibid.

23 Ibid., p. 341.

24 Anon, 'The Historical Romance', *Blackwood's Magazine*, 58 (1845), 341–2, 345–6; reprinted in E. J. Clery and Robert Miles (eds), *Gothic Documents: A Sourcebook 1700–1820* (Manchester: Manchester University Press, 2000), pp. 292–7 (p. 294).

25 Georg Lukács, *The Historical Novel*, trans. Hannah and Stanley Mitchell (1962; Lincoln, NB and London: University of Nebraska Press, 1983).

26 Ibid., p. 30.

27 Avrom Fleishman, *The English Historical Novel: Walter Scott to Virginia Woolf* (Baltimore and London: Johns Hopkins University Press, 1971).

28 Ibid., pp. 3–4.

29 Ibid., p. 15.

30 Anne H. Stevens, *British Historical Fiction before Scott* (Basingstoke: Palgrave Macmillan, 2010), p. 37.

31 Ibid., p. 19.

32 Ibid., p. 7.

33 Richard Maxwell, *The Historical Novel in Europe, 1650–1950* (Cambridge: Cambridge University Press, 2009).

34   Ibid., ch. 3.
35   Jerome de Groot, *The Historical Novel* (London and New York: Rout-
     ledge, 2010), p. 17.
36   Ibid., p. 16.
37   April Alliston, 'Introduction', in Sophia Lee, *The Recess; or, A Tale of
     Other Times*, ed. April Alliston (Lexington: University Press of Ken-
     tucky, 2000), p. xiv.
38   See chapter 2.
39   Leslie Fiedler, *Love and Death in the American Novel* (1960; Harmonds-
     worth: Penguin, 1984), p. 170.
40   Sarah Waters, 'Wolfskins and Togas: Maude Meagher's *The Green
     Scamander* and the Lesbian Historical Novel', *Women: A Cultural Review*,
     7/2 (1996), 176–88, (176).
41   See Robin Gilmour, 'Using the Victorians: the Victorian age in con-
     temporary fiction', in Alice Jenkins and Juliet John (eds), *Rereading
     Victorian Fiction* (Basingstoke and New York: Palgrave, 2000), pp. 189–
     200; Cora Kaplan, '*Fingersmith*'s Coda: Feminism and Victorian Studies,
     Journal of Victorian Culture, 13/1 (2006), 42–55; Lauren Fitzgerald,
     'Female Gothic and the Institutionalisation of Gothic Studies', *Gothic
     Studies*, 6/1 (May 2004), 8–18.
42   Gilmour, 'Using the Victorians', p. 199.
43   Fredric Jameson, *The Political Unconscious: Narrative as a Socially Symbolic
     Act* (1981; London and New York, 2002), p. 67.
44   Linda Hutcheon, *A Poetics of Postmodernism: History, Theory, Fiction*
     (New York and London: Routledge, 1988), p. 5.
45   Ibid.
46   Sally Shuttleworth, 'Natural history: the retro-Victorian novel', in
     Elinor Shaffer (ed.), *The Third Culture: Literature and Science* (New York:
     de Gruyter, 1998), pp. 253–68.
47   Dana Shiller, 'The Redemptive Past in the Neo-Victorian Novel',
     Studies in the Novel, 29/4 (Winter 1997), 538–-60.
48   See Diana Wallace, *The Woman's Historical Novel: British Women Writers,
     1900–2000* (Basingstoke: Palgrave 2005), chs 4 and 8.
49   Hayden White, *Metahistory* (1973; Baltimore and London: Johns Hop-
     kins University Press, 1975), p. 29.
50   Roger Luckhurst (ed.), *Late Victorian Gothic Tales* (Oxford: Oxford
     World's Classics, 2005), p. ix.
51   Michael Cox and Jack Adrian (eds), *The Oxford Book of Historical Stories*
     (Oxford: Oxford University Press, 1995), p. xiii.
52   Allen calls Scott's 'The Two Drovers' 'the first modern short story in
     English': Walter Allen, *The Short Story in English* (Oxford: Oxford
     University Press, 1981), pp. 9–10.

[53] Michael Cox and R. A. Gilbert (eds), *The Oxford Book of English Ghost Stories* (Oxford: Oxford University Press, 1986, p. xii.

[54] Julia Briggs, *Night Visitors: The Rise and Fall of the English Ghost Story* (London: Faber, 1977), p. 23.

[55] Vanessa D. Dickerson, *Victorian Ghosts in the Noontide: Women Writers and the Supernatural* (Columbia and London: University of Missouri Press, 1996), p. 5.

[56] Ibid., p. 8.

[57] Luce Irigaray, *The Irigaray Reader*, ed. Margaret Whitford (Oxford: Blackwell, 1991), pp. 74, 91.

[58] Ellen Moers, *Literary Women* (1976; London: The Women's Press, 1978), p. 90.

[59] Ibid., pp. 91, 92.

[60] Sandra M. Gilbert and Susan Gubar, *The Madwoman in the Attic: The Woman Writer and the Nineteenth-Century Literary Imagination* (1979; New Haven and London: Yale University Press, 1984), p. 360.

[61] For a summary of the debates and key critical works, see Diana Wallace and Andrew Smith, 'Introduction: defining the Female Gothic', in *The Female Gothic: New Directions* (Basingstoke: Palgrave Macamillan, 2009), pp.1–12.

[62] Moers, *Literary Women*, p. 90.

[63] Punter, *Literature of Terror*, p. 52.

[64] Ibid., p. 47.

[65] Clara Reeve, *The Old English Baron* (1777; Oxford: Oxford World's Classics, 2003), p. 2.

[66] Ibid., pp. 5, 3.

[67] Punter, *Literature of Terror*, p. 48.

[68] Norman N. Holland and Leona F. Sherman, 'Gothic Possibilities', *New Literary History*, 8/2 (1977), 279–94 (279).

[69] Claire Kahane, 'The Gothic mirror' (1980), in Shirley Nelson Garner, Claire Kahane and Madelon Spregnether (eds), *The Mother Tongue: Essays in Feminist Psychoanalytic Interpretation* (Ithaca and London: Cornell University Press, 1985), pp. 334–51 (p. 336).

[70] Ibid., p. 347.

[71] Juliann Fleenor (ed.), *The Female Gothic* (Montreal: Eden, 1983).

[72] Anne Williams, *Art of Darkness: A Poetics of Gothic* (Chicago and London: University of Chicago Press, 1995), pp. 102–4.

[73] Avril Horner and Sue Zlosnik, *Daphne du Maurier: Writing, Identity and the Gothic Imagination* (Basingstoke: Macmillan, 1998), pp. 28–9.

[74] Chris Baldick and Robert Mighall, 'Gothic criticism', in David Punter (ed.), *A Companion to the Gothic* (Oxford: Blackwell, 2000), pp. 209–28 (p. 218).

75 Ibid., p. 227.
76 Jane Austen, *Northanger Abbey* (1818; Harmondsworth: Penguin, 1985), p. 123.
77 Margaret Anne Doody, 'Deserts, Ruins and Troubled Waters: Female Dreams in Fiction and the Development of the Gothic Novel', *Genre* 10 (Winter 1977), 562, 560.
78 April Alliston, *Virtue's Faults: Correspondences in Eighteenth-Century British and French Women's Fiction* (Stanford, CA; Stanford University Press, 1996), p. 144, emphasis added.
79 Ibid., p. 146, emphasis added.
80 E. J. Clery, *Women's Gothic: From Clara Reeve to Mary Shelley* (Tavistock: Northcote, 2000), p. 2.
81 Peter Gay, *Freud for Historians* (1985; Oxford: Oxford University Press, 1986), p. 6.
82 Ibid., pp. 212, 211.
83 Ibid., p. 188.
84 Kathleen Woodward, *Aging and Its Discontents: Freud and Other Fictions* (Bloomington and Indianapolis: Indiana University Press, 1991), p. 12.
85 Sally Alexander, 'Feminist History and Psychoanalysis', *History Workshop Journal*, 32/1 (1991), 128–33 (128).
86 Ibid., 132.
87 Lyndall Roper, *Oedipus and the Devil: Witchcraft, Sexuality and Religion in Early Modern Europe* (London and New York: Routledge, 1994); Diane Purkiss, *The Witch in History: Early Modern and Twentieth-Century Representations* (London and New York: Routledge, 1996); Alex Owen, *The Darkened Room: Women, Power and Spiritualism in Late Victorian England* (Chicago and London: University of Chicago Press, 1989). See chs 3 and 6.
88 Irigaray, *Thinking the Difference*, p. 94.
89 Luce Irigaray, *je, tu, nous: Toward a Culture of Difference*, trans. Alison Martin (1990; London: Routledge, 1993), p. 23.
90 Ibid., pp. 24, 27.
91 Ibid., p. 24.
92 Irigaray, *Thinking the Difference*, p. 101.
93 For my purposes here, I define 'patriarchy' as the rule of men over women, institutionalised by legal, social, cultural and linguistic systems.
94 Fleenor, *Female Gothic*, p. 16.
95 Williams, *Art of Darkness*, p. 160.
96 Ibid., p. 43.
97 Ibid., p. 159.

98 Ibid., p. 29.
99 Ibid., p. 31.
100 Irigaray, *Irigaray Reader*, p. 37.
101 Ibid., p. 47.

2: *Sophia Lee's* The Recess

1 Luce Irigaray, *The Irigaray Reader* (Oxford: Blackwell, 1991), pp. 36, 37–8.
2 Quoted in Juliann Fleenor, (ed.), *The Female Gothic* (Montreal: Eden, 1983), p. 7.
3 Sophia Lee, *The Recess; or, A Tale of Other Times*, ed. April Alliston (1783; Lexington: University Press of Kentucky, 2000), p. 157. Further references are given in the main body of the text.
4 Luce Irigaray, *Thinking the Difference: For a Peaceful Revolution*, trans. Karin Montin (1989; London: Athlone, 1994), p. 101.
5 Irigaray, *Reader*, p. 47.
6 Ibid., p. 35.
7 Margaret Anne Doody, 'Deserts, Ruins and Troubled Waters: Female Dreams in Fiction and the Development of the Gothic Novel', *Genre* 10 (Winter 1977), 559.
8 Andrew Becket, review of Anne Fuller, *Alan FitzOsborne, Monthly Review* (September 1787), 190–2, cited in Anne H. Stevens, *British Historical Fiction before Scott* (Basingstoke: Palgrave Macmillan, 2010), p. 127.
9 Jayne Elizabeth Lewis, '"Ev'ry Lost Relation!" Historical Fictions and Sentimental Incidents in Sophia Lee's *The Recess*', *Eighteenth-Century Fiction*, 7/2 (1995), 184.
10 See, for instance, Lewis, '"Ev'ry Lost Relation!"'; Megan Lynn Isaac, 'Sophia Lee and the Gothic of Female Community', *Studies in the Novel*, 28/2 (1996), 200–18; E. J. Clery, *Women's Gothic: From Clara Reeve to Mary Shelley* (Tavistock: Northcote, 2000); Heather Lobban-Viravong, 'Bastard Heirs: The Dream of Legitimacy in Sophia Lee's *The Recess*', *Prose Studies*, 29/2 (August 2007), 204–19; Richard Maxwell, *The Historical Novel in Europe, 1650–1950* (Cambridge: Cambridge University Press, 2009); Stevens, *British Historical Fiction before Scott*.
11 Isaac, 'Sophia Lee and the Gothic of Female Community', 211, 200.
12 Stevens, *British Historical Fiction*, p. 76.
13 David Punter *The Literature of Terror*, vol. I: *The Gothic Tradition*, 2nd edn (London and New York: Longman, 1996), p. 52.

14 J. M. S. Tompkins, *The Popular Novel in England 1770–1800* (1932; London: Methuen, 1969), p. 224.

15 Ibid., p. 227.

16 David H. Richter, 'From medievalism to historicism: representations of history in the Gothic novel and historical romance', in Leslie J. Workman (ed.), *Medievalism in England*, Studies in Medievalism, IV (Cambridge: D. S. Brewer, 1992), p. 88.

17 Hayden White, *Metahistory* (1973; Baltimore and London: Johns Hopkins University Press, 1975), pp. 7, 29.

18 Ibid., p. 8.

19 Juliet Mitchell, *Women: The Longest Revolution* (1966; London: Virago, 1984), p. 108.

20 Stevens, *British Historical Fiction*, p. 90.

21 Clara Reeve, *The Progress of Romance*, in Stephen Regan (ed.), *The Nineteenth-Century Novel: A Critical Reader* (London and New York: Routledge, 2001), pp. 13–22 (p.14).

22 Ian Duncan's *Modern Romance and Transformations of the Novel: The Gothic, Scott and Dickens* (Cambridge; Cambridge University Press, 1992) gives an important and useful account of complex shifts in the meanings of the terms 'romance' and 'novel' slightly later. See my discussion of Radcliffe below.

23 Jane Spencer, *The Rise of the Woman Novelist: From Aphra Behn to Jane Austen* (Oxford: Blackwell, 1986), pp.196, 195.

24 Ibid., p. 200.

25 Ibid.

26 White, *Metahistory*, pp. 9, 10.

27 Richard Maxwell, 'Phantom states: *Cleveland*, *The Recess*, and the origins of historical fiction', in Margaret Cohen and Carolyn Dever (eds), *The Literary Channel: The Inter-National Invention of the Novel* (Princeton and Oxford: Princeton University Press, 2002), p. 152.

28 Harriet Lee, 'Preface', in Harriet and Sophia Lee, *The Canterbury Tales* (1832; London: Pandora, 1989), p. xviii.

29 Richard Maxwell, 'Pretenders in Sanctuary', 61/2 (June 2000), pp. 287–358; Maxwell, 'Phantom States'; Maxwell, *The Historical Novel in Europe*.

30 Maxwell, 'Phantom states', p. 152.

31 Ibid., p. 180.

32 Maxwell, 'Pretenders in Sanctuary', p. 318.

33 Punter, *Literature of Terror*, p. 47.

34 Horace Walpole, *The Castle of Otranto*, in Peter Fairclough (ed.), *Three Gothic Novels* (Harmondsworth: Penguin, 1968), p. 51.

[35] Punter, *Literature of Terror*, p. 46.

[36] Avrom Fleishman, *The English Historical Novel: Walter Scott to Virginia Woolf* (Baltimore and London: Johns Hopkins University Press, 1971), p. 15.

[37] Walpole, *Otranto*, p. 40

[38] James Watt, 'Introduction', in Clara Reeve, *The Old English Baron* (1777; Oxford: Oxford World's Classics, 2003), p. xxiv.

[39] Reeve, *Baron*, p. 110.

[40] Kate Ferguson Ellis, *The Contested Castle: Gothic Novels and the Subversion of Domestic Ideology* (Urbana and Chicago: University of Illinois Press, 1989), p. 57.

[41] Reeve, *Baron*, p. 44.

[42] Alliston, 'Introduction', in Lee, *The Recess*, p. xv.

[43] Madame de La Fayette, *The Princess of Clèves*, trans. Walter J. Cobb (1678; New York: Signet, 1961), p. 16.

[44] Ibid., p. 27.

[45] David Hume, *The History of England* (1757–62; Edinburgh: Peter Hill, 1818), vol. V, p. 420, note KK.

[46] La Fayette, *Princess of Clèves*, p. 32.

[47] Ibid., p. 80.

[48] Ibid., p. 81.

[49] April Alliston's detailed notes in her edition of *The Recess* give a valuable indication of Lee's indebtedness to her historical sources.

[50] Stevens, *British Historical Fiction*, p. 1.

[51] James Chandler, 'History', in Iain McCalman (ed.), *An Oxford Companion to the Romantic Age* (Oxford: Oxford University Press, 1999), p. 354, emphasis added.

[52] David Hume, 'Of the study of history' (1741), in *Essays: Moral, Political and Literary*, ed. Eugene F. Miller (Indianapolis: Liberty Classics, 1987), p. 563.

[53] Ibid., p. 564.

[54] Ibid. Secret histories used hidden personal motive or characteristics to explain conspiracies or power struggles, according to Maxwell, *Historical Novel*, p. 14.

[55] Hume, 'Of the study of history', p. 566.

[56] Ibid., p. 565.

[57] Jane Austen, 'The history of England from the reign of Henry 4th to the death of Charles 1st', in *The Works of Jane Austen*, vol. V: *Minor Works*, ed, R. W. Chapman (London: Oxford University Press, 1959; rev. edn, 1969), pp.138–49 (p.149).

58 Anne H. Stevens, 'Sophia Lee's illegitimate history', in Albert J. Rivero, George Justice and Margo Collins (eds), *The Eighteenth Century Novel*, vol . 3 (New York: AMS Press, 2003), p. 263.

59 William Robertson, *History of Scotland* (1759; Aberdeen: George Clarke, 1847), p. 140.

60 Oliver Goldsmith, *The History of England From the Earliest Times to the Death of George the Second*, Vol. II, 10th edn (London: Johnson et al., 1809), pp. 262–3.

61 Robertson, *History*, p. 139.

62 Ibid., p. 471.

63 Julian Goodare, 'Mary (1542–87), in *Oxford Dictionary of National Biography* (Oxford: Oxford University Press, September 2004), online edn, May 2007, *www.oxforddnb.com/view/article18248*, accessed 17 June 2010, p. 18.

64 Antonia Fraser, *Mary Queen of Scots* (1969; London: Phoenix, 2002), p. 426.

65 Ibid., p. 427.

66 Stevens, 'Illegitimate history', p. 266.

67 Ibid., p. 265.

68 Ibid., p. 286.

69 Hume, *History*, p. 19.

70 Ibid., p. 20.

71 Ibid., p. 319.

72 Ibid., p. 319.

73 Robertson, *History*, p. 334.

74 Hume, *History*, pp. 4, 282.

75 Ibid., p. 450.

76 Robertson, *History*, p.383.

77 Ibid., pp. 383–4.

78 Hume, *History*, p. 83.

79 Jayne Elizabeth Lewis, *Mary Queen of Scots: Romance and Nation* (London and New York: Routledge, 1998), p. 3.

80 Goodare, 'Mary (1542–87)', p. 31.

81 Hume, *History*, p. 15; Robertson, *History*, p. 237.

82 Hume, *History*, p. 222, emphasis added.

83 Diana Wallace, *The Woman's Historical Novel: British Women Writers 190- –2000* (Basingstoke: Palgrave Macmillan, 2005), ch. 3.

84 Irigaray, *Reader*, p. 36.

85 Ibid., p. 36.

86 Ibid., pp. 38–9.

[87] Luce Irigaray, *je, tu, nous: Toward a Culture of Difference*, trans. Alison Martin (1990; London: Routledge, 1993), pp. 24, 27.

[88] Irigaray, *Reader*, p. 37

[89] Ibid., p. 36.

[90] Ibid., p. 37.

[91] Ibid.

[92] Ibid.

[93] Ibid.

[94] Ibid., pp. 37–8.

[95] Ibid., p. 36.

[96] Ibid., p. 38.

[97] Ibid., p. 37

[98] Ibid., p. 44.

[99] Ibid., pp. 43–4.

[100] Ibid., pp. 38–9.

[101] Roland Barthes, *Camera Lucida: Reflections on Photography*, trans. Richard Howard (1980; London: Vintage, 2000), p. 95.

[102] Ibid., pp. 65–6.

[103] Irigaray, *Reader*, p. 40.

[104] Ibid.

[105] Ibid., p. 74.

[106] Ibid., p. 91.

[107] Hume, *History*, p. 445.

[108] Anne Williams, *Art of Darkness: A Poetics of Gothic* (Chicago and London: University of Chicago Press, 1995), p. 104.

[109] April Allison, *Virtue's Faults: Correspondences in Eighteenth-Century British and French Women's Fiction* (Stanford, CA: Stanford University Press, 1996), p. 280, n. 26.

[110] Clery, *Women's Gothic*, p.74.

[111] Rictor Norton, *Mistress of Udolpho: The Life of Ann Radcliffe* (London and New York: Leicester University Press, 1999), p. 253.

[112] Robert Miles, '"Mother Radcliffe": Ann Radcliffe and the Female Gothic', in Diana Wallace and Andrew Smith (eds), *The New Female Gothic: New Directions* (Basingstoke: Palgrave Macamillan, 2009), pp. 45, 44.

[113] Clery, *Women's Gothic*, p. 64.

[114] Georg Lukács, *The Historical Novel*, trans Hannah and Stanley Mitchell (1962; Lincoln and London: University of Nebraska Press, 1983), p. 30.

[115] Ann Radcliffe, *A Sicilian Romance*, ed. Alison Milbank (1790; Oxford: Oxford World's Classics, 1993), p. 3. Further references are given in the main body of the text.

116 Frederick Garber, 'Introduction', in Ann Radcliffe, *The Italian* (1797; Oxford: Oxford World's Classics, 1981), p. x.
117 Norton, *Mistress of Udolpho*, pp. 44, 49.
118 Ibid., pp. 46–9.
119 Ibid., p. 50.
120 Duncan, *Modern Romance and Transformations of the Novel*, p. 13.
121 Reeve, *Baron*, p. 2.
122 Spencer, *Rise of the Woman Novelist*, pp. 192–3.
123 Ibid., p. 207.
124 Ibid., p. x.
125 Norton, *Mistress of Udolpho*, p. 18.
126 Robert Miles, *Ann Radcliffe: The Great Enchantress* (Manchester: Manchester University Press, 1994), p. 131.
127 Alison Milbank, 'Introduction', in Radcliffe, *A Sicilian Romance*, p. xxiii.
128 Ibid., p. xxiv.
129 Miles, *Ann Radcliffe*, pp. 93–4.
130 Clery, *Women's Gothic*, p. 68.
131 Ibid.
132 Milbank confirms the basis of this in Brydone's *A Tour through Sicily and Malta*. See Radcliffe, *Sicilian Romance*, p. 206.
133 Fleishman, *English Historical Novel*, p. 15.
134 Miles, *Ann Radcliffe*, p. 87.
135 Ibid., p. 98.
136 Reeve, *Baron*, p. 136.
137 White, *Metahistory*, p. 10.
138 Ibid., p. 11.
139 Duncan, *Modern Romance and Transformations of the Novel*, p. 13.
140 Lukács, *The Historical Novel*, p. 13.

3: Elizabeth Gaskell's Gothic Historical Tales

1 Letter to Mary Green, January 1854, quoted in Jenny Uglow, *Elizabeth Gaskell: A Habit of Stories* (1993; London: Faber, 1994), p. 236.
2 J. A. V. Chapple, *Elizabeth Gaskell: A Portrait in Letters* (Manchester and New York: Manchester University Press, 2007), p. 1.
3 Avrom Fleishmann devotes just two sentences to *Sylvia's Lovers* in *The English Historical Novel* (Baltimore and London: Johns Hopkins University Press, 1971), while Gaskell is mentioned only in passing by Jerome de Groot in *The Historical Novel* (London and New York:

Routledge, 2010) and Richard Maxwell in *The Historical Novel in Europe, 1650–1950* (Cambridge: Cambridge University Press, 2009). There are, however, useful chapters in Andrew Rance, *The Historical Novel and Popular Politics in Nineteenth-Century England* (London: Vision, 1975) and Andrew Sanders, *The Victorian Historical Novel 1840–1880* (London and Basingstoke: Macmillan, 1978).

4 Patsy Stoneman, *Elizabeth Gaskell* (Brighton: Harvester, 1987), p. 9.

5 Uglow, *Elizabeth Gaskell*, p. 120.

6 Marion Shaw, '*Sylvia's Lovers* and other historical fiction', pp. 75–89, and Shirley Foster, 'Elizabeth Gaskell's shorter pieces', pp. 108–30, both in Jill Matus (ed.), *The Cambridge Companion to Elizabeth Gaskell* (Cambridge: Cambridge University, 2007).

7 Jean Pickering, 'Time and the short story', in Clare Hanson (ed.), *Re-reading the Short Story* (London: Macmillan, 1989), p. 48.

8 Ibid., p. 49.

9 Nadine Gordimer, 'The flash of fireflies', in Charles May (ed.), *The New Short Story Theories* (Athens: Ohio University Press, 1994), pp. 264–5.

10 Walter Scott, 'The Two Drovers' in *Chronicles of the Canongate*, ed. Clare Lamont (London: Penguin, 2003), pp. 124–46.

11 Walter Scott, 'On the Supernatural in Fictitious Composition' (1827), quoted in Julia Briggs, *Night Visitors: The Rise and Fall of the English Ghost Story* (London: Faber, 1977), p. 13.

12 Briggs, *Night Visitors*, p. 117.

13 Gordimer, 'The flash of fireflies', p. 265.

14 Elizabeth Bowen, 'Preface', in *A Day in the Dark and Other Stories* (London: Jonathan Cape, 1965), p. 9.

15 Clare Hanson (ed.), *Re-reading the Short Story* (London: Macmillan, 1989), p. 2.

16 Ibid., p. 6.

17 Carol A. Martin, 'Gaskell's Ghosts: Truths in Disguise', *Studies in the Novel*, 21/1 (1989), 27–40 (33).

18 Maureen T. Reddy, 'Gaskell's "The Grey Woman": A Feminist Palimpsest', *Journal of Narrative Technique*, 15 (1985), 183–93 (183, 192).

19 Clare Hanson, '"Things out of words": towards a poetics of short fiction', in *Re-reading the Short Story*, pp. 22–33 (p. 24).

20 Hanson, 'Things out of words', p. 31.

21 Ibid., pp. 27, 31.

22 Elizabeth Gaskell, 'The Poor Clare', in *Gothic Tales* (London: Penguin, 2000), pp. 49–102, (p. 49); 'Lois the Witch', in *Gothic Tales*, pp. 139–226 (p. 139); 'The Grey Woman', in *Gothic Tales*, pp. 287–340 (p. 295). Further references are given in the main body of the text.

[23] Shaw, '*Sylvia's Lovers* and other historical fiction', p. 77.

[24] Chapple, *Elizabeth Gaskell*, p. 35, emphasis added.

[25] Jill Matus, '*Mary Barton* and *North and South*', in *The Cambridge Companion to Elizabeth Gaskell*, pp. 27–45 (p. 35).

[26] Ibid., p. 42.

[27] Eve Kosofsky Sedgwick, *The Coherence of Gothic Conventions* (1980; New York and London: Methuen, 1986).

[28] Elizabeth Gaskell, 'Clopton House', in *The Works of Elizabeth Gaskell*, vol. I: *Journalism, Early Fiction and Personal Writings*, ed. Joanne Shattock (London: Pickering and Chatto, 2005), pp. 39–41 (p. 39). Further references are given in the main body of the text.

[29] Sigmund Freud, 'The uncanny', in *Art and Literature*, The Penguin Freud Library, 14 (1985; London: Penguin, 1990), p. 366.

[30] Ibid., p. 367.

[31] Ibid., p. 356.

[32] Angus Easson, *Elizabeth Gaskell* (London, Boston and Henley: Routledge and Kegan Paul, 1979), p. 228.

[33] Samuel Rogers, 'Italy: 22 Ginevra', *poemhunter.com/best-poems/Samuelrogers/italy-22ginevra/*, accessed 17 March 2011.

[34] Nickianne Moody, 'Visible margins: women writers and the English ghost story', in Sarah Sceats and Gail Cunningham (eds), *Image and Power: Women in Fiction in the Twentieth Century* (London and New York: Longman, 1990), p. 78.

[35] Thomas Carlyle, *Heroes and Hero-Worship*, in *Selected Writings* (London: Penguin, 1986), p. 233, emphasis added.

[36] Thomas Carlyle, 'On Sir Walter Scott' (1838), in *The Complete Works of Thomas Carlyle*, vols I and II (New York: Thomas Y. Crowell, 1869), pp. 400–60, pp. 417, 416.

[37] Ibid., p. 417.

[38] Ibid., p. 427 .

[39] J. R. Watson, 'Elizabeth Gaskell: Heroes and Heroines and *Sylvia's Lovers*', *Gaskell Society Journal*, 18 (2004), 81–94.

[40] Suzanne Lewis, 'Introduction', in Elizabeth Gaskell, *The Moorland Cottage and Other Stories* (Oxford: Oxford World's Classics, 1995), p. xxi.

[41] Jane Austen, *Northanger Abbey* (1818; Harmondsworth: Penguin, 1985), p. 123.

[42] Ibid.

[43] A. W. Ward suggested that 'nothing is more likely' than that the legend of Charlotte Clopton inspired Shakespeare's treatment of Juliet's death. See Elizabeth Gaskell, 'Clopton House', *www/lang.nagoya-u.ac/~matsuoka/EG-Clopton.html*, accessed 2 July 2010.

44 Carlyle, 'On History', in *Selected Writings*, p. 51.
45 Christine L. Krueger discusses Lady Ludlow as a 'female paternalist' historian: 'The "female paternalist" as historian: Elizabeth Gaskell's *My Lady Ludlow*', in Linda M. Shires (ed.), *Rewriting the Victorians: Theory, History and the Politics of Gender* (New York and London: Routledge, 1992), pp. 166–83. My own reading of Lady Ludlow is more positive because I think that Gaskell is most interested not in her conservative 'paternalism' but in her capacity to change through listening to others' 'stories'.
46 Elizabeth Gaskell, 'Morton Hall', in *The Moorland Cottage and Other Stories*, pp. 167–203 (p. 167). Further page references are given in the main body of the text.
47 Foster, 'Elizabeth Gaskell's shorter pieces', p. 127.
48 Claiming to be based on real events, Jemima Luke's *The Female Jesuit* told the story of Marie, who posed as a runaway nun in order to infiltrate a Protestant family. Timothy Verhoeven notes that the novel was praised by American reviewers for alerting Americans to the dangers of female Jesuits. See Timothy Verhoeven, *Transatlantic Anti-Catholicism: France and the United States in the Nineteenth Century* (New York: Palgrave, 2010), p. 115.
49 Lewis, 'Introduction', p. xix.
50 Elizabeth Gaskell, *The Life of Charlotte Brontë* (1857; London: Dent, 1908), p. 375.
51 Uglow, *Elizabeth Gaskell*, p. 399.
52 Gaskell, *Life of Charlotte Brontë*, pp. 237–8.
53 Ibid., p. 238.
54 Walter Scott, 'The Highland Widow', in *Chronicles of the Canongate* (London: Penguin, 2003), pp. 68–122.
55 Gaskell, *Gothic Tales*, p. 349.
56 Elizabeth Gaskell, 'Lois the Witch', in *Gothic Tales*, pp. 139–226.
57 Shaw, '*Sylvia's Lovers* and other historical fiction', pp. 81–3; Deborah Wynne, 'Hysteria Repeating Itself: Elizabeth Gaskell's *Lois the Witch*', *Women's Writing*, 12/1 (2005), 85–97; Louise Henson, '"Half Believing, Half Incredulous": Elizabeth Gaskell, Superstition and the Victorian Mind', *Nineteenth-Century Contexts*, 24/3 (2002), 251–69; Rebecca Styler, '"Lois the Witch": A Unitarian Tale', *Gaskell Society Journal*, 21 (2007), 73–85.
58 Wynne, 'Hysteria Repeating Itself', 85–97.
59 Charles Upham, *Lectures on Witchcraft, comprising a History of the Delusion in Salem in 1692* (Boston: Carter, Hendee and Babcock, 1831). See pp. 127–9, and Gaskell, 'Lois the Witch', pp. 224–5. Gaskell also uses

almost verbatim Upham's description of the son who effects his mother's escape from prison and secretes her in 'the Blueberry swamp . . . until after the delusion had passed away': 'Lois the Witch', pp. 218–19, and Upham, *Lectures*, pp. 35–6.

[60] Harriet Martineau, 'On Witchcraft', *Monthly Repository*, n.s., 6 (1832), 545–55 (554–5).

[61] Ibid., 555.

[62] A. W. Ward (ed.), *The Works of Mrs Gaskell*, vol. 7 (London: Smith, Elder, 1906), p. xxiii.

[63] Shaw, '*Sylvia's Lovers* and other historical fiction', p. 83.

[64] Lyndall Roper, *Oedipus and the Devil: Witchcraft, Sexuality and Religion in Early Modern Europe* (London and New York: Routledge, 1994), p. 201.

[65] Nathaniel Hawthorne, 'The Minister's Black Veil', in *The Celestial Railroad and Other Stories* (New York: Signet, 1980), pp.101–14.

[66] Frances Hill, *A Delusion of Satan: The Full Story of the Salem Witch Trials* (London: Penguin, 1997), p. 32.

[67] Upham, *Lectures*, p. 18, emphasis added.

[68] Hill, *A Delusion of Satan*, p. 36.

[69] Ibid., p. 229.

[70] Paul Boyer and Stephen Nissenbaum, *Salem Possessed: The Social Origins of Witchcraft* (Cambridge, MA and London: Harvard University Press, 1974).

[71] Ibid., pp. 146–7.

[72] Diane Purkiss, *The Witch in History: Early Modern and Twentieth-Century Representations* (London and New York: Routledge, 1996), p. 9.

[73] Ibid., p. 19.

[74] Ibid., p. 2.

[75] Roper, *Oedipus and the Devil*, p. 216.

[76] Ibid., p. 217.

[77] Purkiss, *The Witch in History*, p. 81.

[78] Ibid., p. 82.

[79] Ibid., p. 60

[80] Upham, *Lectures*, p. 270.

[81] Hill, *A Delusion of Satan*, pp. 22, 37.

[82] Ibid., p. 22, 38.

[83] Purkiss, *The Witch in History*, p. 2.

[84] Charles Perrault, 'The Blue Beard', in Iona and Peter Opie, *The Classic Fairy Tales* (1974; London: Granada, 1980), pp.137–41; the Brothers Grimm, 'Fitcher's Bird' and 'The Robber Bridegroom',

trans. Margaret Taylor (1848), *classic lit.about.com/library/bl-etexts/grimm/ bl-grimm-fitcher.htm*, accessed 30 March 2011.

[85] Reddy, 'Gaskell's "The Grey Woman"', 185.

[86] J. S. Mill, *On Liberty and The Subjection of Women* (London: Penguin, 2006), p. 133. Alan Ryan notes that Mill had finished the MS by 1861 but waited until 1869 to publish it (p. xviii).

[87] Beard, *Woman as Force in History*, p. 103.

[88] Mill, *Subjection of Women*, p. 220.

[89] Ibid., p. 170.

[90] Elizabeth Gaskell, 'French Life', in Ward (ed.), *The Works of Mrs Gaskell*, vol.7, pp. 604–80.

[91] J. G. Sharps notes a version in Dumas the Elder, *Crimes Célèbres* (1839–40), vols II–III, translated into English as Alexander Dumas, *Celebrated Crimes* (London: Chapman and Hall, 1843). Other possible sources he notes include François Gayot de Pitaval, *Causes Célèbres* (1734–43) and Charlotte Smith's reworking of this in *The Romance of Real Life*, 3 vols (London: T. Cadell, 1787), vol 1. See J. G. Sharps, *Mrs Gaskell's Observations and Inventions: A Study of Her Non-Biographic Works* (Sussex: Linden Press, 1970), pp. 465–7. Ann Radcliffe refers to 'Guyot de Pitaval' as the source of her story of Pierre de la Motte in the opening of *The Romance of the Forest*, although Chloe Chard notes that her novel does not follow any of the stories in either collection exactly. See Radcliffe, *The Romance of the Forest*, ed. Chloe Chard (Oxford: Oxford World's Classics, 1986), p. 1, with note on p. 367.

[92] Gaskell, 'French Life', p. 665

[93] Ibid., p. 672.

[94] Ibid., p. 667.

[95] Ibid., p. 669.

[96] Ibid., p. 679.

[97] Grimm, 'Fitcher's Bird', p. 2.

[98] Sir William Blackstone, *Commentaries on the Laws of England*, quoted in Mary Beard, *Woman as Force in History* (New York: Macmillan, 1946), p. 78.

[99] Dickerson, *Victorian Ghosts in the Noontide*, p. 11.

[100] Anne Williams, *Art of Darkness: A Poetics of Gothic* (Chicago and London: University of Chicago Press, 1995), p. 43.

[101] Reddy, 'Gaskell's "The Grey Woman"', 186.

[102] Ibid.

4: *Vernon Lee's Fantastic Stories*

1   Vernon Lee, 'Puzzles of the Past', *Hortus Vitae: Essays on the Gardening of Life*, 2nd edn (London and New York: John Lane: The Bodley Head, 1904), pp.189–197 (pp. 196-7).

2   Ibid., p. 189.

3   Ibid., p. 191.

4   Vernon Lee, 'In praise of old houses', in *Limbo and Other Essays* (1897; Doyleston, PA: Wildside, n.d.), pp. 21–34 (p. 33).

5   Vernon Lee, 'Amour Dure', in *Hauntings and Other Fantastic Tales*, ed. Catherine Maxwell and Patricia Pulham (Peterborough, Ontario: Broadview, 2006), pp.41–76 (p. 41). Further references are given in the main body of the text.

6   The scholarly edition of Lee's *Hauntings and Other Fantastic Tales*, edited by Catherine Maxwell and Patricia Pulham, is particularly welcome since it makes these texts available for teaching.

7   Vineta Colby, *Vernon Lee: A Literary Biography* (Charlottesville and London: University of Virginia Press, 2003), p. 92.

8   Ibid., p. 308.

9   Rosemary Jackson, *Fantasy: The Literature of Subversion* (1981: London and New York: Routledge, 1998), p. 4.

10 Vernon Lee, 'Faustus and Helena: notes on the supernatural in art', in *Hauntings*, pp. 291–319 (p. 312).

11 Ibid., p. 313.

12 Ibid., p. 319.

13 Ibid., p. 312.

14 Angela Leighton, 'Resurrections of the body: women writers and the idea of the Renaissance' in Alison Chapman and Jane Stabler (eds), *Unfolding the South: Nineteenth-Century British Women Writers and Artists in Italy* (Manchester and New York: Manchester University Press, 2003), pp. 222–38 (p. 235).

15 See, for instance, Martha Vicinius, 'The Adolescent Boy: Fin de Siècle Femme Fatale?' *Journal of the History of Sexuality*, 4/11 (1994), 90–114; Kathy Psomiades, '"Still burning from this strangling embrace": Vernon Lee on desire and aesthetics', in Richard Dellamora (ed.), *Victorian Sexual Dissidence* (Chicago and London: University of Chicago Press, 1999), pp. 21–41; Sally Newman, 'The Archival Traces of Desire: Vernon Lee's Failed Sexuality and the Interpretation of Letters in Lesbian History', *Journal of the History of Sexuality*, 14/1–2 (January/April 2005), 51–75.

[16] Vernon Lee, *The Handling of Words and Other Studies in Literary Psychology* (London: John Lane, 1923), p. 298.

[17] Ibid., p. 301.

[18] Colby, *Vernon Lee*, p. 2.

[19] Christa Zorn, *Vernon Lee: Aesthetics, History and the Victorian Female Intellectual* (Athens: Ohio University Press, 2003), p. xxix.

[20] Lee, *Hauntings*, p. 41.

[21] Roger Luckhurst (ed.), *Late Victorian Gothic Tales* (Oxford: Oxford World's Classics, 2005).

[22] Bram Dijkstra, *Idols of Perversity: Fantasies of Feminine Evil in Fin-de-Siècle Culture* (Oxford: Oxford University Press, 1986).

[23] Vicinus, 'The Adolescent Boy'.

[24] Catherine Maxwell and Patricia Pulham (eds), 'Introduction', in *Vernon Lee: Decadence, Ethics, Aesthetics* (Basingtsoke: Palgrave, 2006), p. 6.

[25] Emily Harrington, 'The Strain of Sympathy: A. Mary F. Robinson, *The New Arcadia*, and Vernon Lee', *Nineteenth-Century Literature*, 61/1 (2006), 66–98.

[26] Hilary Fraser, 'Regarding the eighteenth century: Vernon Lee and Emilia Dilke construct a period', in Francis O'Gorman and Katherine Turner (eds), *The Victorians and the Eighteenth Century: Reassessing the Tradition* (Aldershot and Burlington, VT: Ashgate, 2004), pp. 223–49 (p. 232).

[27] Lee, quoted ibid., p. 232.

[28] Ibid.

[29] Vernon Lee, *Euphorion* (London: T. Fisher Unwin, 1884), p.79, quoted in Zorn, *Vernon Lee*, p 35.

[30] Patricia Pulham, *Art and the Transitional Object in Vernon Lee's Supernatural Tales* (Aldershot: Ashgate, 2008), ch. 1.

[31] Vernon Lee, 'Dionea', 'Oke of Okehurst', 'A Wicked Voice', in *Hauntings and Other Fantastic Tales*, ed. Catherine Maxwell and Patricia Pulham (Peterborough, Ontario: Broadview, 2006), pp. 77–104, 105–53, 154–81. Further references are given in the main body of the text.

[32] Colby, *Vernon Lee*, ch. 9.

[33] Christa Zorn, 'Aesthetic Intertextuality as Cultural Critique: Vernon Lee Rewrites History through Walter Pater's "La Gioconda"', *The Victorian Newsletter*, 91 (1997), 4–10 (10).

[34] Ibid., 4–10.

[35] Vernon Lee, *Gospels of Anarchy and Other Contemporary Studies* (London and Leipzig: T. Fisher Unwin, 1908), p. 286.

[36] Ibid., p. 294.

37 Ibid., p. 263.

38 Ibid., p. 296.

39 Margaret Stetz, 'The snake lady and the bruised Bodley Head: Vernon Lee and Oscar Wilde in the *Yellow Book*', in Maxwell and Pulham (eds), *Vernon Lee*, pp. 112–22 (p. 117).

40 Jane Hotchkiss, '(P)revising Freud: Vernon Lee's castration phantasy', in Carola M. Kaplan and Anne B. Simpson (eds), *Seeing Double: Revisioning Edwardian and Modernist Literature* (New York: St. Martin's Press, 1996), pp. 21–38.

41 Mary Patricia Kane, 'The Uncanny Mother in Vernon Lee's "Prince Alberic and the Snake Lady', *Victorian Review*, 32/1 (2006), 41–62.

42 Vernon Lee, 'Prince Alberic and the Snake Lady', in *Hauntings*, pp. 182–228 (p. 182). Further references are given in the main body of the text.

43 Maxwell and Pulham note the significance of 1701 as the start of the War of Spanish Succession (*Hauntings*, p. 182, n. 2).

44 Maria, referring to the mother of Christ, and Balthasar, the name traditionally given to one of the three Wise Men.

45 Algernon Charles Swinburne, 'Notes on designs of the Old Masters at Florence', in *Hauntings*, pp. 279–81 (p. 280).

46 E. T. A. Hoffmann, *The Golden Pot and Other Tales*, trans. Ritchie Robertson (Oxford: World's Classics, 1992). The importance of the Melusina legend for women writers is suggested by the fact that it is used in two other recent historical novels about female genealogies: A. S. Byatt's *Possession* (1990; London: Vintage, 1991), and Philippa Gregory's *The White Queen* (2009; London: Simon and Schuster, 2010).

47 Luce Irigaray, *The Irigaray Reader* (Oxford: Blackwell, 1991), pp. 38–9.

48 Hotchkiss, '(P)revising Freud', p. 22.

49 Kane, 'The Uncanny Mother', 56.

50 Catherine Maxwell, 'From Dionysus to "Dionea": Vernon Lee's Portraits', *Word and Image*, 13/3 (July–September 1997), 253–69 (260).

51 Vernon Lee, 'Dionysus in the Euganean Hills: W. H. Pater in Memoriam', *Contemporary Review*, 120 (September 1921), 346–53 (348).

52 Ibid., 349.

53 Maxwell, 'From Dionysus to "Dionea"', 265.

54 Marianna Torgovnick, 'Discovering Jane Harrison', in Carola M. Kaplan and Anne B. Simpson (eds), *Seeing Double: Revisioning Edwardian and Modernist Literature* (New York: St. Martin's Press, 1996), pp.131–48 (p. 138). Colby records Lee reading Jane Harrison's work in the 1920s (*Vernon Lee*, p. 316) but it seems likely she knew it earlier.

55 E. H. Blakeney, *A Smaller Classical Dictionary* (London and Toronto: J. M. Dent, 1910), p. 196.

56 Vernon Lee, 'The Doll', in *For Maurice: Five Unlikely Tales* (1927), reprinted in *Hauntings: The Supernatural Stories*, ed. David G. Rowlands (Ashcroft, British Columbia: Ash-Tress, 2002), pp. 277–83.

57 Peter Gunn, *Vernon Lee: Violet Paget, 1856–1935* (London: Oxford University Press, 1964), p. 168.

58 Ibid., p. 86.

59 Vernon Lee, *Penelope Brandling: A Tale of the Welsh Coast in the Eighteenth Century* (London: T. Fisher Unwin, 1903), p. 28. Further references are given in the main body of the text.

60 Marie Trevelyan, *Folk-Lore and Folk-Stories of Wales* (London: Elliot Stock, 1909), p.65. I am indebted to Jane Aaron for drawing my attention to Trevelyan's work.

61 Alan Hall, *St Donat's Castle: A Guide and History* (St Donat's, 2002), p. 26.

62 Ibid.

63 Marie Trevelyan, *Glimpses of Welsh Life and Character* (1893; London: John Hogg, n.d), pp. 312–17.

64 Hall, *St Donat's Castle*, p. 20.

65 Enfys McMurray, *Hearst's Other Castles* (Bridgend: Seren, 1999), p. 27.

66 Ibid., p. 24.

67 Rachel Blau DuPlessis, *Writing beyond the Ending: Narrative Structures of Twentieth Century Women Writers* (Bloomington: Indiana University Press, 1985).

68 Angela Carter, *The Bloody Chamber* (London: Virago, 1979).

69 Lee, *The Handling of Words*, p. 301.

70 Ibid., p. 298.

71 See Anne H. Stevens, 'Sophia Lee's illegitimate history', in Albert J. Rivero, George Justice and Margo Collins (eds), *The Eighteenth Century Novel*, vol. 3 (New York: AMS Press, 2003), pp. 263–91 (p. 286).

72 Ellen Moers, *Literary Women* (1976; London: The Women's Press, 1978), pp. 254–7.

73 Ibid., p. 254.

74 Ibid., p. 255.

75 Vernon Lee, *Genius Loci: Notes on Places* (London: Grant Richards, 1897).

76 Vernon Lee, 'The Hidden Door', in *Vanitas: Polite Stories* (London: Heineman, 1892), reprinted in *Hauntings,* ed. Rowlands, pp. 321–8.

77 'Marsyas in Flanders', in *For Maurice,* reprinted in *Hauntings*, ed. Rowlands, pp. 221–30.

78 Pulham, *Art and the Transitional Object*, p. 49.
79 Ibid., p. 51.
80 Trevelyan, *Glimpses of Welsh Life*, p. 315.
81 Vernon Lee, letter to Eugene Lee-Hamilton, quoted in Maxwell and Pulham, *Vernon Lee*, p. 32.

5: Daphne du Maurier and the Modern Gothic

1   Daphne du Maurier, *Rebecca* (1938; London: Pan, 1975), p. 8. Further references are given in the main body of the text.
2   Ronald Bryden, 'Queen of the Wild Mullions', *The Spectator*, 20 April 1962, p. 514; Joanna Russ, 'Somebody's Trying to Kill Me and I Think It's My Husband: The Modern Gothic', *Journal of Popular Culture*, 6 (Spring 1973), 666–91 (666).
3   Victoria Holt, *The Legend of the Seventh Virgin* (1965; London and Glasgow: Fontana, 1967), jacket blurb. Further references are given in the main body of the text.
4   Patsy Stoneman, *Brontë Transformations: The Cultural Dissemination of Jane Eyre and Wuthering Heights* (Hemel Hempstead: Prentice Hall/ Harvester Wheatsheaf, 1996), p. 4.
5   Ibid., p. 4.
6   Ibid.
7   Ibid., pp. 4, 5.
8   Mary Ann Doane, *Femmes Fatales: Feminism, Film Theory, Psychoanalysis* (New York and Routledge, 1991), p. 91.
9   Ian Jack, 'Introduction', in Emily Brontë, *Wuthering Heights* (1847; Oxford: World's Classics, 1981), p. ix.
10 April Alliston, *Virtue's Faults: Correspondences in Eighteenth-Century British and French Women's Fiction* (Stanford, CA: Stanford University Press, 1996), pp. 278–9.
11 Janina Nordius, 'A Tale of Other Places: Sophia Lee's *The Recess* and Colonial Gothic', *Studies in the Novel*, 34/2 (Summer 2002), 162–77 (162).
12 Eve Kosofsky Sedgwick, *The Coherence of Gothic Conventions* (1980; London: Methuen, 1986).
13 Norman N. Holland and Leona F. Sherman, 'Gothic Possibilities', *New Literary History*, 8/2 (1977), 279–94 (279).
14 Avril Horner and Sue Zlosnik, *Daphne du Maurier: Writing, Identity and the Gothic Imagination* (Basingstoke: Macmillan, 1998), pp. 28–9.
15 Ibid., p. 29.

16 Margaret Forster, *Daphne du Maurier* (1993; London: Arrow, 1994), p. 222.

17 Daphne du Maurier, *Myself When Young: The Shaping of a Writer* (1977; London: Virago, 2004), p. 54.

18 Ibid., p. 11.

19 Bruno Bettelheim, *The Uses of Enchantment* (1976: London: Penguin, 1991).

20 Du Maurier, *Myself When Young*, p. 11.

21 Ibid., p. 57.

22 Ibid., p. 130.

23 Ibid., p. 132.

24 Tania Modleski, *The Women Who Knew Too Much: Hitchcock and Feminist Theory* (New York and London: Routledge, 1988), p. 46.

25 Karen Hollinger, 'The Female Oedipal Drama of *Rebecca* from Novel to Film', *Quarterly Review of Film and Video*, 14/4 (1993), 17–30 (27, 27–8).

26 Daphne du Maurier, *Jamaica Inn* (1936: London: Arrow, 1992), pp. 200, 18. Further references are given in the main body of the text.

27 Vernon Lee, *Penelope Brandling* (London: T. Fisher Unwin, 1903), p. 57. Further references are given in the main body of the text.

28 Joanna Russ, 'Somebody's Trying to Kill Me', 669.

29 Luce Irigaray, *The Irigaray Reader* (Oxford: Blackwell, 1991), p. 47.

30 Anne Williams, *Art of Darkness: A Poetics of Gothic* (Chicago and London: University of Chicago Press, 1995), p. 43.

31 Russ, 'Somebody's Trying to Kill Me', 668.

32 Daphne du Maurier, 'The house of secrets' (1946), in *The Rebecca Notebooks and Other Memories* (London: Victor Gollancz, 1981), pp. 130–40.

33 Ibid., p. 140.

34 Ibid., p. 130.

35 Ian Roy, 'Sir Richard Grenville', *The Oxford Dictionary of National Biography*. *www.oxforddnb.com/articles/11/11495-article.html*, accesssed 22 February 2005.

36 Judith Cook, *Daphne: A Portrait of Daphne du Maurier* (London: Transworld, 1991), p. 178.

37 Daphne du Maurier, *The King's General* (1946; London: Pan, 1974), p. 7. Further references are given in the main body of the text.

38 Roy, 'Sir Richard Grenville', p. 4.

39 Ian Roy suggests this comes from the Dutch for 'rascal'. Roy, 'Sir Richard Grenville', p. 2.

40 Horner and Zlosnik, *Daphne du Maurier*, p. 96.

41 The 'Defence against All Aspersions of Malignant Persons', published by Grenville in the Netherlands in 1654 (Roy, 'Sir Richard Grenville', p. 4).

42 Horner and Zlosnick, *Daphne du Maurier*, pp. 141–2.

43 Daphne du Maurier, *My Cousin Rachel* (1951; London: Arrow, 1992), p. 5. Further references are given in the main body of the text.

44 Horner and Zlosnik, *Daphne du Maurier*, p. 134.

45 Ibid., pp. 143, 144.

46 Ibid., p. 145.

47 Eric Pace, 'Gothic Novels for Women Prove Bonanza for Publishers', *The New York Times*, Monday 18 June 1973, pp 31, 34.

48 Pace, 'Gothic Novels for Women', p. 34.

49 Emma Mai Ewing, 'Gothic Mania', *New York Times Book Review*, 11 May 1975, p. 11.

50 Catherine Bennett, 'The Prime of Miss Jean Plaidy', *The Guardian*, 4 July 1991, p. 3.

51 Richard Dalby, 'All about Jean Plaidy', *Book and Magazine Collector*, 10 (April 1993), *jeanplaidy.tripod.com/id17.htm*, accessed 7 April 2011.

52 Both Martha Duffy and Emma Mai Ewing note that Holt dominated the field: Martha Duffy, 'On the Road to Manderley', *Time*, Monday 12 April 1971, pp. 65–6; Ewing, 'Gothic Mania', 11.

53 Marketing copy at the back of the Fontana editions of Victoria Holt novels.

54 Ewing, 'Gothic Mania', 11.

55 Bennett, 'The Prime of Miss Jean Plaidy,' 3.

56 Ibid., 4.

57 Juliann Fleenor, 'Introduction', in *The Female Gothic* (Montreal and London: Eden, 1983), p. 4.

58 Lesley Henderson (ed.), *Twentieth Century Romance and Historical Writers* (Chicago and London: St James Press, 1990), p. 403.

59 The exceptions are *Bride of Pendorric* (1963), set in the 1960s, *The Queen's Confession* (1968), about Marie Antoinette, and *My Enemy the Queen* (1978), about Lettice Knollys and Elizabeth I.

60 Phyllis Whitney, *Thunder Heights* (1960; London: Coronet, 1973), p. 19.

61 Victorian Holt, *Mistress of Mellyn* (1960: London: Fontana, 1963). Further references are given in the main body of the text.

62 Bennett, 'The Prime of Miss Jean Plaidy', 1.

63 Victoria Holt, *Menfreya* (1966; London and Glasgow: Fontana, 1968). Further references are given in the main body of the text.

64 Bennett, 'The Prime of Miss Jean Plaidy', 3.

65 Joanne Shattock, *The Oxford Guide to British Women Writers* (Oxford: Oxford University Press, 1993), p. 212.

66 Diana Wallace, *Sisters and Rivals in British Women's Fiction, 1914–39* (Basingstoke: Macmillan, 2000), pp. 50–1.
67 Russ, 'Somebody's Trying to Kill Me', 684.
68 Ibid., 668, 669.
69 Jean Plaidy, *Together They Ride* (London: Gerald S. Swan, 1945).
70 Ibid., pp.92, 93.
71 Victoria Holt, *Kirkland Revels* (1962; Glasgow: Fontana, 1964). Further references are given in the main body of the text.
72 Daphne du Maurier, 'Introduction', in Jane Austen, *Northanger Abbey* (1818; London: Williams and Norgate, 1948), pp. x–xi.
73 Louise C. Weston and Josephine A. Ruggiero, 'Male–Female Relationships in Best-Selling "Modern Gothic" Novels', *Sex Roles*, 4/5 (1978), 647–55.
74 Ibid., 654.
75 Pace, 'Gothic Novels for Women', 31.
76 Ibid., 34.
77 Tania Modleski, *Loving with a Vengeance* (London: Routledge, 1982), pp. 69, 70.
78 Victoria Holt, *Bride of Pendorric* (1963; London: Fontana, 1965), p. 283. Further references are given in the main body of the text.
79 Sigmund Freud, 'The uncanny', in *Art and Literature*, The Penguin Freud Library, 14 (1985; London: Penguin, 1990), p. 366.
80 Ibid., p. 367.
81 Modleski, *Loving with a Vengeance*, p. 71.
82 Ibid.
83 Ibid.
84 Nora Johnson, 'The Captivity of Marriage', *Atlantic Monthly*, 207/6 (June 1961), 38–42 (38).
85 Ibid., pp. 39, 38.
86 Ibid., p. 40.
87 Mary Wings, '*Rebecca redux*: tears on a lesbian pillow', in Liz Gibbs (ed.), *Daring to Dissent: Lesbian Culture from Margin to Mainstream* (London and New York: Cassell, 1994), pp. 12–13.
88 Du Maurier, 'Introduction', p. xi.
89 Charlotte Brontë, *Jane Eyre* (1847; London; Pan, 1967), p. 331.
90 Du Maurier, *Rebecca*, p. 283.
91 Du Maurier, 'Introduction', p. xi.
92 Philippa Carr, *Lament for a Lost Lover* (1977; London: Fontana, 1978), p. 10.
93 Philippa Carr, *The Miracle at St Bruno's* (1972: London: Fontana, 1974). Further references are given in the main body of the text.

94 Williams, *Art of Darkness*, p. 29.
95 Carolyn Steedman, 'True romances', in Raphael Samuel (ed.), *Patriotism: The Making and Unmaking of British National Identity*, vol. I: *History and Politics* (London and New York: Routledge, 1989), pp. 26–35.
96 Sigmund Freud, 'Family romances' (1909), in *The Standard Edition of the Complete Psychological Works*, vol. IX (London: Hogarth, 1959), pp. 237–41 (p. 239).
97 Steedman, 'True romances', p. 27.
98 Ibid., pp. 32–3.

6: Sarah Waters's Gothic Historical Novels

1   Sarah Waters, *Affinity* (London: Virago, 1999), p. 7. Further references are given in the body of the text.
2   Queer: 1. strange, odd, eccentric; of questionable character, shady, out of sorts, giddy, faint . . . 2. homosexual 3. spoil, put out of order (*OED*).
3   Sarah Waters, 'Wolfskins and togas: lesbian and gay historical fictions, 1870 to the present' (unpublished Ph.D. thesis, Queen Mary and Westfield College, University of London, 1995), 8.
4   Sarah Waters, 'Wolfskins and Togas: Maude Meagher's *The Green Scamander* and the Lesbian Historical Novel', *Women: A Cultural Review*, 7/2 (1996), 177–88, (177).
5   Paulina Palmer, *Lesbian Gothic: Transgressive Fictions* (London and New York: Cassell, 1999), p. 9.
6   Ibid., p. 8.
7   Lucie Armitt, 'Garden Paths and Blindspots' (review of *The Little Stranger*), *New Welsh Review*, 85 (Autumn 2009), 28–35 (34).
8   Terry Castle, *The Apparitional Lesbian: Female Homosexuality and Modern Culture* (New York: Columbia University Press, 1993), pp. 2, 4
9   Sarah Waters, *Fingersmith* (London: Virago, 2002); Sarah Waters, *The Night Watch* (London: Virago, 2006); Sarah Waters, *The Little Stranger* (London: Virago, 2009); Sarah Waters, *Tipping the Velvet* (London: Virago, 1998), p. 279. Further references to all novels are given in the main body of the text.
10 Although most critics use the term 'neo-Victorian', Kate Mitchell argues that *Affinity* and *Fingersmith* are 'Faux-Victorian' novels in that they refuse to mark their difference from the Victorian tradition 'in the characteristically parodic mode of historiographic metafiction':

History and Cultural Memory in Neo-Victorian Fiction (Basingstoke and New York: Palgrave Macmillan, 2010), p. 117.

11 Cora Kaplan, *Victoriana: Histories, Fictions, Criticisms* (Edinburgh: Edinburgh University Press, 2007), p. 114.

12 Lucie Armitt, Interview with Sarah Waters (CWWN conference. University of Wales, Bangor, 22 April 2006), *Feminist Review*, 85 (2007), 116–27 (120).

13 Important studies here, all of which reference Waters, include: Jeannette King, *The Victorian Woman Question in Contemporary Feminist Fiction* (Basingstoke and New York: Palgrave Macmillan, 2005); Kaplan, *Victoriana*; Tatiana Kontou, *Spiritualism and Women's Writing: From the Fin de Siècle to the Neo-Victorian* (Basingstoke and New York: Palgrave Macmillan, 2009); Ann Heilmann and Mark Llewellyn, *Neo-Victorianism: The Victorians in the Twenty-First Century, 1999–2009* (Basingstoke and New York: Palgrave Macmillan, 2010); Mitchell, *History and Cultural Memory in Neo-Victoran Fiction*; Louisa Hadley, *Neo-Victorian Fiction and Historical Narrative: The Victorians and Us* (Basingstoke and New York: Palgrave Macmillan, 2010); Rosario Arias and Patricia Pulham (eds), *Haunting and Spectrality in Neo-Victorian Fiction: Possessing the Past* (Basingstoke and New York: Palgrave Macmillan, 2010).

14 Waters, 'Wolfskins and togas' (Ph.D. thesis), 249.

15 Ibid.

16 Abigail Dennis, '"Ladies in Peril"; Sarah Waters on Neo-Victorian Narrative Celebrations and Why She Stopped Writing about the Victorian Era', *Neo-Victorian Studies*, 1/1 (Autumn 2008), 41–52 (48).

17 Sarah Waters, 'My Hero: Angela Carter', *The Guardian*, Saturday Review, 3 October 2009, p. 5.

18 Angela Carter, *The Sadeian Women: An Exercise in Cultural History* (London: Virago, 1979), p. 9.

19 Naomi Mitchison, *You May Well Ask: A Memoir 1920–1940* (London: Victor Gollancz, 1979), p. 179.

20 Waters, 'Maude Meagher's *The Green Scamander*', 188.

21 Christian Gutleben, *Nostalgic Postmodernism: The Victorian Tradition and the Contemporary British Novel* (Amsterdam and New York: Rodopi, 2001), pp. 11–12, original emphasis.

22 Ibid., p. 12.

23 Jacket blurb, Waters, *Fingersmith*.

24 Waters, 'Maude Meagher's *The Green Scamander*', 188.

25 Alex Owen, *The Darkened Room: Women, Power and Spiritualism in Late Victorian England* (1989; Chicago and London: University of Chicago Press, 2004).

26 Waters, 'Wolfskins and togas' (Ph.D. thesis), 185.
27 Owen, *Darkened Room*, p. xx.
28 Ibid., p. 206.
29 Kontou, *Spiritualism and Women's Writing*, pp. 172–92.
30 Owen, *Darkened Room*, p. 52,
31 Ibid., p. 216.
32 Ibid., p. 222.
33 Ibid., pp. 96–106, 228
34 Ibid., p. 18.
35 Paul Boyer and Stephen Nissenbaum, *Salem Possessed: The Social Origins of Witchcraft* (Cambridge, MA and London: Harvard University Press, 1974), pp. 27–30.
36 King, *The Victorian Woman Question*, p. 90.
37 Fredric Jameson, *The Political Unconscious* (1981; London and New York: Routledge, 2002), p. 67.
38 Owen, *Darkened Room*, pp. 33–8.
39 Dennis, '"Ladies in Peril"', 45.
40 Cora Kaplan, 'Introduction', in Elizabeth Barrett Browning, *Aurora Leigh with Other Poems* (London: The Women's Press, 1978), pp. 5–36 (p.36).
41 Ibid.
42 Ibid.
43 Kaplan, *Victoriana*, p. 133.
44 Palmer, *Lesbian Gothic*, p.10.
45 Luce Irigaray, *The Irigaray Reader*, ed. Margaret Whitford (Oxford: Blackwell, 1991), p. 47.
46 Sheridan Le Fanu, *The Rose and the Key* (1871; New York: Dover, 1982), p. 60.
47 Ibid.
48 Nadine Muller, 'Not My Mother's Daughter: Matrilinealism, Third Wave Feminism and Neo-Victorian Fiction', *Neo-Victorian Studies* 2/2 (Winter 2009/10), 109–36.
49 Ibid., 131.
50 Jameson, *Political Unconscious*, p. 67.
51 Angela Carter, *The Bloody Chamber* (London: Virago, 1979).
52 Angela Carter, in John Haffenden, *Novelists in Interview* (London and New York: Methuen, 1985), p. 84.
53 Kaplan, *Victoriana*, p. 113.
54 Cora Kaplan, '*Fingersmith*'s Coda: Feminism and Victorian Studies', *Journal of Victorian Culture*, 13/1 (2008), 42–55 (53).

55 Both Cora Kaplan and Kathleen A. Miller have also made this point. See Kaplan, '*Fingersmith*'s Coda', and Kathleen A. Miller, 'Sarah Waters' *Fingersmith*: Leaving Women's Fingerprints on Victorian Pornography', *Nineteenth-Century Gender Studies*, 4/1 (Spring 2008), *www.ncgsjournal.com/issue41/miller.htm*, accessed 20 July 2011,

56 Dennis, '"Ladies in Peril"', p.60.

57 Carter, *Sadeian Woman*, pp. 3–4.

58 Ibid., pp. 6–7.

59 Waters, 'Maude Meagher's *The Green Scamander*', 181.

60 See Waters' own analysis, 'Wolfskins and togas' (Ph.D. thesis), ch. 9.

61 Castle, *Apparitional Lesbian*, p. 7.

62 Norman Jones, *Gay and Lesbian Historical Fiction: Sexual Mystery and Post-secular Narrative* (Basingstoke and New York: Palgrave Macmillan, 2007), p. 96.

63 Ibid., p. 97.

64 Castle, *Apparitional Lesbian*, p. 74.

65 Waters, 'Maude Meagher's *The Green Scamander*', 177.

66 Sylvia Townsend Warner, *Summer Will Show* (1936; London: Virago, 1987), p. 274.

67 Le Fanu, *The Rose and the Key*, p. 359.

68 Ibid., p. 358.

69 Elaine Showalter, *The Female Malady: Women, Madness and English Culture, 1830–1980* (London: Virago, 1987), p. 25.

70 Irigaray, *The Irigaray Reader*, p. 35.

71 Ibid., p. 36.

72 Ibid., p. 39.

73 Ibid., p. 40.

74 Ibid., pp. 44–5.

75 Ibid., p. 37.

76 In *The End of History and the Last Man* (London: Hamish Hamilton, 1992), Francis Fukuyama argued that the collapse of communism signalled the triumph of democratic capitalism and the establishment of a global consensus, and thus the end of history as a Hegelian process of dialectical evolution.

77 Sarah Waters, 'Romance among the Ruins', *The Guardian, Saturday Review*, 28 January 2006, pp. 4–6 (5).

78 John Mullan, 'Guardian Book Club: Sarah Waters on Writing *The Little Stranger*', *The Guardian Review*, 7 August 2010, p. 5.

79 'Sarah Waters on *The Little Stranger*', The Man Booker Prizes, *www.themanbookerprize.com/perspectice/articles/1261*, accessed 6 October 2009.

⁸⁰ Sarah Waters, 'The Lost Girl', *The Guardian*, 30 May 2009, *www/. guardian.co.uk/books/2009/may/30/sarah-waters-books/print*, accessed 6 October 2009.

⁸¹ 'Sarah Waters', Man Booker Prizes, p. 2

⁸² Sarah Waters, 'The Lost Girl'.

⁸³ Josephine Tey, *The Franchise Affair* (1948; London: Penguin, 1951), p. 10.

⁸⁴ Norman N. Holland and Leona F. Sherman, 'Gothic Possibilities', *New Literary History*, 8/2 (1977), 279–94 (279).

⁸⁵ Lucie Armitt, 'Garden Paths', 35.

⁸⁶ Mullan, 'Guardian Book Club', 5.

⁸⁷ Ibid.

⁸⁸ Agatha Christie, *The Murder of Roger Ackroyd* (1926; London: Harper Collins, 2002), pp. 239, 174.

⁸⁹ Anne Williams, *Art of Darkness: A Poetics of Gothic* (Chicago and London: University of Chicago Press, 1995), pp.105–6.

⁹⁰ Ibid., p. 107.

⁹¹ Robert McCrum, 'What Lies Beneath' (interview with Sarah Waters), *The Observer*, Sunday 10 May 2009, *guardian.co.uk/books/2009/may/ 10/books-sarah-waters/*, accessed 6 October 2009, p. 4.

⁹² Ibid., 5.

⁹³ Scott Bravmann, quoted in Waters, 'Wolfskins and togas' (Ph.D. thesis), 255.

Afterword

¹ Walter Benjamin, 'Theses on the philosophy of history', in *Illuminations* (1940; London: Fontana, 1973), p. 255.

² Abigail Dennis, '"Ladies in Peril"; Sarah Waters on Neo-Victorian Narrative Celebrations and Why She Stopped Writing about the Victorian Era', *Neo-Victorian Studies* 1/1 (Autumn 2008), 41–52 (48).

³ Virginia Woolf, 'Women and fiction' (1929), in *On Women and Writing*, ed. Michèle Barrett (London: The Women's Press, 1979), p. 44.

⁴ Alex Owen, *The Darkened Room: Women, Power and Spiritualism in Late Victorian England* (Chicago and London: University of Chicago Press, 1989), p. 242.

Bibliography

Primary sources

Austen, Jane, *Northanger Abbey* (1818; Harmondsworth: Penguin, 1985).
Brontë, Charlotte, *Jane Eyre* (1847; London; Pan, 1967).
Brontë, Emily, *Wuthering Heights*, ed. Ian Jack (1847; Oxford: Oxford World's Classics, 1981).
Carr, Philippa, *The Miracle at St Bruno's* (1972: London: Fontana, 1974).
Carr, Philippa, *Lament for a Lost Lover* (1977; London: Fontana, 1978).
Carter, Angela, *The Bloody Chamber* (London: Virago, 1979).
Christie, Agatha, *The Murder of Roger Ackroyd* (1926; London: Harper Collins, 2002).
du Maurier, Daphne, *Jamaica Inn* (1936: London: Arrow, 1992).
du Maurier, Daphne, *Rebecca* (1938; London: Pan, 1975).
du Maurier, Daphne, *The King's General* (1946; London: Pan, 1974).
du Maurier, Daphne, *My Cousin Rachel* (1951; London: Arrow, 1992).
Gaskell, Elizabeth, 'French Life', in *The Works of Mrs Gaskell*, ed. A.W. Ward, vol. 7 (London: Smith, Elder, 1906), pp. 604–80.
Gaskell, Elizabeth, *The Moorland Cottage and Other Stories*, ed. Suzanne Lewis (Oxford: Oxford World's Classics, 1995).
Gaskell, Elizabeth, *Gothic Tales*, ed. Laura Kranzler (London: Penguin, 2000).
Gaskell, Elizabeth, *The Works of Elizabeth Gaskell*, vol. 1: *Journalism, Early Fiction and Personal Writings*, ed. Joanne Shattock (London: Pickering and Chatto, 2005).
Hawthorne, Nathaniel, *The Celestial Railroad and Other Stories* (New York: Signet, 1980).

Hoffmann, E. T. A., *The Golden Pot and Other Tales*, trans. Ritchie Robertson (Oxford: Oxford World's Classics, 1992).

Holt, Victoria, *Mistress of Mellyn* (1960: London: Fontana, 1963).

Holt, Victoria, *Kirkland Revels* (1962; Glasgow: Fontana, 1964).

Holt, Victoria, *Bride of Pendorric* (1963; London: Fontana, 1965).

Holt, Victoria, *The Legend of the Seventh Virgin* (1965; London and Glasgow: Fontana, 1967).

Holt, Victoria, *Menfreya* (1966; London and Glasgow: Fontana, 1968).

Holt, Victoria, *The Curse of the Kings* (1973; Glasgow: Fontana, 1975).

Holt, Victoria, *The House of a Thousand Lanterns* (1974; London and Glasgow: Fontana, 1976).

La Fayette, Madame de, *The Princess of Clèves*, trans. Walter J. Cobb (1678; New York: Signet, 1961).

Lee, Harriet and Sophia Lee, *The Canterbury Tales* (1832; London: Pandora, 1989).

Lee, Sophia, *The Recess; or, A Tale of Other Times*, ed. April Alliston (1783–5; Lexington: University Press of Kentucky, 2000).

Lee, Vernon, *Penelope Brandling: A Tale of the Welsh Coast in the Eighteenth Century* (London: T. Fisher Unwin, 1903).

Lee, Vernon, *Hauntings: The Supernatural Stories*, ed. David G. Rowlands (Ashcroft, British Columbia: Ash-Tree, 2002).

Lee, Vernon, *Hauntings and Other Fantastic Tales*, ed. Catherine Maxwell and Patricia Pulham (Peterborough, Ontario: Broadview, 2006).

Le Fanu, Sheridan, *The Rose and the Key* (1871; New York: Dover, 1982).

Lewis, Matthew, *The Monk* (1796; Oxford: Oxford World's Classics, 1998).

Plaidy, Jean, *Together They Ride* (London: Gerald S. Swan, 1945).

Radcliffe, Ann, *A Sicilian Romance*, ed. Alison Milbank (1790; Oxford: Oxford World's Classics, 1993).

Radcliffe, Ann, *The Romance of the Forest*, ed. Chloe Chard (1791; Oxford: Oxford World's Classics, 1986).

Radcliffe, Ann, *The Mysteries of Udolpho*, ed. Bonamy Dobrée (1794; Oxford: Oxford World's Classics, 1980).

Radcliffe, Ann, *The Italian*, ed. Frederick Garber (1797; Oxford: Oxford World's Classics, 1981).

Radcliffe, Ann, *Gaston de Blondeville*, ed. Frances Chiu (1826; Chicago: Valancourt, 2006).

Reeve, Clara, *The Old English Baron*, ed. James Watt (1777; Oxford: Oxford World's Classics, 2003).

Scott, Walter, *Waverley; or, 'Tis Sixty Years Since* (1814; Oxford: Oxford World's Classics, 1998).

Bibliography

Scott, Walter, *Chronicles of the Canongate*, ed. Clare Lamont (London: Penguin, 2003).

Tey, Josephine, *The Franchise Affair* (1948; London: Penguin, 1951).

Walpole, Horace, *The Castle of Otranto*, in Peter Fairclough (ed.), *Three Gothic Novels* (Harmondsworth: Penguin, 1968).

Warner, Sylvia Townsend, *Summer Will Show* (1936; London: Virago, 1987).

Waters, Sarah, *Tipping the Velvet* (London: Virago, 1998).

Waters, Sarah, *Affinity* (London: Virago, 1999).

Waters, Sarah, *Fingersmith* (London: Virago, 2002).

Waters, Sarah, *The Night Watch* (London: Virago, 2006).

Waters, Sarah, *The Little Stranger* (London: Virago, 2009).

Whitney, Phyllis, *Thunder Heights* (1960; London: Coronet, 1973).

Secondary sources

Alexander, Sally, 'Feminist History and Psychoanalysis', *History Workshop Journal*, 32/1 (1991), 128–33.

Allen, Walter, *The Short Story in English* (Oxford: Oxford University Press, 1981).

Allerdice, Lisa, 'Uncharted Waters' (Interview with Sarah Waters), *The Guardian*, Thursday 1 June 2006. Available at *books.guardian.co/print/0,,329493754-120824,00.html*, accessed 30 November 2007.

Alliston, April, *Virtue's Faults: Correspondences in Eighteenth-Century British and French Women's Fiction* (Stanford, CA: Stanford University Press, 1996).

Anon., 'The Historical Romance', *Blackwood's Magazine*, 58 (1845), 341–2; reprinted in E. J. Clery and Robert Miles (eds), *Gothic Documents: A Sourcebook 1700–1820* (Manchester: Manchester University Press, 2000), pp. 292–7.

Arias, Rosario and Patricia Pulham (eds), *Haunting and Spectrality in Neo-Victorian Fiction: Possessing the Past* (Basingstoke and New York: Palgrave Macmillan, 2010).

Armitt, Lucie, 'Interview with Sarah Waters (CWWN conference. University of Wales, Bangor, 22 April 2006), *Feminist Review*, 85 (2007), 116–27.

Armitt, Lucie, 'Garden Paths and Blindspots' (review of *The Little Stranger*), *New Welsh Review*, 85 (Autumn 2009), 28–35.

Austen, Jane, 'The history of England from the reign of Henry 4th to the death of Charles 1st', in *The Works of Jane Austen*, vol. VI: *Minor Works*, ed. R. W. Chapman (London: Oxford University Press, 1959; rev. edn, 1969), pp. 138–49.

Baldick, Chris and Robert Mighall, 'Gothic criticism', in David Punter (ed.), *A Companion to the Gothic* (Oxford: Blackwell, 2000), pp. 209–28.

Barthes, Roland, *Camera Lucida: Reflections on Photography*, trans. Richard Howard (1980; London: Vintage, 2000).

Beard, Mary R., *Woman as Force in History* (New York: Macmillan, 1946).

Benjamin, Walter, *Illuminations* (1940; London: Fontana, 1973).

Bennett, Catherine, 'The Prime of Miss Jean Plaidy', *The Guardian*, 4 July 1991, p. 3.

Bettelheim, Bruno, *The Uses of Enchantment* (1976: London: Penguin, 1991).

Blakeney, E. H., *A Smaller Classical Dictionary* (London and Toronto: J. M. Dent, 1910).

Boulding, Elise, *The Underside of History: A View of Women through Time* (Boulder, CO: Westview, 1976).

Bowen, Elizabeth, 'Preface', in *A Day in the Dark and Other Stories* (London: Jonathan Cape, 1965).

Boyer, Paul, and Stephen Nissenbaum, *Salem Possessed: The Social Origins of Witchcraft* (Cambridge, MA and London: Harvard University Press, 1974).

Briggs, Julia, *Night Visitors: The Rise and Fall of the English Ghost Story* (London: Faber, 1977).

Bryden, Ronald, 'Queen of the Wild Mullions', *The Spectator*, 20 April 1962, p. 514.

Carlyle, Thomas, *Selected Writings* (London: Penguin, 1986).

Carlyle, Thomas, *The Complete Works of Thomas Carlyle*, vols I and II (New York: Thomas Y. Crowell, 1869).

Carter, Angela, *The Sadeian Women: An Exercise in Cultural History* (London: Virago, 1979).

Castle, Terry, *The Apparitional Lesbian: Female Homosexuality and Modern Culture* (New York: Columbia University Press, 1993).

Chandler, James, 'History', in Iain McCalman (ed.), *An Oxford Companion to the Romantic Age* (Oxford: Oxford University Press, 1999), pp. 354–61.

Chapple, J. A. V., *Elizabeth Gaskell: A Portrait in Letters* (Manchester and New York: Manchester University Press, 2007).

Clery, E. J., *Women's Gothic: From Clara Reeve to Mary Shelley* (Tavistock: Northcote, 2000).

Colby, Vineta, *Vernon Lee: A Literary Biography* (Charlottesville and London: University of Virginia Press, 2003).

Bibliography

Cook, Judith, *Daphne: A Portrait of Daphne du Maurier* (London: Transworld, 1991).

Cox, Michael and Jack Adrian (eds), *The Oxford Book of Historical Stories* (Oxford: Oxford University Press, 1995).

Cox, Michael and R. A. Gilbert (eds), *The Oxford Book of English Ghost Stories* (Oxford; Oxford University Press, 1986).

Crosby, Christina, *The Ends of History: Victorians and 'the woman question'* (New York and London: Routledge, 1991).

Dalby, Richard, 'All about Jean Plaidy', *Book and Magazine Collector*, 10 (April 1993), *jeanplaidy.tripod.com/id17.htm*, accessed 7 April 2011.

Dennis, Abigail, '"Ladies in Peril"; Sarah Waters on Neo-Victorian Narrative Celebrations and Why She Stopped Writing about the Victorian Era', *Neo-Victorian Studies*, 1/1 (Autumn 2008), 41–52.

Dickerson, Vanessa D., *Victorian Ghosts in the Noontide: Women Writers and the Supernatural* (Columbia and London: University of Missouri Press, 1996).

Dijkstra, Bram, *Idols of Perversity: Fantasies of Feminine Evil in Fin-de-Siècle Culture* (Oxford: Oxford University Press, 1986).

Doane, Mary Ann, *Femmes Fatales: Feminism, Film Theory, Psychoanalysis* (New York and London: Routledge, 1991).

Doody, Margaret Anne, 'Deserts, Ruins and Troubled Waters: Female Dreams in Fiction and the Development of the Gothic Novel', *Genre*, 10 (Winter 1977), 527–72.

Duffy, Martha, 'On the Road to Manderley', *Time*, Monday 12 April 1971, pp. 65–6.

du Maurier, Daphne, 'Introduction', in Jane Austen, *Northanger Abbey* (London: Williams and Norgate, 1948), pp. x–xi.

du Maurier, Daphne, *Myself When Young: The Shaping of a Writer* (1977; London: Virago, 2004).

du Maurier, Daphne, *The Rebecca Notebooks and Other Memories* (London: Victor Gollancz, 1981).

Duncan, Ian, *Modern Romance and Transformations of the Novel: The Gothic, Scott and Dickens* (Cambridge: Cambridge University Press, 1992).

DuPlessis, Rachel Blau, *Writing beyond the Ending: Narrative Structures of Twentieth Century Women Writers* (Bloomington: Indiana University Press, 1985).

Easson, Angus, *Elizabeth Gaskell* (London, Boston and Henley: Routledge and Kegan Paul, 1979).

Ellis, Kate Ferguson, *The Contested Castle: Gothic Novels and the Subversion of Domestic Ideology* (Urbana and Chicago: University of Illinois Press, 1989).

Ewing, Emma Mai, 'Gothic Mania', *New York Times Book Review*, 11 May 1975, pp. 10, 11–12.

Fiedler, Leslie, *Love and Death in the American Novel* (1960; Harmondsworth: Penguin, 1984).

Fitzgerald, Lauren, 'Female Gothic and the Institutionalisation of Gothic Studies', *Gothic Studies*, 6/1 (May 2004), 8–18.

Fleenor, Juliann (ed.), *The Female Gothic* (Montreal and London: Eden, 1983).

Fleishman, Avrom, *The English Historical Novel: Walter Scott to Virginia Woolf* (Baltimore and London: Johns Hopkins University Press, 1971).

Forster, Margaret, *Daphne du Maurier* (1993; London: Arrow, 1994).

Foster, Shirley, 'Elizabeth Gaskell's shorter pieces', in Jill Matus (ed.), *The Cambridge Companion to Elizabeth Gaskell* (Cambridge: Cambridge University Press, 2007), pp. 108–30.

Fraser, Antonia, *Mary Queen of Scots* (1969; London: Phoenix, 2002).

Fraser, Hilary, 'Regarding the Eighteenth Century: Vernon Lee and Emilia Dilke Construct a Period', in Francis O. Gorman and Katherine Turner (eds), *The Victorians and the Eighteenth Century: Reassessing the Tradition* (Aldershot and Burlington, VT: Ashgate, 2004), pp. 223–49.

Freud, Sigmund, 'Family romances' (1909) in *The Standard Edition of the Complete Psychological Works*, vol. IX (London: Hogarth, 1959), pp. 237–41.

Freud, Sigmund, 'The uncanny' (1919), *Art and Literature*, The Penguin Freud Library, 14 (1985; London: Penguin, 1990), pp. 339–76.

Fukuyama, Francis, *The End of History and the Last Man* (London: Hamish Hamilton, 1992).

Gaskell, Elizabeth, *The Life of Charlotte Brontë* (1857; London: Dent, 1908).

Gay, Peter, *Freud for Historians* (1985; Oxford: Oxford University Press, 1986).

Gilbert, Sandra M. and Susan Gubar, *The Madwoman in the Attic: The Woman Writer and the Nineteenth-Century Literary Imagination* (1979; New Haven and London: Yale University Press, 1984).

Gilmour, Robin, 'Using the Victorians: the Victorian age in contemporary fiction', in Alice Jenkins, and Juliet John (eds), *Rereading Victorian Fiction* (Basingstoke and New York; Palgrave, 2000), pp. 189–200.

Goldsmith, Oliver, *The History of England from the Earliest Times to the Death of George the Second*, vol. II, 10th edn (London: Johnson et al., 1809).

Goodare, Julian, 'Mary (1542–87)', *Oxford Dictionary of National Biography* (Oxford University Press, September 2004), online edn, May 2007, *www.oxforddnb.com/view/article18248*, accessed 17 June 2010.

Gordimer, Nadine, 'The flash of fireflies', in Charles May (ed.), *The New Short Story Theories* (Athens: Ohio University Press, 1994), pp. 264–5.

Groot, Jerome de, *The Historical Novel* (London and New York: Routledge, 2010).

Gunn, Peter, *Vernon Lee: Violet Paget, 1856–1935* (London: Oxford University Press, 1964).

Gutleben, Christian, *Nostalgic Postmodernism: The Victorian Tradition and the Contemporary British Novel* (Amsterdam and New York: Rodopi, 2001).

Hadley, Louisa, *Neo-Victorian Fiction and Historical Narrative: The Victorians and Us* (Basingstoke and New York: Palgrave Macmillan, 2010).

Haffenden, John, *Novelists in Interview* (London and New York: Methuen, 1985).

Hall, Alan, *St Donat's Castle: A Guide and History* (St Donat's, 2002).

Hanson, Clare (ed.), *Re-reading the Short Story* (London: Macmillan, 1989).

Hanson, Clare, '"Things out of words": towards a poetics of short fiction', in Clare Hanson (ed.), *Re-reading the Short Story* (London: Macmillan, 1989), pp. 22–33.

Harrington, Emily, 'The Strain of Sympathy: A. Mary F. Robinson, *The New Arcadia*, and Vernon Lee', *Nineteenth-Century Literature*, 61/1 (2006), 66–98.

Heilmann, Ann and Mark Llewellyn, *Neo-Victorianism: The Victorians in the Twenty-First Century, 1999–2009* (Basingstoke and New York: Palgrave Macmillan, 2010).

Henderson, Lesley (ed.), *Twentieth Century Romance and Historical Writers* (Chicago and London: St James Press, 1990).

Henson, Louise, '"Half Believing, Half Incredulous": Elizabeth Gaskell, Superstition and the Victorian Mind', *Nineteenth-Century Contexts*, 24/3 (2002), 251–69;

Hill, Frances, *A Delusion of Satan: The Full Story of the Salem Witch Trials* (London: Penguin, 1997).

Holland, Norman N. and Leona F. Sherman, 'Gothic Possibilities', *New Literary History*, 8/2 (1977), 279–94.

Hollinger, Karen, 'The Female Oedipal Drama of *Rebecca* from Novel to Film', *Quarterly Review of Film and Video*, 14/4 (1993), 17–30.

Horner, Avril and Sue Zlosnik, *Daphne du Maurier: Writing, Identity and the Gothic Imagination* (Basingstoke: Macmillan, 1998).

Hotchkiss, Jane, '(P)revising Freud: Vernon Lee's castration phantasy', in Carola M. Kaplan and Anne B. Simpson (eds), *Seeing Double: Revisioning Edwardian and Modernist Literature* (New York: St. Martin's Press, 1996), pp. 21–38.

Hume, David, 'Of the study of history' (1741), in *Essays:Moral, Political and Literary*, ed. Eugene F. Miller (Indianapolis: Liberty Classics, 1987), pp. 563–8.

Hume, David, *The History of England from the Invasion of Julius Caesar, to the Revolution in 1688* (1757–62; Edinburgh: Peter Hill, 1818), vol. V.

Hutcheon, Linda, *A Poetics of Postmodernism: History, Theory, Fiction* (New York and London: Routledge, 1988).

Irigaray, Luce, *Thinking the Difference: For a Peaceful Revolution*, trans. Karin Montin (1989; London: Athlone, 1994).

Irigaray, Luce, *je, tu, nous: Toward a Culture of Difference*, trans. Alison Martin (1990; London: Routledge, 1993).

Irigaray, Luce, *The Irigaray Reader*, ed. Margaret Whitford (Oxford: Blackwell, 1991).

Isaac, Megan Lynn, 'Sophia Lee and the Gothic of Female Community', *Studies in the Novel*, 28/2 (1996), 200–18.

Jackson, Rosemary, *Fantasy: The Literature of Subversion* (1981; London and New York: Routledge, 1998).

Jameson, Fredric, *The Political Unconscious: Narrative as a Socially Symbolic Act* (1981; London and New York, 2002).

Johnson, Nora, 'The Captivity of Marriage', *Atlantic Monthly*, 207/6 (June 1961), 38–42.

Jones, Norman, *Gay and Lesbian Historical Fiction: Sexual Mystery and Post-Secular Narrative* (Basingstoke and New York: Palgrave Macmillan, 2007).

Kahane, Claire, 'The Gothic mirror' (1980), in Shirley Nelson Garner, Claire Kahane and Madelon Sprengether (eds), *The Mother Tongue: Essays in Feminist Psychoanalytic Interpretation* (Ithaca and London: Cornell University Press, 1985), pp. 334–51.

Kane, Mary Patricia, 'The Uncanny Mother in Vernon Lee's "Prince Alberic and the Snake Lady"', *Victorian Review*, 32/1 (2006), 41–62.

Kaplan, Cora, 'Introduction', in Elizabeth Barrett Browning, *Aurora Leigh with Other Poems* (London: The Women's Press, 1978), pp. 5–36.

Kaplan, Cora, *Victoriana: Histories, Fictions, Criticisms* (Edinburgh: Edinburgh University Press, 2007).

Kaplan, Cora '*Fingersmith*'s Coda: Feminism and Victorian Studies', *Journal of Victorian Culture*, 13/1 (2008), 42–55.

King, Jeannette, *The Victorian Woman Question in Contemporary Feminist Fiction* (Basingstoke and New York; Palgrave Macmillan, 2005).

Kontou, Tatiana, *Spiritualism and Women's Writing: From the Fin de Siècle to the Neo-Victorian* (Basingstoke and New York: Palgrave Macmillan, 2009).

Krueger, Christine L., 'The "female paternalist" as historian: Elizabeth Gaskell's *My Lady Ludlow*', in Linda M. Shires (ed.), *Rewriting the Victorians: Theory, History and the Politics of Gender* (New York and London: Routledge, 1992), pp. 166–83.

Lee, Vernon, *Genius Loci: Notes on Places* (London: Grant Richards, 1897).

Lee, Vernon, *Limbo and Other Essays* (1897; Doyleston, PA; Wildside, n.d.).

Lee, Vernon, *Hortus Vitae: Essays on the Gardening of Life*, 2nd edn (London and New York: John Lane, The Bodley Head, 1904).

Lee, Vernon, *Gospels of Anarchy and Other Contemporary Studies* (London and Leipzig: T. Fisher Unwin, 1908).

Lee, Vernon, 'Dionysus in the Euganean Hills: W. H. Pater in Memoriam', *Contemporary Review*, 120 (September 1921), 346–53.

Lee, Vernon, *The Handling of Words and Other Studies in Literary Psychology* (London: John Lane, 1923).

Leighton, Angela, 'Resurrections of the body: women writers and the idea of the Renaissance', in Alison Chapman and Jane Stabler (eds), *Unfolding the South: Nineteenth-Century British Women Writers and Artists in Italy* (Manchester and New York: Manchester University Press, 2003), pp. 222–38.

Lewis, Jayne Elizabeth, '"Ev'ry Lost Relation!" Historical Fictions and Sentimental Incidents in Sophia Lee's *The Recess*', *Eighteenth-Century Fiction*, 7/2 (1995), 165–85.

Lewis, Jayne Elizabeth, *Mary Queen of Scots: Romance and Nation* (London and New York: Routledge, 1998).

Lobban-Viravong, Heather, 'Bastard Heirs: The Dream of Legitimacy in Sophia Lee's *The Recess*', *Prose Studies*, 29/2 (August 2007), 204–19.

Luckhurst, Roger (ed.), *Late Victorian Gothic Tales* (Oxford: Oxford World's Classics, 2005).

Lukács, Georg, *The Historical Novel*, trans. Hannah and Stanley Mitchell (1962; Lincoln, NB and London: University of Nebraska Press, 1983).

Martin, Carol A., 'Gaskell's Ghosts: Truths in Disguise', *Studies in the Novel*, 21/1 (1989), 27–40.

Martineau, Harriet, 'On Witchcraft', *Monthly Repository*, n.s., 6 (1832), 545–55.

Matus, Jill (ed.), *The Cambridge Companion to Elizabeth Gaskell* (Cambridge: Cambridge University Press, 2007).

Matus, Jill, '*Mary Barton* and *North and South*', in Jill Matus (ed.), *The Cambridge Companion to Elizabeth Gaskell* (Cambridge: Cambridge University Press, 2007), pp. 27–45.

Maxwell, Catherine, 'From Dionysus to "Dionea": Vernon Lee's Portraits', *Word and Image*, 13/3 (July–September 1997), 253–69.

Maxwell, Catherine and Patricia Pulham (eds), *Vernon Lee: Decadence, Ethics, Aesthetics* (Basingstoke: Palgrave, 2006).

Maxwell, 'Pretenders in Sanctuary', *Modern Language Quarterly*, 61/2 (June 2000), 287–358.

Maxwell, Richard, 'Phantom states: *Cleveland*, *The Recess*, and the origins of historical fiction', in Margaret Cohen and Carolyn Dever (eds), *The Literary Channel: The Inter- National Invention of the Novel* (Princeton and Oxford: Princeton University Press, 2002), pp. 151–82.

Maxwell, Richard, *The Historical Novel in Europe, 1650–1950* (Cambridge: Cambridge University Press, 2009).

May, Charles (ed.), *The New Short Story Theories* (Athens: Ohio University Press, 1994).

McCrum, Robert, 'What Lies Beneath' (interview with Sarah Waters), *The Observer*, Sunday 10 May 2009, *guardian.co.uk/books/2009/may/10/books-sarah-waters/* , accessed 6 October 2009.

McMurray, Enfys, *Hearst's Other Castles* (Bridgend: Seren, 1999).

Miles, Robert, *Ann Radcliffe: The Great Enchantress* (Manchester: Manchester University Press, 1994).

Miles, Robert, '"Mother Radcliffe": Ann Radcliffe and the Female Gothic', in Diana Wallace and Andrew Smith (eds), *The New Female Gothic: New Directions* (Basingstoke: Palgrave Macmillan, 2009), pp. 42–59.

Mill, J. S., *On Liberty and The Subjection of Women*, ed. Alan Ryan (London: Penguin, 2006).

Miller, Kathleen A., 'Sarah Waters' *Fingersmith*: Leaving Women's Fingerprints on Victorian Pornography', *Nineteenth-Century Gender Studies*, 4/1 (Spring 2008), *www.ncgsjournal.com/issue41/miller.htm.*, accessed 20 July 2011.

Mitchell, Juliet, *Women: The Longest Revolution* (1966; London: Virago, 1984).

Mitchell, Kate, *History and Cultural Memory in Neo-Victorian Fiction* (Basingstoke and New York: Palgrave Macmillan, 2010).

Mitchison, Naomi, *You May Well Ask: A Memoir 1920–1940* (London: Victor Gollancz, 1979).

Modleski, Tania, *Loving with a Vengeance* (London: Routledge, 1982).

Modleski, Tania, *The Women Who Knew Too Much: Hitchcock and Feminist Theory* (New York and London: Routledge, 1988).

Moers, Ellen, *Literary Women* (1976; London: The Women's Press, 1978).

Moody, Nickianne, 'Visible margins: women writers and the English ghost story', in Sarah Sceats and Gail Cunningham (eds), *Image and Power;*

Women in Fiction in the Twentieth Century (London and New York: Longman, 1990), pp.77−90.

Mullan, John, 'Guardian Book Club: Sarah Waters on Writing *The Little Stranger*', *The Guardian Review*, 7 August 2010, p. 5.

Muller, Nadine, 'Not My Mother's Daughter: Matrilinealism, Third Wave Feminism and Neo-Victorian Fiction', *Neo-Victorian Studies* 2/2 (Winter 2009/10), 109−36.

Newman, Sally, 'The Archival Traces of Desire: Vernon Lee's Failed Sexuality and the Interpretation of Letters in Lesbian History', *Journal of the History of Sexuality*, 14/1−2 (January−April 2005), 51−75.

Nordius, Janina, 'A Tale of Other Places: Sophia Lee's *The Recess* and Colonial Gothic', *Studies in the Novel*, 34/2 (Summer 2002), 162−77.

Norton, Rictor, *Mistress of Udolpho: The Life of Ann Radcliffe* (London and New York: Leicester University Press, 1999).

Opie, Iona and Peter, *The Classic Fairy Tales* (1974; London: Granada, 1980).

Owen, Alex, *The Darkened Room: Women, Power and Spiritualism in Late Victorian England* (Chicago and London: University of Chicago Press, 1989).

Pace, Eric, 'Gothic Novels for Women Prove Bonanza for Publishers', *The New York Times*, Monday 18 June 1973, pp.31, 34.

Palmer, Paulina, *Lesbian Gothic: Transgressive Fictions* (London and New York: Cassell, 1999).

Pickering, Jean, 'Time and the short story', in Clare Hanson (ed.), *Re-reading the Short Story* (London: Macmillan, 1989), pp. 45−54.

Psomiades, Kathy, '"Still burning from this strangling embrace": Vernon Lee on desire and aesthetics', in Richard Dellamora (ed.), *Victorian Sexual Dissidence* (Chicago and London: University of Chicago Press, 1999), pp. 21−41.

Pulham, Patricia, *Art and the Transitional Object in Vernon Lee's Supernatural Tales* (Aldershot: Ashgate, 2008).

Punter, David, *The Literature of Terror*, vol. I: *The Gothic Tradition*, 2nd edn (London and New York: Longman, 1996).

Purkiss, Diane, *The Witch in History: Early Modern and Twentieth-Century Representations* (London and New York: Routledge, 1996).

Rance, Andrew, *The Historical Novel and Popular Politics in Nineteenth-Century England* (London: Vision, 1975).

Reddy, Maureen T., 'Gaskell's "The Grey Woman": A Feminist Palimpsest', *Journal of Narrative Technique*, 15 (1985), 183−93.

Reeve, Clara, 'From *The Progress of Romance*', in Stephen Regan (ed.), *The Nineteenth-Century Novel: A Critical Reader* (London and New York: Routledge, 2001), pp. 13−22.

Richter, David H., 'From medievalism to historicism: representations of history in the Gothic novel and historical romance', in Leslie J. Workman (ed.), *Medievalism in England*, Studies in Medievalism, IV (Cambridge: D. S. Brewer, 1992), pp. 79–104.

Robertson, William, *The History of Scotland during the Reigns of Queen Mary, and of King James VI* (1759; Aberdeen: George Clarke, 1847).

Rogers, Samuel, 'Italy: 22 Ginevra', *poemhunter.com/best-poems/Samuel-rogers/italy- 22ginevra/*, accessed 17 March 2011.

Roper, Lyndall, *Oedipus and the Devil: Witchcraft, Sexuality and Religion in Early Modern Europe* (London and New York: Routledge, 1994).

Rowbotham, Sheila, *Hidden from History: Rediscovering Women in History from the Seventeenth Century to the Present* (1973; New York: Vintage, 1976).

Roy, Ian, 'Sir Richard Grenville', *The Oxford Dictionary of National Biography*, *www.oxforddnb.com/articles/11/11495-article.html*, accessed 22 February 2005.

Russ, Joanna, 'Somebody's Trying to Kill Me and I Think It's My Husband: The Modern Gothic', *Journal of Popular Culture*, 6 (Spring 1973), 666–91.

Sabatini, Rafael, *A Century of Historical Stories* (London: Hutchinson, 1936).

Sanders, Andrew, *The Victorian Historical Novel 1840–1880* (London and Basingstoke: Macmillan, 1978).

Scott, Joan Wallach, 'After History', *Common Knowledge*, 5/3 (1996), 9–25.

Sedgwick, Eve Kosofsky, *The Coherence of Gothic Conventions* (1980; New York and London: Methuen, 1986).

Sharps, J. G., *Mrs Gaskell's Observations and Inventions: A Study of Her Non-Biographic Works* (Sussex: Linden Press, 1970).

Shattock, Joanne, *The Oxford Guide to British Women Writers* (Oxford: Oxford University Press, 1993).

Shaw, Marion, '*Sylvia's Lovers* and other historical fiction', in Jill Matus (ed.), *The Cambridge Companion to Elizabeth Gaskell* (Cambridge: Cambridge University, 2007), pp.75–89.

Shiller, Dana, 'The Redemptive Past in the Neo-Victorian Novel', *Studies in the Novel*, 29/4 (Winter 1997), 538–60.

Showalter, Elaine, *The Female Malady: Women, Madness and English Culture, 1830–1980* (London: Virago, 1987).

Shuttleworth, Sally, 'Natural history: the retro-Victorian novel', in S. Shaffer (ed.), *The Third Culture: Literature and Science* (Berlin and New York: W. de Gruyther, 1998), pp. 253–68.

Smith, Bonnie G., *The Gender of History: Men, Women and Historical Practice* (Cambridge, MA and London: Harvard University Press, 1998).

Spencer, Jane, *The Rise of the Woman Novelist: From Aphra Behn to Jane Austen* (Oxford: Blackwell, 1986).

Spongberg, Mary, *Writing Women's History since the Renaissance* (Basingstoke: Palgrave Macmillan, 2002).

Steedman, Carolyn, 'True romances', in Raphael Samuel (ed.), *Patriotism: The Making and Unmaking of British National Identity*, vol. I: *History and Politics* (London and New York: Routledge, 1989), pp. 26–35.

Stevens, Anne H., 'Sophia Lee's illegitimate history', in Albert J. Rivero, George Justice and Margo Collins (eds), *The Eighteenth Century Novel*, vol. 3 (New York: AMS Press, 2003), pp. 263–91.

Stevens, Anne H., *British Historical Fiction before Scott* (Basingstoke: Palgrave Macmillan, 2010).

Stoneman, Patsy, *Elizabeth Gaskell* (Brighton: Harvester, 1987).

Stoneman, Patsy, *Brontë Transformations: The Cultural Dissemination of Jane Eyre and Wuthering Heights* (Hemel Hempstead: Prentice Hall/ Harvester Wheatsheaf, 1996).

Styler, Rebecca, '"Lois the Witch": A Unitarian Tale', *Gaskell Society Journal*, 21 (2007), 73–85.

Summers, Montague, *The Gothic Quest: A History of the Gothic Novel* (1938; London: Fortune Press, 1968).

Tompkins, J. M. S., *The Popular Novel in England 1770–1800* (1932: London: Methuen, 1969).

Torgovnick, Marianna, 'Discovering Jane Harrison', in Carola M. Kaplan and Anne B. Simpson (eds), *Seeing Double: Revisioning Edwardian and Modernist Literature* (New York: St. Martin's Press, 1996), pp. 131–48.

Trevelyan, Marie, *Glimpses of Welsh Life and Character* (1893; London: John Hogg, n.d.).

Trevelyan, Marie, *Folk-Lore and Folk-Stories of Wales* (London: Elliot Stock, 1909).

Uglow, Jenny, *Elizabeth Gaskell: A Habit of Stories* (1993; London: Faber, 1994).

Upham, Charles, *Lectures on Witchcraft, comprising a History of the Delusion in Salem in 1692* (Boston: Carter, Hendee and Babcock, 1831).

Varma, Devendra P., *The Gothic Flame* (1957; New York: Russell and Russell, 1966).

Verhoeven, Timothy, *Transatlantic Anti-Catholicism: France and the United States in the Nineteenth Century* (New York: Palgrave, 2010).

Vicinus, Martha, 'The Adolescent Boy: Fin de Siècle Femme Fatale?' *Journal of the History of Sexuality*, 4/11 (1994), 90–114.

Wallace, Diana, *Sisters and Rivals in British Women's Fiction, 1914–39* (Basingstoke: Macmillan, 2000).

Wallace, Diana, *The Woman's Historical Novel: British Women Writers 1900–2000* (Basingstoke: Palgrave, 2005).

Wallace, Diana, and Andrew Smith (eds), *The Female Gothic: New Directions* (Basingstoke: Palgrave Macmillan, 2009).

Waters, Sarah, 'Wolfskins and togas: lesbian and gay historical fictions, 1870 to the present' (unpublished Ph.D. thesis, Queen Mary and Westfield College, University of London, 1995).

Waters, Sarah, 'Wolfskins and Togas: Maude Meagher's *The Green Scamander* and the Lesbian Historical Novel', *Women: A Cultural Review*, 7/2 (1996), 177–88.

Waters, Sarah, 'Romance among the Ruins', *The Guardian, Saturday Review*, 28 January 2006, pp. 4–6.

Waters, Sarah, 'My Hero: Angela Carter', *The Guardian, Saturday Review*, 3 October 2009, p. 5.

Waters, Sarah, 'Sarah Waters on *The Little Stranger*', The Man Booker Prizes, *www.themanbookerprize.com/perspectice/articles/1261*, accessed 6 October 2009.

Waters, Sarah ,'The Lost Girl', *The Guardian*, 30 May 2009, *www/. guardian.co.uk/books/2009/may/30/sarah-waters-books/print*, accessed 6 October 2009.

Watson, J. R., 'Elizabeth Gaskell: Heroes and Heroines and *Sylvia's Lovers*', *Gaskell Society Journal*, 18 (2004), 81–94.

Waugh, Patricia, *Metafiction* (London and New York: Routledge, 1984).

Weston, Louise C. and Josephine A. Ruggiero, 'Male–Female Relationships in Best-Selling "Modern Gothic" Novels', *Sex Roles*, 4/5 (1978), 647–55.

White, Hayden, *Metahistory: The Historical Imagination in Nineteenth-Century Europe* (1973; Baltimore and London: Johns Hopkins University Press, 1975).

White, Hayden, *Tropics of Discourse* (1978; Baltimore and London: Johns Hopkins University Press, 1985).

Williams, Anne, *Art of Darkness: A Poetics of Gothic* (Chicago and London: University of Chicago Press, 1995).

Wings, Mary, '*Rebecca redux*: tears on a lesbian pillow', in Liz Gibbs (ed.), *Daring to Dissent: Lesbian Culture from Margin to Mainstream* (London and New York: Cassell, 1994), pp. 12–13.

Woodward, Kathleen, *Aging and its Discontents: Freud and Other Fictions* (Bloomington and Indianapolis: Indiana University Press, 1991).

Woolf, Virginia, *A Room of One's Own* (1929; London: Granada, 1977).

Woolf, Virginia, 'Women and fiction' (1929), in *On Women and Writing*, ed. Michèle Barrett (London: The Women's Press, 1979).

Wynne, Deborah, 'Hysteria Repeating Itself: Elizabeth Gaskell's *Lois the Witch*', *Women's Writing*, 12/1 (2005), 85–97.

Zorn, Christa, 'Aesthetic Intertextuality as Cultural Critique: Vernon Lee Rewrites History through Walter Pater's "La Gioconda"', *The Victorian Newsletter*, 91 (1997), 4–10.

Zorn, Christa, *Vernon Lee: Aesthetics, History and the Victorian Female Intellectual* (Athens: Ohio University Press, 2003).

Index